THE CHALLENGE OF CHRISTIAN DISCIPLESHIP

William Cosgrave

The Challenge of
Christian Discipleship

the columba press

First published in 2012 by
the columba press
55A Spruce Avenue, Stillorgan Industrial Park,
Blackrock, Co Dublin

Cover by Bill Bolger
Origination by The Columba Press
Printed by Gemini International Ltd, Dublin

ISBN 978-1-85607-765-1

Contents

Acknowledgements   6
Introduction   7

1.   The Emotions in the Moral Life   9

2.   Emotional Intelligence:
      Its Meaning and Practical Implications   37

3.   Understanding and Managing Anger   63

4.   The Virtue Model of the Christian Moral Life   76

5.   Men and Women are equal:
      But how do they complement each other?   95

6.   The Christian Life:
      Relating its Spiritual and Moral Dimensions   118

7.   Happiness: Challenge and Blessing   135

8.   The Mid-Life Transition   145

9.   What Theologians Today are saying about Sin   163

10.   Reconciliation:
      The Struggle to Repent and Forgive   177

11.   The Decline of Confessions:
      Disaster or Return to Normal?   196

12.   Models of the Priesthood Today   205

13.   Structures of Authority in the Church   220

14.   The Diocesan Clerical System:
      How it shapes the Clergy within it   248

15.   The Cost of Discipleship   275

16.   Understanding Baptism:
      Changes of Emphasis Today   286

17.   Concelebration: Values and Drawbacks   292

18.   Eucharistic Devotions:
      Understanding their Decline   298

19.   Mass Offerings: Issues in Theology and Practice   307

Acknowledgements

The publisher gratefully acknowledges the use of the following material:

Chapter 1: 'The Emotions in the Moral Life' brings together three articles from *Doctrine and Life*, January, 2005, pp 12-20, February, 2005, pp 20-28, and March, 2005, pp 7-18; **Chapter 2**: 'Emotional Intelligence: its Meaning and practical Implications' consists of three articles in *Doctrine and Life*, January, 2009, pp 9-16, February, 2009, pp 12-23, and March, 2009, pp 14-23. **Chapter 3**: 'Understanding and Managing Anger', *The Furrow*, September 2007, pp 480-490; **Chapter 4**: 'The Virtue Model of the Christian Moral Life', *Doctrine and Life*, April 2011, pp 30-48; **Chapter 5**: 'Men and Women are Equal: But how do they complement each other?', *Doctrine and Life*, November 2010, pp 40-54 and December 2010, pp 28-35. **Chapter 6**: 'The Christian Life: Relating its Spiritual and Moral Dimensions', *Doctrine and Life*, May/June 2009, pp 23-38. **Chapter 7**: 'Happiness: Challenge and Blessing', *The Furrow*, January 2011, pp 39-47. **Chapter 8**: 'The Mid-Life Transition', *The Furrow*, April 1995, pp 210-219 and *Intercom*, October 1993, pp 30-31. **Chapter 9**: 'What Theologians Today are saying about Sin', *Doctrine and Life*, May/June 2000, pp 287-295 and *The Furrow*, April 2008, pp 218-223. **Chapter 10**: 'Reconciliation: The Struggle to Repent and Forgive' is an expanded version of my article 'Repent and Forgive', *The Furrow*, February, 2003, pp 82-92. **Chapter 11**: 'The Decline of Confessions: Disaster or Return to Normal?', *The Furrow*, March 1994, pp 158-162. **Chapter 12**: 'Models of the Priesthood Today', *Doctrine and Life*, July/August 1997, pp 356-361 and September 1997, pp 417-424. **Chapter 13**: 'Structures of Authority in the Church', in Seán MacRéamoinn, Editor, *Authority in the Church*, The Columba Press, Dublin, 1995, pp 26-47. **Chapter 14**: 'The Diocesan Clerical System: How it shapes the Clergy within it', *Doctrine and Life*, October 2005, pp 5-19 and November, 2005, pp 13-26. **Chapter 15**: 'The Cost of Discipleship', *The Furrow*, February 2005, pp 67-76. **Chapter 16**: 'Understanding Baptism: Changes of Emphasis Today', *The Furrow*, April 2009, pp 223-228. **Chapter 17**: 'Concelebration: Values and Drawbacks', *The Furrow*, April 1993, pp 236-239. **Chapter 18**: 'Eucharistic Devotions: Understanding their Decline', *The Furrow*, October 1996, pp 536-542. **Chapter 19**: 'Mass Offerings: Issues in Theology and Practice', *The Furrow*, February 2008, pp 77-85.

Introduction

This volume of essays in moral and pastoral theology has been nearly twenty years in the making. It contains articles that for the most part were originally published in church magazines between 1993 and 2011. They are presented here in the belief that they contain some ideas that are valuable today as in earlier years and will inform the reader about some of the latest theological and pastoral thinking that has been done in the church in recent decades. I have done some light revision in nearly all the original essays to take account of the latest insights that I have come across, but substantially the chapters are as they originally appeared.

Like every other theologian and pastoral writer I am indebted to numerous experts in these fields. To a large degree I have learned from and used the insights of our best moral, spiritual and pastoral writers, as will be clear to any reasonably well informed reader of church books and magazines and as the sources I have used and footnoted will indicate. I wish to thank all these learned thinkers and I hope that my use and arrangement of their reflections will help to make their valuable work more easily and more widely available.

This book is aimed at readers who have some interest in and are somewhat informed about church matters and the thinking going on in church circles in the last few years. There is little here for theological, spiritual or pastoral experts, though it is possible some of them might find some ideas here that might have some relevance to undergraduate courses and lectures. Some ideas might also have value at second level and even for the busy preacher running short of inspiration for his homily / sermon! I have tried to write clearly, positively and logically, so that the reader may be helped to understand somewhat better his/her own experience and the Christian message in the areas of morality, spirituality and the pastoral life of the church. The hope then is that this will assist readers to progress in the struggle for more dedicated Christian living and a deeper commitment to the Christian gospel and its vision, ideals and values.

William Cosgrave

CHAPTER ONE

The Emotions in the Moral Life

If you were asked to mention a significant element or aspect of the moral life generally and, in particular, of the moral life of the Christian, it is not very likely that you or I or anyone else would pick out our emotions or feelings as such an element. In fact the emotions would probably not figure at all in the list of things one might draw up in response to such a request. We'd be more inclined to focus on such obvious things as conscience, sin, virtue, vice, injustice, the church's teaching, etc. This is not surprising, given the long tradition in western ethics and in Christian moral reflection of either paying little attention to our emotions or of discussing them in very negative terms or both.[1]

Today, however, this tradition and tendency are being rethought and renewed and, as we come to understand our emotional life better and take a more positive view of its place and function in our lives generally, moralists and others are beginning to recognise the very significant and indeed central role our emotions play in our lives as persons-in-relationship-and-in-community and so in our moral lives. This is quite a new emphasis and area of discussion, especially in Catholic moral thinking, certainly at its more practical or pastoral level.

In this chapter we will present some of the main ideas that are being given currency today in regard to our emotional life and its role in and impact on the moral life of the Christian. We will attempt to make the case that our emotions play a very significant part in our moral lives and spell out in a little detail what that part is, indicating also some of the consequences of this for us as we seek to follow the Christian way of life. It will become clear, we hope, that we will need to take our emotional life and its development more seriously, if we are to reach the goal or ideal of moral maturity which our calling as human beings and as disciples of Christ lays upon us.

---

1. Cosgrave, William, *Christian Living Today: Essays in Moral and Pastoral Theology* (Columba Press, Dublin, 2001), pp 42-3.

WHAT ARE THE EMOTIONS?[2]

As the word itself indicates, our emotions are movements of feeling within us that tend to move us out of ourselves (e-motion). As such they may be said to be in essence or by their nature impulses to act, to do something. This becomes clearer when we look at the findings of modern physiology in relation to the bodily changes that each emotion brings about in us. When, for example, we experience the feeling of anger, that is, become angry, our heart rate increases, blood flows to our hands and feet, adrenalin is released to provide added energy and our face becomes red or even white (with rage). All this represents the body, the person, preparing for action, whether it be a verbal confrontation with someone, a heated argument or a physical fight with fists and/or weapons. In the case of the feeling of fear the blood flows to our limbs to prepare us for flight, if need be, the face loses its colour as the blood rushes off to the limbs and a flood of hormones puts the body on high alert for a rapid response. In relation to the positive emotion of love or tender feelings we experience the opposite of the flight or fight response. The body feels calm and contented and this moves the person towards relationship and cooperation with the loved one.[3]

Our ordinary experience confirms all this data from the human sciences and makes it clear that our emotions are powerful forces within us that move us to respond to situations and people in ways that can often be very significant for ourselves and/or for our relationships, whether positively or negatively. Our experience of anger and aggression, of fear and fright,

---

2. Diana Fritz Cates, in her book *Aquinas and The Emotions: A Religious-Ethical Inquiry*, Georgetown University Press, Washington DC, 2009, says: 'There are significant differences in philosophical ways of describing or representing emotions,' p 1; '… it is not easy to specify a working definition of emotion in face of (this) significant philosophical disagreement.' To do so, she says, would require 'delving into major philosophical issues,' p 13. Here, then, we confine ourselves to the more practical aspects of the study of emotion.

3. Daniel Goleman, *Emotional Intelligence: Why it can matter more than IQ* (Bloomsbury, London, 1996) pp 6-7 (hereinafter referred to as *EI*); Francis Wilks, *Intelligent Emotions: How to succeed through transforming your feelings* (Arrow Books, London, 1998), p 76; Pat Collins CM, *Intimacy and the Hungers of the Heart* (Columba Press, Dublin, 1991), p 44.

makes this clear, but we know its truth also from having experienced feelings like sadness, guilt, shame, sorrow, enjoyment, love, surprise and shock.

From what has been said here, it is not too difficult to understand that our emotions are sources of energy within us that can, in a sense personal to each of us, move mountains, as it were. This is psychic energy that is generated in response to our perceptions of the realities and especially the people we encounter and that touch us in ways that are significant. The power and strength of this energy can be seen particularly when we are in the grip of an emotion like sexual infatuation or have fallen in love, when we are filled with anger and rage, when we are carried away with joy and happiness or when panic or terror lay hold of us. Action usually follows such deep and powerful emotions and very dramatic action it may be, as experience again confirms. So our emotions and their accompanying energy can be life-transforming for better or for worse. All this is normal and to be expected in our daily lives. The problem is usually to harness and channel this emotional energy in constructive and appropriate ways so that one's own and others' welfare and happiness are promoted and enhanced. This is the task of emotional growth and maturity, as we will see later.

Experts tell us that how we handle the psychic energy of our emotions is very important for our emotional health and growth and consequently for our relationships with others and our general welfare and happiness as persons. We have a variety of psychic mechanisms for dealing with this energy. One unhealthy one is called repression. Repression is usually an unconscious process by which we banish from our conscious awareness certain 'unacceptable' or 'bad' experiences or feelings. It is a method of emotional self-regulation in which we automatically tune out certain disturbing feelings as a way of defending ourselves against the upset we feel they would cause us. One can understand it as a form of denial that renders one unaware of the feelings that one represses. This may happen in relation to feelings of anger and hostility towards a parent or authority figure like a teacher, priest or bishop or a celibate may repress sexual or genital feelings because he/she assumes they are 'bad'.

Psychic repression such as we are here considering, though

often finding a place in people's ordinary lives, comes at a cost and this is the point we want to emphasise here. Such repression is emotionally or psychically unhealthy and damaging, because it buries the emotions involved within one's unconscious. But these emotions still retain their psychic energy; in other words, they are buried alive rather than dead and they, therefore, continue to seek an outlet, some form of expression. Preventing such an outlet or expression uses up some of one's ordinary resources of psychic energy and renders it more difficult for a person to be one's true self in an emotionally mature way. In addition, the buried energy will probably seep out in disguise, as it were, and result in the person becoming, e.g. irritable, angry, frustrated, moody, etc. or even developing physical symptoms of illnesses like colds, fevers, ulcers, skin diseases or even more serious complaints.[4] Clearly it will be very important for our emotional health to avoid or at least overcome any tendency we may have to repression. But that is far from easy as repression is unconsciously done and one may well require help from others to overcome it.

Experience shows that our emotional reactions tend to be much more rapid than those of our rational mind. This speed is the result of a long process of evolution and its purpose was to give the individual person a better chance of escaping the threats to his/her life in the very dangerous world of millions of years ago. This same instantaneous emotional reaction is still with us today and can be either a benefit or a problem depending on the situation. It can appear, therefore, that in a sense we have two minds or two aspects of the one mind, the emotional and the rational. While this is true, these two normally operate in tight harmony with our emotions feeding into and informing the operations of the rational mind and the rational mind refining and sometimes vetoing the inputs or tendencies of the emotions.[5]

Scholars are now able to tell us what is happening in the brain when these emotional and rational operations are taking

---

4. Goleman, EI, 75-77; William F. Kraft, *Sexual Dimensions of the Celibate Life* (Gill & Macmillan, Dublin, 1979), 64-68; Cosgrave, 107.
5. Goleman, EI, 5; Daniel Goleman, *Working with Emotional Intelligence* (Bloomsbury, London, 199), 73-78 (hereinafter referred to as WWEI); Gael Lindenfield, *Emotional Confidence* (Thorsons, London, 1997), 12-21.

place. The two parts of the brain that are most involved are the amygdala and the neo-cortex. The *amygdala* (from the Greek word for almond) is an almond-shaped structure in the pre-frontal lobes. It is situated above the brainstem near the bottom of the limbic ring. The neo-cortex evolved much later than the amygdala. It too is part of the limbic system; it surrounds the brainstem and is placed above the amygdala. To put it at its simplest we can say that the amygdala is the seat of our emotions and the neo-cortex is the seat of our thinking. The former is the emotional brain; the latter is our rational brain. These two elements of our mental life normally work together, as we have already mentioned. But the amygdala can react to a perception quicker than the neo-cortex and so occasionally we have an emotional reaction to a perceived threat, attraction or opportunity that escapes the control of the neo-cortex. As a result such a reaction may turn out to be inappropriate or even primitive. Some refer to these occurrences as emotional hijacks in which our reason is overwhelmed, our emotions take over, declare an emergency and take some drastic and perhaps quite unhelpful, exaggerated or even destructive action. It could be some form of aggression or violence or fear or fright, triggered, maybe, by some emotional memory from one's past.[6]

THE EMOTIONS AND INSIGHT

What has been said so far is concerned largely with our emotions as observable phenomena, as physical or bodily realities. This is important but more needs to be said about them. Our emotions have an inner aspect, what we could call an inward experience that has often been overlooked but is of major and indeed primary significance for our general understanding of our feelings and particularly for throwing light on the role of our emotions in our moral lives.

We are bodily beings and our emotions are part of that bodiliness. Now, since it is through the body that we are in the world and participate in what goes on there, we can say that our emotions put us in touch with our world; through them we participate in the world and are attuned to it. In a sense we breathe in the world through our feelings and these feelings are rooted ultimately in our

6. Goleman, EI, 8-29.

being-in-the-world, or more exactly, in our being-with-others-in-the-world. These feelings are directed towards situations in the world and are responses to what one perceives in one's world. They are not, therefore, purely subjective. They have a real reference to objective events; they attune us to reality.[7]

Feelings are very specific and differ according to the situations which evoke them. One situation gives rise to fear, for example, while another evokes anger and yet another joy or hope or sadness or shame, etc. Now this indicates that each of these feelings carries within it an awareness, an understanding, however vague and unarticulated, of the situation to which it refers and from which it arises. At least implicitly, it asserts that the situation has a certain character, e.g. a feeling of fear carries an awareness of some threat, one of anger contains an awareness of some hurt, frustration or injustice. And so with other feelings. While this awareness or insight is not often made explicit or put into words, it is, nevertheless, there. Hence, we can say that there are no *mere* feelings but only feelings or emotions that give us to understand something and make some assertion or disclose something about the situation from which they arise. In other words, our feelings give us an insight into a situation and it is an insight that is neither purely subjective nor is it completely objective like something we hear or see or touch. What is disclosed by our feelings transcends this distinction between subjective and objective and is referred to by some as existential or primordial.[8]

What we have just been saying in the preceding paragraphs is important as it makes it clear that it is false to oppose understanding and emotion to each other as has, unfortunately, been done in philosophy and even in Christian ethics over the centuries. We see now, however, that our emotions have a cognitive element and function; they can and do give us knowledge and insight, not just into particular situations but also through those situations into the values that are to be found in those situations and indeed in the whole of the moral life.[9]

7. John Macquarrie, *Existentialism* (Penguin, Middlesex, 1973), 118-24; Collins, 46-47.
8. John Macquarrie, *Existentialism, Studies in Christian Existentialism* (SCM Press, London, 1965), 144.
9. Linda Hogan, *Confronting the Truth: Conscience in the Catholic Tradition* (DLT, London, 2001), 144.

We may spell out this last point on the moral life a little more fully.

Our insight into values, moral values included, and our understanding and appreciation of them come to us, first of all, through our feelings. We appreciate values or goods emotionally, to begin with. What we love we value; where our heart is, there is our treasure. We do, of course, come to appreciate some values intellectually but unless we feel a value in our heart, as it were, then that value will be for us more a notional than a real one. It won't move or inspire us; we'll lack the moral energy to pursue that value and realise it in our actions or make it part of our character. This implies too that our appreciation of and commitment to the various virtues are also emotional, and need to be, if those virtues are not to remain for us impersonal ideals rather than attitudes and values which touch our hearts, which we are committed to practising in our daily lives as Christians and which come to form significant dimensions of our moral character. To put this in other words, the springs of morality and of one's moral life are in the heart, and the origins or roots of our moral experience are in our feelings or affections.

It is important to add here that the insight into values and virtues that our emotions provide or contain has also an evaluative element or a kind of judgment. We encounter values or goods in specific situations in which people are involved and our feelings are often stirred in response to a particular action or situation that has a moral dimension to it. Thus we bristle and feel anger, if we discern injustice in some situation, especially if we feel we ourselves are being unjustly treated. Many people seem to feel a negative affective response to the idea of storing the sperm of superior people like Einstein or Lincoln in order to breed better people in the future.[10] People are outraged when they discover that top political figures have lied about or covered up scandals in matters of public interest or when church leaders are discovered to have done similar things in relation to sex abuse of children by priests.

---

10. Daniel Maguire, *The Moral Choice* (Winston Press, Minneapolis, 1979), 283

In such situations the evaluations or judgments we discover in and through our feelings are moral in character. Such judgements are quite common in our daily lives as, for example, when we react, negatively or positively, to various situations and express a moral judgment on them without always being able to articulate any very adequate reasons for our conclusion. So we can see that here our emotions provide us with an initial moral assessment of or judgment on the actions under discussion and that these preliminary assessments have significant value and importance for the moral choices we will make in these cases. Whether these affective moral responses are confirmed by subsequent moral reflection and logical analysis or not, the point here is that emotion pervades all our moral knowledge and contains an important element of moral understanding and evaluation.

From what has been said in the preceding paragraphs it would seem right to say that most of the moral judgments we make in the ordinary run of our lives are of the sort discussed above. They are affective and intuitive and only later, if at all, do we put our reasoning powers to work to articulate reasons for the choice we have made.[11] It may happen that this reasoning process leads us to modify or even reverse our initial moral assessment. But in most cases, certainly the more routine ones, our emotional evaluation is confirmed and generally acted upon, sometimes without being backed up by what others would consider very weighty rational considerations. This shows us the power and importance of our initial emotional response to the situations we meet in daily life and the significance for each of us personally of our preliminary moral evaluation of those situations. However, this does not mean that we are irrational creatures content to let our emotions dictate our moral judgments and choices. We do that on occasions, it has to be admitted. But frequently these initial affective judgements will be right, because they will have a wisdom of their own that comes from the moral experience of living for years in relationship and in community and making moral evaluations and choices with great frequency and usually with due discernment and care. This

---

11. Maguire, 284-5; Cosgrave, 34.

holds particularly when the person having the insights and following his/her initial emotional moral assessments has achieved a good level of emotional maturity and wisdom. In the light of this, then, we can say that emotional intelligence or maturity is a very important requirement for the making of good decisions of any sort and especially moral decisions, that is, decisions involving the welfare of some person or persons, oneself included.[12]

THE EMOTIONS AND REASON

We have stated earlier that we should not conceive of reason and emotion as simply opposed to each other and in the previous section we have at least begun to show why this is so. Now we will seek to spell this out in a little more detail and see how the relationship between these two vitally important dimensions of the human psyche should be understood, especially as they are operative in making moral decisions and, hence, in building moral character. We will do this in two main stages:[13]

i) Reason judges and shapes our moral reasoning process, our intuitions and emotions.
There is no argument about the fact that we should struggle to the best of our intellectual ability to think as well and as rationally as we can in the process of any decision-making and especially moral decision-making. This should involve us in questioning our own reasoning processes and the arguments we bring to support a particular conclusion we may have tentatively drawn, perhaps as a result of intuition or past experience. The usual rational criteria of good thinking must, therefore, be applied, e.g. consistency, logic, clarity, coherence, etc.[14]

More importantly from our perspective here, we can and should also rationally judge, assess and shape the emotions which affect us as we wrestle with our moral decisions. In the first place, the search for and the commitment to finding moral

---

12. Cosgrave, 43-50; Goleman, EI, 42-5 and chapters 4-8.
13. Here we are drawing on Sidney Callahan, *In Good Conscience: Reason and Emotion in Moral Decision-Making* (HarperSanFrancisco, 1991), 124-138.
14. Callahan, 125, 127.

truth are fuelled and energised by emotions we feel or induce. These emotions can be appropriate and so give rise to real interest, care and the desire for truth, or they can be weak and flat with the result that our commitment to making the right decision may leave something to be desired. Then we may settle for a decision that makes for a quiet life, provides an easier option or doesn't interfere with our ambitions, civil or ecclesiastical. Or we may search only for evidence that confirms what we want to believe or that doesn't require us to revise or even abandon a position we have long held.

In this context there can be what the New Testament refers to as a 'hardening of the heart'. This means that a person sets up emotional barriers against outside influences, usually in relation to a particular subject, habit, attitude, person, community or institution. This hardening may take place because the person feels defensive or fearful or perceives that his/her self-serving interests are being threatened. Or it may occur out of a desire to dominate and control. These barriers may be erected, then, to defend one's intellectual position or way of acting against specific rational arguments, new evidence and/or a particular experience or experiences. So, clearly, such a hardening of the heart is a negative thing both emotionally and morally. The result of taking this emotional stance is, of course, that one's mind is closed and one refuses to listen, learn or change anything further in the area in question. Not a few people, it may be assumed, have had experience of such a 'hard heart' in others and suffered not a little frustration, anger, pain and hurt as a result. One may even discern it in oneself, at least looking back at one's attitudes and/or behaviour.[15]

The root problem here is one's lack of real commitment to knowing and doing the truth. That is an emotional lack or deficit and it can sometimes be very difficult to reverse or overcome. But overcome it we must, if we are to choose rightly, make truly moral decisions and live in a virtuous and Christian manner.[16]

---

15. Callahan, 188
16. Callahan, 127, 188.

It may also happen that in the course of our moral decision-making we experience emotions that may sway us in our reasoning but which may not be based on correct or sufficient evidence. These feelings could be ones like disgust, joy, anger or relief at particular facts, implications, conclusions or proposed solutions to one's moral dilemma. Here too reason has to assess these emotional reactions and judge whether they are well grounded, excessive, inappropriate, etc.[17]

Examples are not hard to find. Anxiety may accompany one's belief that one may not pass a particular important examination. Fear will tend to result from the belief that one is likely to be attacked by a threatening group of men close by or that one has a serious disease. Such negative feelings, if not properly controlled by reason, can upset and diminish one's capacity to use one's abilities, intellectual and otherwise.[18] On the other hand, contentment and gratitude will tend to be the feelings one will have if one believes one is a good moral person and/or is loved by God. Joy tends to spring from the feeling that one is well loved by some other people. Hope and optimism characterise people who believe that they can achieve their goals. Such positive feelings generally enhance one's performance.[19]

This adjudicating role of reason will also be necessary in case of emotions that arise in specific situations and that need to be evaluated in relation to our overall moral vision and value system. In this context we may conclude that feelings like envy, contempt or cowardice are to be judged negatively and so not allowed to persist or exercise their influence, while we may take a positive view of emotions like good will, care, empathy and love. It may happen too that we find that we have little or no emotional response to evil and immoral practices or acts. Here there may well be cause for serious moral concern. It would seem that in such an eventuality our moral sense itself is somehow impaired and we are not really open to the moral imperative as we should be. In such a case our reason may well judge that the absence of emotion in relation, say, to things like cheating, stealing, torture,

17. Callahan, 128.
18. Goleman, EI, 83-87.
19. Goleman, EI, 87-90.

racial discrimination etc is a sign of moral numbness and perhaps even of psychopathic tendencies.

On the positive side experience shows that we are normally able to manage and control our emotions by rational means or strategies. This is a sign of maturity as a person. Such control may include inducing particular feelings in a specific situation, e.g. sadness at a bereavement or joy at a celebration, especially by deciding to pay attention to that situation and remaining attentive to it, so as to act in an appropriate and constructive manner there.[20] We may exercise our control of our feelings also by, e.g. recalling particular emotions or states of feeling which we experienced in the past and so induce these or similar feelings in the present. We could think, e.g. of the particular feelings we had when being punished for some wrongdoing or being punished in the wrong, being rewarded for some act of kindness or generosity, or being ridiculed for our ethnic background. Such recall of feelings, now rationally reflected on, can help one, in the present, to be more sensitive to others in similar situations. We could also bring to mind some of our beliefs, moral, religious or others, and these too could stir up or give rise to emotional responses.

It will be clear from these ways in which we can shape and control our feelings that reason can and does exercise extensive sway over our emotional life. In fact it can and should judge, shape and tutor our emotions in every situation. Exceptions are possible, however. Emotional hijacks do take place in certain situations or we may lack appropriate emotions in some cases or we may fail to apply our rational powers so that they can do their job in relation to our emotions. Still, the ability to engage in reflective rational testing and managing of our reasoning, intuitions and emotions belongs to most adult people. And what's more we can develop and improve that ability. When we do exercise it in a regular, consistent and mature way, then it can be said that we are acting in an adult and constructive manner and that means that one is a person well advanced in the formation of a good moral character.[21]

---

20. Callahan, 120, 129.
21. See Callahan, 129.

ii) Emotions test and tutor reason

We are reasonably familiar with the ideas in the previous sub-section. But the heading of the present section will seem novel and to some debatable. But we have earlier made points very similar to what is being asserted here, when we said that our emotions provide us with moral insight into and moral evaluation of the situations we find ourselves in. Thus they give us a preliminary moral judgment or assessment of particular actions that we are contemplating doing. Examples have been given and these show clearly that our emotional evaluations of particular actions do offer us moral guidance for our daily lives and contain a wisdom that is indispensable for right moral decisions and good moral living. Here we may add some points by way of expansion in relation to the role of emotion in testing and guiding reason as it operates in the moral life.

Take the case of the psychopath. (S)he is not lacking in knowledge of right and wrong nor in the intellectual ability to distinguish one from the other. What is missing is the emotional capacity to enable the psychopath to care for another person and that person's welfare or good. The psychopath is bereft of emotion or feeling for others. He or she is unable to love or have empathy for others and so is unable to make any commitment to the good of those others or to avoiding evil in their regard. As a result of this deficiency he or she can do the most horrendously evil deeds and feel no qualms of conscience about the harm thus done to some other person(s). We can say, in fact, that the psychopath has no moral conscience, no moral sense; he or she is not just immoral but amoral.

But the point to note here is that this is due to an emotional deficit or lack, not to any rational difficulty or inability. The absence of feeling for others is the root of the moral problem here and that makes the person quite unable to use her/his rational powers to make moral judgements or commitments to the good. In a word, then, without a properly functioning emotional life one is incapable of being a person with a moral sense; one is prevented from committing him/herself to the good or against the evil. This would seem to suggest, more positively, that our emotions provide us with the capacity to live in a truly moral way, because they give us the ability to care for, to empathise with and to love others (and to hate others too) and so to commit ourselves to goods and values that arise from the foundational value of respect for the person, which itself is also intuited or appreciated emotionally or not at all.[22]

Another example will confirm the essential role of our emotional life in making morality possible for us and thus allowing reason to function as it ought in relation to our moral life generally. Contemporary neurologists tell us[23] that if a person has had significant damage done to the amygdala in the pre-frontal lobes in the brain, the amygdala, being, as we have already noted, the seat of the emotions, then that person, while being intellectually quite unimpaired, is rendered practically incapable of making any decisions, including moral decisions. The reason for this is that such a person seems to have lost access to his/her emotional memory and the emotional learning and wisdom that was stored there. As a consequence this person can no longer make a commitment to or a choice of good nor a rejection of evil. Indeed she/he seems to have lost the capacity to choose between any options presented to him/her. The reason for this has again to do with the emotional life. Choice is impossible here because the person no longer has any emotional reaction, positive or negative, to any options placed before him/her. He or she has no feelings for or against anything and so can't decide or choose or make a commitment in regard to anything either inside or outside the moral sphere. From this we can again conclude that feelings are indispensable for making choices and commitments of a moral nature and that without them reason is in practice rendered inoperable in relation both to morality and to the daily choices that are such a regular and unavoidable feature of ordinary living.

A further point needs to be made here. It is our emotions that alert us, in the first place, to the presence of a moral dimension or problem in a particular situation. In other words, our emotions can sharpen and guide our perceptions,[24] and this in a negative and in a positive way. It may happen, for example, that in

---

22. Richard M. Gula, *Moral Discernment* (Paulist Press, NY, 19-7), 37-8; Maguire, 263-6; Callahan, 41-2; Goleman, EI, 107-10.
23. See Goleman, EI, 27-8, 52-4.
24. Gula, 88-9.

a specific case we experience negative feelings about a proposed action or moral judgement or argument for some moral conclusion. These feelings may range from strong to mild emotional reactions but either way they function as signals from our deeper self, from the heart, you could say, that we are morally uneasy about or even hostile to the proposed action or line of argument, e.g. the use of torture, the harvesting of organs from living bodies, abortion, the refusal to treat AIDS patients, etc.[25] When we experience such negative feelings, we may not be able to articulate any reasons why we feel as we do. But our emotional aversion may induce us to withhold consent and continue looking beyond the proposed action or arguments in the search for a solution that we find acceptable. Later, we may be able to spell out why we felt negatively in the case.

Here we see an example of the way in which our emotions can sharpen and guide our moral perceptions and in which, then, reason can clarify and spell out the rational content or meaning of our original emotional response.[26]

Turning to the importance of positive emotions experienced in particular situations we can say that they too can alert us to the moral dimension of a situation and in particular to moral obligations there that would not otherwise have been discerned. Such positive moral feelings are more likely to be experienced by people who are morally good and wise and who, as a result, are more morally sensitive than others.[27] One example is righteous anger at unfair or oppressive treatment of oneself or others. Another is empathy that can alert one to the presence of discrimination or the violation of the human rights of hitherto neglected or oppressed groups like slaves, women, workers, ethnic minorities, the handicapped, sexually abused children or even in regard to the environment and God's creation itself. Perhaps we can see emotion sharpening and guiding our moral perception most clearly of all in the case of love.

The emotion of love is the great moral educator, Callahan says,[28] because it makes us pay attention to and value what we

25. Callahan, 130.
26. Callahan, 130-1.
27. Callahan, 131.
28. Callahan, 132.

love. Love in its true sense, as distinct from infatuation, mere sexual attraction, or plain insensitivity, engenders attention, care and concern for others. It motivates fine and careful perception or, in more ordinary language, it opens our eyes to moral needs and obligations that those who don't love may not discern. In this sense love is the opposite of being blind. In fact it enables us to see more clearly and more deeply, both in regard to the persons loved, their qualities and goodness, and in regard to moral obligations which arise in relation to those we love. Here we discover the famous 'reasons of the heart' which reason or the head cannot know.[29] This point about love is perhaps best illustrated by reflecting on the love of a parent for her/his child or that of a spouse for her/his beloved. Such love will inspire and motivate care, attention and self-sacrifice but it can also enable the loving person to discern important but subtle personal needs of the loved one and subtle ways in which these and other needs can be better responded to and met. In other words, love can sharpen and guide our moral perceptions so that we can care and help even more effectively.[30]

This can come about in another way too. It can happen that, because we love and appreciate another person, we are able to discern and be inspired to imitate the good moral qualities of that person. Here again love opens our eyes, morally speaking, and motivates us to grow in virtue and goodness. This can occur in any loving human relationship and for the Christian, most significantly of all, in one's relationship with Christ.[31]

To conclude this sub-section about our emotions testing and tutoring our reason we may sum up in the words of Sidney Callahan:

> The most adequate moral decision-making of conscience must achieve congruence or a fusion of thinking, feeling and willing into a unified whole … It is unlikely that an amoral or evil person could make consistently wise and good ethical judgments and give good moral counsel.[32]

---

29. Callahan, 131; see Maguire, 87-8, 288-90, 298, 305.
30. Callahan, 188-9.
31. Callahan, 132-3, 188-90.
32. 134, 135, 137.

As a rule only the person who is emotionally mature and is of good moral character will be well placed consistently to make such judgements and give such counsel.

Our reflections on the emotions in the moral life in the preceding pages have brought to our attention some points that are very significant but which have not been given the importance they deserve and demand in our thinking on Christian morality and in our Christian living. This is particularly true in relation to the insight or understanding we discover in our emotions and the manner in which our emotions test and guide our moral perceptions, so that without those emotions we are gravely handicapped in regard to our moral sense generally and especially in regard to our capacity to discern moral obligations and make moral decisions.

THE EMOTIONS AND MORAL COMMITMENT

One of the most important things about our emotions is that they enable us to commit ourselves to value and especially to persons, and to reject or refuse commitment to what we perceive as disvalues or evils in relation to persons. If we had no feelings, we'd be unable to commit ourselves to anyone or anything. We would be quite incapable of caring, empathising, loving or hating, for that matter. In a word, commitments and especially moral commitments are a matter of the heart. Our emotions, then, provide us with the insight to discern values and they also give us the energy to care for and commit ourselves to them and to make choices in their regard.

The point here may become clearer if we note the difference between a moral judgment on a specific action by an ethical theorist and the actual choice and performance of that action by a particular person. While the theorist's judgment will be influenced by emotional and rational factors as indicated above, it won't involve the theorist in any personal moral commitment to the action assessed. But the person doing the action will necessarily have to make a personal commitment of her/himself to the good or value the action. Her/his heart is in the choice that is made and the action that is done. That's what makes it a personal and moral choice. The agent makes an emotional (and intellectual or rational) commitment to the value in the action;

both her/his heart and head are engaged. But without this en-gaging of the agent's emotions, there is no real moral commit-ment and no real moral decision. The person appreciates the values(s) emotionally and hence makes a personal moral com-mitment to it/them in his/her action.[33] Central to moral com-mitment are two realities that are also in the area of our emo-tions or have a significant emotional dimension. These are one's perception and appreciation of values and one's motivation or willpower. Some comments on each will be appropriate here.

Appreciation of value
We have said that specific values, moral and non-moral, are, in the first place, discerned and appreciated in the heart, that is, by our emotions with their built-in insight and judgment. After this initial discernment we will likely come to an intellectual or ra-tional appreciation of values like justice, peace, truthfulness, freedom, courage, temperance, chastity, etc., though there are varying degrees of such appreciation and also differing depths of commitment to these values. We can, of course, sharpen our appreciation of any particular value by reflecting on, reading or hearing about it and its importance and implications. But per-haps the most powerful and effective way that we come to ap-preciate values is by personal experience in specific situations and cases. In such cases one's heart is involved and is often touched in deep ways, so that one's appreciation of and commit-ment to particular values are transformed or at least deepened notably.

Examples are not far to seek. It would seem true to say that in many, if not all, cases having a child of one's own is a very pow-erful and deeply touching way of bringing a person to a greater appreciation and valuing of the human person and of the per-son's intrinsic worth and dignity. Having a child with a disabili-ty can move one to deep compassion for those with similar or other disabilities. Discovering through and in another person the pearl of true human love not merely enriches one but often opens one's eyes to appreciate what love really is. It can motiv-ate one to do all one can to love others and enrich their lives too. Experiencing the horrors of war or violence can shock one into

---

33. Callahan, 19-23, 116.

profound appreciation of and love for life itself, health, good human relationships and true peace and justice. First-hand exposure to poverty, famine and hunger in the Third World can transform one from a complacent tourist from the rich and self-indulgent First World to a committed and wholehearted campaigner for world justice, for basic human rights and equality for all, and for a good living standard especially for those most in need.

The reason why such personal experiences can affect these kinds of transformation in people is precisely because these experiences are personal and not just intellectual or academic. In other words, they touch the heart; they stir our feelings and so they move and inspire the person to make some deeper commitment to practical action on behalf of others. It is easy to see that such deepened and strengthened appreciation and awareness are necessary, if one is to improve one's moral commitment to realising these and other values in one's daily life. And that appreciation and awareness are primarily matters of the heart as well as being matters of the head.

Motivation
In relation to motivation our emotions are basic and essential. The words motivation and emotion come from the same Latin word, *movere* (to move) and this link points to the close connection between the two realities these words refer to and name. We may note too that in daily living motivation is closely related to what we call willpower. To have the willpower to give up smoking or excessive drinking, for example, means effectively to have the motivation to do so, despite the difficulty involved.

Scholars today tell us that being able to motivate oneself to persist in one's efforts despite difficulty and setbacks is a basic requirement for any sort of real achievement in life from sport to spirituality, from the university to the workplace. What seems to set apart those at the top of competitive pursuits like sport, study, playing a musical instrument, etc. from others of roughly equal ability is the degree to which they can pursue an arduous practice routine for years and years. And that persistence and

---

34. Daniel Goleman, EI, 79-80. See this whole chapter in Goleman, 78-95.

determination depend on emotional traits, namely, enthusiasm, commitment and perseverance; in a word, on motivation or willpower.[34]

So one can say with Goleman (p 80) that to the degree that our emotions get in the way of or enhance our ability to think and plan, to pursue training for a distant goal, to solve problems and the like, they define the limits of our capacity to use our innate mental abilities and so determine how we do in life. This can turn out very positively for some and they can achieve major success or growth. For others things can go wrong and that can result in significant problems or even failure. But whatever the outcome, the point is that one's motivation and its depth and strength or lack of these is of enormous importance in and for one's moral living. One can see this in things like the struggle to overcome habits of sin, persevere in prayer, remain faithful to an unloving spouse, cope with unrelieved pain and suffering, etc.

The basic point we are making here is, then, that our moral commitments are not just rational, intellectual choices involving the head only. Rather they are personal choices that involve our emotions, the heart, at two crucial points: our appreciation of value and our motivation for what we do and don't do, and how we build and form our moral character. Here again we can clearly see the centrality and the power of our emotions in relation to our moral lives.

THE RELIGIOUS DIMENSION OF THE EMOTIONS

Cates tells us that, 'Just as our emotions can be of moral significance, they can also be of religious significance.'[35] Scholars, it seems, find it no easy task to articulate how the religious dimension of Christianity impacts on its moral dimension. While it is agreed that Christians have to do their morality in fidelity to their own religious myth or story or theology and that the moral life is transfigured by Christian faith, it is not fully agreed what

35. Cates, p 7.
36. Vincent MacNamara, 'Christian Moral Life', *An Irish Reader in Moral Theology: The Legacy of the last Fifty Years, Volume 1: Foundations,* edited by Enda McDonagh and Vincent MacNamara, Columba Press, Dublin, 2009, 205, 188-191; Vincent MacNamara, 'The Distinctiveness of Christian Morality', *Christian Ethics: An Introduction,* edited by Bernard Hoose, Cassell, London, 1998, 146-60.

the impact of this religious story is on the Christian moral life and how exactly the religious and the moral aspects of our Christian faith are related.[36] In this context it is no surprise to learn that scholars struggle to explain how our emotions have religious significance and how our religious faith affects our emotions.

One thing is certain, though. There are religious emotions or emotions that have a religious dimension. Examples are not far to seek. Faith, hope and love are human realities or virtues but clearly they become religious or acquire a religious depth or dimension for the Christian. Similarly with gratitude, repentance, forgiveness, reconciliation, fear, grief, anger, etc. Here one focuses on some human or created reality but in and through that one focuses on God. Thus we can speak of religious emotions or affections.[37]

> Religious thoughts, intuitions and questions can condition a wide array of emotions. They can condition emotions that are about God or divine things ... or the way things are going in our lives, where we suspect that something unusually deep or significant is happening ... Some emotions are partly a matter of religion ... some emotions are composed, at least in part, of religious beliefs, assumptions, intuitions, wonder and concern.[38]

> It is part of the business of religion to evoke or redirect people's emotions to bring about desired ends. By working with the emotions, religions can affect in profound ways the quality of peoples' lives and in the way they get along – or fail to get along.[39]

EMOTIONAL GROWTH AND THE MORAL LIFE

All that has been said in the preceding pages about the central place and importance of emotion in our moral lives makes it clear that there is no such thing as a purely intellectual moral decision or choice. A truly reasonable moral choice will be based on emotion, intuition and reason working together in harmony,

---

36. Cates, 45-61, 217-220.
38. Cates, 57-58.
39. Cates, 56.

to which will be added for the Christian the Bible, the Christian tradition and the teaching of the church.

It seems a fairly obvious conclusion from this and from what we have said earlier about the vital role of emotion in our moral lives that we need to pay much more attention to our emotional life and our level of emotional growth than in the past, if we are to be truly serious about good moral living and about doing our best to make good moral decisions and so to build a good moral character. It is clear now that there is a close connection between our level of emotional development and our level of moral development. The more emotionally mature we are, the better moral life we will be enabled to live and the better moral choices we will be able to make. But to the extent that we are emotionally immature our level of moral maturity will be restricted and we will have difficulty in consistently making wise and mature choices in the area of morality as in every other area of life.

The message here, then, is quite obvious. We are called as moral beings to attend conscientiously to our emotional development or lack of it and to take whatever steps are required to bring about the emotional growth that we may need, in order that we may live the Christian moral life better. This is a focus or concern that we have not heard much about in our Christian formation at any level, but it is one that we must now take on board as an essential requirement for good moral living and character building. This will present many of us, especially men, with not inconsiderable difficulty, both because some of us are not very aware of our emotional life and its level of development and because emotional growth of any sort is far from easy and will demand plenty of time and effort and maybe a good deal of help from others. So problems may arise on two levels, that of awareness and that of growth itself. And of course not a few will feel at a loss in regard to how to go about achieving progress in either area, while others may find themselves struggling with their motivation to undertake the tasks involved in the whole project of emotional growth.

We may illustrate the links between our emotional life and our moral life that we have been reflecting on by discussing an issue that is very much part of our moral and indeed our spiritual lives, namely, overcoming our habits of sin. Then we will devote some attention to outlining the central elements of emotional maturity itself.

Overcoming our habits of sin[40]
Experience teaches us that it is very difficult and in practice often impossible to uproot many of our habits of sin like using vulgar language, being aggressive and having poor control of one's anger, jealousy, bossiness, exhibiting attitudes of superiority, etc.

Modern psychology provides us with important insights here. It indicates that our sins, and especially our habits of sin, often have their roots in our emotional lives and in particular in the emotional wounds most of us have picked up over the course of our upbringing.

Common sense tells us that, if we don't get to the root of a problem, moral or otherwise, we are very unlikely to solve it. And so it is here. We need to heal the emotional wounds we have been mentioning, if we are to get rid of the habits of sin which arise from those wounds.

In line with this viewpoint, it will be clear that the remedy at the pastoral level for these habits of sin will be to deal with the emotional problem first and then one can hope for significant progress at the moral level.

We can see the same sort of relationship between the emotional and the spiritual life in some difficulties in prayer, contemplation, etc. An approach similar to that taken above will be needed in resolving these problems.[41]

THE MAIN ELEMENTS OF EMOTIONAL MATURITY

It will be important to clarify, at least to some extent, what we are talking about when we speak of emotional maturity or, to use a more modern term, emotional intelligence. We may outline what is in question here under the following five headings:[42]

---

40. See Cosgrave, 81-2; and also my articles, 'The Roots of Sin', *Intercom*, May 1994, 12-4, and 'To Repent and Forgive', *The Furrow*, February 2003, 85-8, and, in addition, chapter 9 below for a fuller treatment of this issue.
41. Cosgrave 82. See also Tony Baggot, 'Getting the Spiritual Life Together', *The Furrow*, November 1991, 628-635.
42. See Cosgrave, 45-50; Goleman, EI, chapters 4-8; Goleman, WWEI, 317-8.

i) Awareness of one's emotions as they occur[43]

Here we are talking about self-awareness and central to that is awareness of our feelings as they are occurring within us. This is essential for good psychological insight into oneself and for managing one's emotions constructively and appropriately. It will be of great significance also in relation to making moral decisions, as will be very clear from our earlier discussion of the relation between these two areas of our lives. Related to but different from self-awareness is self-knowledge. This means knowing about one's personality and character with their qualities and abilities, their strengths and weaknesses. Such self-knowledge is very important for the quality of one's living but is not a substitute for the self-awareness that is under discussion in the present context.

ii) Managing our emotions appropriately

This presupposes and is dependent on the awareness of our emotions which we have just been talking about. The greater our self-awareness the better we will be able to manage our emotions and so the better chance we will have of achieving emotional balance or maturity and of making progress towards moral maturity. Poor emotional awareness will make management of our emotions more difficult and will expose us to being often enough at the mercy of our moods with all the negative consequences that can flow from that.

iii) Controlling impulse and motivating oneself

Here we have two vitally important emotional skills that facilitate the full use of our talents and abilities. Without them success in any area of life will tend to elude us; with them we are well set to be successful, whether in sport or prayer or whatever. Controlling our impulses means one has a specific goal in mind and in order to achieve it restrains one's tendency to make a dash for quick results or to seek instant gratification by some impulsive action, perhaps only partially thought out and likely to do more harm than good. Motivation has been discussed

---

43. See Ron Yeung, *Emotional Intelligence*, The New Rule Series, Marshall Cavendish Business, London, 2009, 13-40. These elements of emotional maturity are given more extensive treatment in chapter 2 below.

earlier and its importance is clear. It will be especially necessary when the going gets tough as one seeks some end or goal that is difficult to attain, whether in the moral or spiritual life or in business or sport, etc. Motivating oneself is the real engine or source of energy in all our commitments, moral ones included.

iv) Empathy: being sensitive to others' feelings

While empathy is a relatively new word, its meaning is clear and its importance in human relationships is immense. It means feeling for another or being able to put oneself in another's emotional shoes, as it were. In a word, to be empathic means to be sensitive to others' feelings and needs. Given this understanding, it is not hard to see that there will very likely be a close link between one's level of empathy and one's level or depth of caring for others. To empathise with another is the root of caring for that person. The implication is clear, then, that the degree of one's empathy will shape significantly the morality one lives by. In a sense the roots of morality are to be found in empathy and this again is an emotional skill; it is a reality of the heart. So we see here another clear link between our emotional life and our moral life: the more empathic one is, the more moral one is likely to be and vice versa.[44] We may add that the empathic person is one who is likely to be good at and in human relationships and friendships; she or he is likely to be a loving and a well loved person. It must be said that women in general are better at this kind of empathy than men, though they have no monopoly on it.

v) Handling emotions in relationships

Empathy is the foundation of being able to notice and manage emotions in other people and so in relationships. If one can do this, one will shine in the use of social skills and display great social competence. This art is central to being able to make and keep good relationships with others at various levels. It will involve things like putting others at ease, soothing their bruised feelings, influencing and persuading them, inspiring them to action, setting the tone in interpersonal meetings, making friends, loving others, leading and organising people in groups, resolving conflicts.

---

44. Cosgrave, 52.

This brief outline of the main elements of emotional maturity makes clear how important such maturity is for human living. It reminds us again of the very close links between our emotional life and our moral life. Only the person who has achieved a reasonable degree of growth and maturity in relation to her/his feelings will be able to be really successful and happy in life and, in addition, only he/she will be able to arrive at a good level of moral maturity. Thus we arrive at the conclusion that only the emotionally mature or intelligent person will have the capacity to live a full and truly human and Christian life.

THE STRUGGLE FOR EMOTIONAL GROWTH

Our discussion in the foregoing pages has shown us the close, if to some perhaps surprising, links between the moral life and the emotional life. It is now clear that to live the moral life well, whether one is a Christian or not, requires one to attend to the state of one's emotions and to do all one can to further emotional growth and become as emotionally mature as possible. Implied in this is the important additional insight that, since the moral life is a central element of one's spiritual life, our Christian spirituality demands that we cultivate emotional growth and maturity so that we may attain the highest level we can in the spiritual life. At this point the question becomes very practical as we have to ask: how is this to be done? What is required in order that we grow emotionally and make progress towards emotional maturity? This is not a question many people will have asked themselves, though in recent times there seems to be a major increase in concern for emotional health, if one is to judge by the huge number of self-help books and magazines on the shelves these days and by the notable increase in the number of counsellors and those seeking their help in recent years. It looks as if people in the western world are more emotionally troubled than ever, despite never having had it so good economically in recent years. The frightening increase in the number of suicides in Ireland and elsewhere in the West may also be a sign of this. No doubt the current recession will only add to their emotional (and other) woes. So, we turn to the crucial issue of the method and means by which emotional growth can be furthered so that the Christian moral and spiritual life can be lived that much better. Only some brief pointers will be given here.

i) Promoting self-awareness

The ancient Greek Socrates recognised the importance of this when he advised his fellow citizens to 'know yourself'. As already noted in relation to emotional maturity this is absolutely basic and essential for emotional growth. Some people, especially women, are very much in touch with their feelings; others, men in particular, are not. But the good news is that we can improve in this matter, if we are motivated enough to set about doing so. There is no easy way to do the job, though. Paying attention to your feelings, especially your gut feelings, is a habit you can cultivate, and listening to what others say about you can be illuminating, if not a little upsetting at times. Writing a journal can help too as can taking time off for reflection or meditation; good also is sharing with a friend who is in touch with her/his feelings and can model for you how to do it.[45]

ii) Healing your emotional wounds

This presupposes good self-awareness so that one knows what these wounds are. Some have been mentioned already. Central to them is low self-esteem, which is at the root of many of our bad habits and faults. Sharing the problem with someone will be essential here, whether that is a friend or a counsellor. Taking to heart the encouraging things said by that person and others will be a big help too. Positive thinking about yourself will be valuable also as will giving up comparing yourself with others.[46]

iii) Growing in self-confidence

What has been said just now will be helpful here too, though like healing the wounds, this building of confidence is usually a long hard battle that will with perseverance bring a gradual but real growth over time. It will be important to be clear that loving yourself, regarded by some as selfish and wrong, is in fact an essential requirement for loving others and loving God and, far from being wrong, it is the basis on which self-confidence must be built. So one needs to treat oneself well, think positively, though realistically, about oneself and take seriously the praise and compliments one gets from others. This will help one to

---

45. See Goleman, EI, chapter 4; Goleman, WWEI, chapter 4.
46. See Gael Lindenfield, *Emotional Confidence*, (Thorsons, London, 1997), 49-98; Gael Lindenfield, *Self-Esteem* (Thorsons, London, 1995).

come to believe in one's abilities and skills and so to use them better. As one's self-confidence grows one will become able to assert oneself, make good decisions despite uncertainties and pressures and face new challenges.[47]

iv) Developing the other elements of emotional maturity

Having already mentioned self-awareness as an essential for emotional maturity and growth, it will be obvious that working to develop the other four elements of emotional maturity we outlined in the previous section will be necessary so as to promote emotional growth. These are, as listed above, managing one's emotions appropriately, controlling impulse and motivating oneself, working to deepen one's empathy and handling sensibly the emotions of others in relationships.

CONCLUSION

Our rather lengthy discussion in this chapter of the place and role of the emotions in the moral life will, hopefully, have alerted the reader to a number of insights that are fresh and significant. It is hoped also that the practical implications of what we have been outlining will be clear and will perhaps move some to take specific steps to achieve the goal of emotional growth towards emotional maturity. This will help to ensure better moral living and further development of one's spiritual life as a Christian in the church.

47. See Goleman, *WWEI*, 68-72; Lindenfield, *Self-Esteem*, 21-27; Tony Humphries, *Self-Esteem: Key to your Child's Education* (Gill & Macmillan, Dublin, 1996), chapter 5.

CHAPTER TWO

Emotional Intelligence:
Its Meaning and Practical Implications

In recent years there has been quite a lot of writing and discussion about emotional intelligence (EI). It is a rather new idea that is often contrasted with IQ (intelligence quotient). We are told that, while IQ is important in its own way, it won't get you very far without a significant amount of EI. Indeed EI can matter more than IQ[1] and without it even a person with a very high IQ can be very unsuccessful in his/her career and life generally. It is said also that it is not just to individuals that this applies, but it holds as well in the context of relationships like friendship, marriage, the family and the workplace and also in groups and organisations, in particular in relation to those who are leaders in them. We are even told that people who are far from distinguished in the usual intellectual sense can become real stars in life, if they rate highly in EI terms.

Obviously, the critical or key word in this context is emotional. We don't often associate intelligence with emotion. In fact the opposite has long been an almost taken for granted viewpoint in the western philosophical tradition, in the Christian moral and spiritual traditions and among people generally. Nowadays, however, this position has been shown to be unsustainable and numerous studies of human emotion[2] have presented us with a very positive and significant understanding of our emotions, showing their profound importance for all aspects of human living. 'Emotions, science now tells us, are part of rationality, not

---

1. Subtitle of Daniel Goleman's book, *Emotional Intelligence: Why it can matter more than IQ* (Bloomsbury, London, 1996), henceforth referred to as Goleman, EI.
2. For example, Edward Collins Vacek, 'Passions and Principles: A Sketch of an Effective Foundation for Morality', *Milltown Studies*, Dublin, No 52, 2003, 67-94; William Cosgrave, 'The Emotions in the Moral Life', *Doctrine and Life*, Dublin, January 2005, 12-20; ibid., 'The Emotions and Reason', *Doctrine and Life*, February, 2005, 20-28; ibid., 'The Emotions and Moral Commitment', *Doctrine and Life*, March 2005, 7-18; These three articles are brought together in chapter 1 above.

opposed to it', says Goleman *et al.*[3] The major emphasis on EI today aims to take this basic insight with the utmost seriousness and to spell out what it means and involves. Its fundamental meaning is captured in the phrase 'emotional intelligence' itself. This implies that our emotions have an intelligence of their own that is quite different from IQ, i.e. academic intelligence, and that is of vital importance for the quality of our lives.

In this chapter the intention is to explain how this is true. Attention will be focused at the beginning on EI itself as we explore what it is and how it relates to IQ. Then its core or essential elements will be discussed and explained. With this understanding we can then move on to look at some areas of life to see how they are to be understood in EI terms and how living in these areas can be transformed when one takes an emotionally intelligent approach to them. We begin, however, with a discussion of the nature of EI, its relation to IQ and its core elements.

EMOTIONAL INTELLIGENCE: WHAT IT IS AND HOW IT RELATES TO IQ

We are all well aware of the fact that we human beings are gifted with intelligence, popularly referred to as 'brains'. We are intelligent persons. This intelligence, as usually understood, enables us to understand all manner of things from mathematical formulae to how complicated machines operate, from abstract philosophical concepts to what is involved in playing a particular game. This is our academic, rational intelligence, which is, of course, a great blessing and a distinctively human endowment. We are, then, rational beings who can remember, think, understand, be self-aware and make choices and thus live a rich and happy life. This kind of intelligence is generally referred to as IQ.

Today, however, some scholars are saying that we need to understand human intelligence in a wider and perhaps deeper sense than this. They call this wider and deeper kind of intelligence or rationality emotional intelligence (EI).

Central to this view of things is the statement that our emotions are an element or dimension of our rationality. They are

---

3. Daniel Goleman, Richard Boyatzis and Annie McKee, *The New Leaders: Transforming the Art of Leadership into the Science of Results* (Little, Brown, London 2002), 42, henceforth referred to as Goleman, TNL.

not, then, opposed to our reasoning powers or IQ; rather they have an intelligence or rationality that it is essential to take account of and develop, if our reasoning powers are to function well and in a truly human manner.

EI, then, is the form of human intelligence that you acquire as you grow towards emotional maturity. As you advance along that road, you become able to integrate your emotions into your personality and character and use their warmth and energy to enrich your own life and the lives of those people with whom you relate. Then we discover that our emotions have wisdom; they guide our thinking, our valuing and our decision-making and even our very survival.[4]

Hence, without EI one cannot live a truly human life and only with it can one become the loving and mature person that God calls one to be. So, EI is human intelligence in its full sense, the kind that one has to arrive at, if one is to live to the fullest of one's potential as a human person and child of God. Only emotionally intelligent people can love their neighbour and their God in the manner in which Jesus did and to which he calls all of us to aspire. It will be obvious from this view of things that we must avoid any dualistic presentation of reason and emotion or head and heart as if they were adversaries in conflict with each other. Rather the life task for each and all of us is to harmonise reason and emotion in our personality and character, so that they complement and enrich each other and thus enable the person to live a fully intelligent life, one that is rational in the full sense, where reason and emotion work together and are brought to full maturity, each playing its own positive and essential role. Only thus will we be enabled to be fulfilled, successful and happy people with our potential at least substantially realised.

OUR EMOTIONS CONTRIBUTE TO INTELLIGENT LIVING[5]

Experts tell us today that our IQ or academic intelligence contributes at most about 25% to the factors that determine success in life. In other words, 'brains' accounts only for about a quarter

4. Goleman, EI, XIV.
5. The following two paragraphs are quoted with minor alterations from William Cosgrave, *Christian Living Today: Essays in Moral and Pastoral Theology* (Columba Press, Dublin, 2001), 44-5.

of what we may call a happy and successful life but perhaps much less.[6] At least 75% of that success and happiness is due to other factors. This fact alone would seem to indicate that we have dramatically over estimated the importance of IQ in and for our lives; we have placed too much emphasis on the rational or intellectual dimension of our personality and too little on the other factors, most of which are in the emotional area and which we are calling emotional intelligence or simply affective maturity. We may note too that academic intelligence has little to do with one's emotional life or level of happiness, as is clear from many instances of very intelligent people being quite unsuccessful in their careers and unhappy in their life generally. Of course many people of high IQ are very successful in life but many are not and the reason for this lies in the 75% of factors just referred to. Central to these is the issue of how we handle our emotions.

Experience shows that some people are more emotionally mature or adept than others and many studies highlight the fact that this maturity or adeptness is crucial to understanding why one person thrives in life, while another, of equal or even greater academic intelligence, fails or under-achieves. It seems clear, then, that emotional development and skill are basic in determining how well we can use whatever skills we have, including our 'brains'. There is now plenty of evidence that people who have acquired significant emotional maturity are at an advantage in all areas of life and are more likely to be content and effective whatever they choose to do in life. On the other hand, those who are under-developed in their emotional life find that they are hamstrung as far as using even their intellectual gifts is concerned. Success and happiness tend to elude them.

THE CORE ELEMENTS OF EMOTIONAL INTELLIGENCE

The question here is, then, what does one have to do to live an emotionally intelligent life? What is involved and required for one to become an emotionally intelligent person? Obviously, what will be needed will be in the area of one's emotions and will call for development in a variety of aspects of one's emotional life. The challenge here is to manage one's emotions with

6. Goleman, Daniel, Working with Emotional Intelligence, (Bloomsbury, London, 1998), 19 (hereinafter referred to as Goleman, WWEI.)

intelligence. When one does that, one's emotions will have real wisdom and will provide guidance and insight for one's whole life. If one does not manage one's emotions well, then the opposite will be likely to happen.

It would seem that the main emotional abilities or competencies that go to make up EI are the following four: Self-awareness, self-management, awareness of others in relationships and relationship management.[7] These will now be explained in turn.

Self-awareness[8]
There are three elements of self-awareness that call for reflection here.

i) Being in touch with one's emotions:
What is in question here is that one make an effort to respond to the principle enunciated long ago by the Greek philosopher, Socrates: know yourself! Being aware of oneself in the present context means recognising one's feelings as they occur; being in touch with what is going on in one's emotional life from moment to moment. This is emotional self-awareness. In this sense self-awareness is considered to be the keystone of EI, the fundamental emotional competence on which the other emotional abilities are based. As will be made clear shortly this self-awareness means more than self-knowledge. Having good self-awareness brings many benefits and much richness to one's life. A person who is well aware of his/her emotions will tend, other things being equal, to be sure about his/her boundaries, be in good psychological health, have a positive outlook on life, be clear about what feels right for her/him in relation to job opportunities and personal relationships, etc. and be independent in one's approach to life generally.[9]

On the other hand, being out of touch with one's feelings has a major impact of a negative kind on all aspects of one's life. Of course there are degrees of emotional self-awareness but few are

---

7. Goleman, TNL, 37ff; Cosgrave, 45-50; See Rob Yeung, *Emotional Intelligence*, The New Rule Series. (Marshall Cavendish Business, London, 2009, 13-160 (hereinafter referred to as Yeung, EI).
8. Goleman, EI, 43 and chapter 4; ibid., *TNL*, 40-45, 253-254; ibid., *WWEI*, chapter 4; Cosgrave, 46; Yeung, EI, 13-40.
9. Goleman, EI, 54; Cosgrave, 46.

totally lacking it. One who is out of touch with her/his emotions is rendered unable to make decisions and can't use her/his reasoning powers in any adequate way. In addition, one's emotions will tend to escape one's control and may do a lot of damage to relationships and even to oneself. One who completely lacks emotional self-awareness will appear to others as quite emotionally flat or dull, will seem unresponsive to feelings in others, personally remote or unengaged and will find it difficult to develop and maintain any worthwhile personal relationships.[10]

It may be noted here that solving this problem of poor self-awareness will be made more difficult by the fact that a person may be quite unaware of this lack of self-awareness and so will be in no position to tackle it and work towards overcoming it. This can persist for a long time and can even be lifelong, though some may be jolted into awareness by a variety of circumstances, eg. falling in love, a major bereavement, marital breakdown. It may be added that the most telling and important sign of good self-awareness is a tendency for self-reflection and thoughtfulness.[11] The reflective person who regularly looks within is much more likely to be in touch with her/his deeper self - though this is not guaranteed – and so to be more aware of his/her feelings deep down.

In this context it may be mentioned that what are often referred to as gut feelings or intuitions can have a major and positive role in one's judgments and choices in all areas of one's life and especially in regard to one's relationships. These feelings arise from one's store of information and wisdom in one's emotional memory and can have great value. They can provide significant insights that should not be ignored as one decides and chooses. Experience will bear this out, above all in regard to one's judgments or hunches concerning people and their character and qualities. Such hunches are usually intuitive and based on gut feelings. When one is in touch with one's feelings, such hunches or gut feelings are frequently insightful and may well bring one to correct judgments that are right for the person making them.[12]

---

10. Goleman, EI, 54; Cosgrave, 46.
11. Goleman, TNL, 40; ibid., WWEI, chapter four.
12. Goleman, WWEI, 49-54.

ii) Self-knowledge

Self-awareness also involves self-knowledge, i.e. having knowledge about oneself and the sort of person one is, eg. being aware of one's strengths and weaknesses, one's values and principles, one's goals and motives, one's limitations and faults, one's personality and character. If one has arrived at such an accurate self-assessment, that will be of great importance and positive benefit, especially in regard to decision-making about one's direction in life and one's career but also in regard to one's relationships. If one is deficient in self-knowledge, one may well make decisions and take on tasks that may not be very suitable and one may enter relationships and groups that may turn out to be less than positive and enriching. One can, of course, grow in knowledge of oneself, especially by reflecting on one's own experience with its successes and failures and also by listening to feedback from others and indeed by soliciting it. So good self-knowledge as an element of self-awareness and so of EI has major significance for one's progress in life. Its absence can make one's use of one's academic intelligence far less positive and wise than it ought to be.[13]

iii) Self-confidence

This is a reality that arises from or is based on how one feels about oneself. It is an emotional reality that enables one to believe in, to value and to trust oneself. It is considered to be an element of self-awareness because it is essential if one's self-awareness and self-knowledge are to bear fruit in one's life and work as they should. On the other hand, without good self-awareness and good self-knowledge one's self-confidence will very likely be unrealistic, i.e. not based on the true reality that is oneself. Then one may present oneself as feeling confident in one's ability to take on, say, a particular role or task, when in reality one is unsuited for it, a fact of which others may be quite well aware. This is a false self-confidence and may be damaging for oneself and those close at hand. But true realistic self-confidence is a precious gift that enables one to accept and to be oneself, to develop and use one's talents to the full, to make and keep significant relationships, to love self, others and God well

---

13. Goleman, *WWEI*, 61-67.

and to accept love from others, to take initiatives and be assertive in one's dealings with others including authority figures, so that problems won't be pushed under the carpet and justice will be done and be seen to be done.

From all that has been said here under the heading of self-awareness it will be clear that the three elements of being in touch with one's emotions, self-knowledge and self-confidence are rightly considered to be required for genuine emotional self-awareness. These three may be called emotional competencies or abilities that are vital in order that one be truly emotionally intelligent.

Managing one's emotions[14]
The self-awareness that has just been discussed is an essential prerequisite for good management of one's emotions. If one is deficient in that awareness, it will be very difficult to manage and control one's emotions well, since the person will be out of touch with him/herself at the emotional level. If this is the case, one may, for example, be poor at anger and aggression management or be frequently moody and contrary, but (s)he will not be aware of this or at best will be unable to do much about it. In a word, then, awareness precedes control and control requires awareness. Without that awareness it is very likely that our emotions will control us; we'll be at the mercy of our moods and subject to emotional hijack.

Managing one's emotions is a skill that enables one to steer a middle course between the extremes of emotional repression and letting one's emotions run wild. Good management will enable one to experience appropriate emotion in whatever circumstances one finds oneself. This good management may be referred to as integrating one's feelings into one's personality, so as to live a balanced, mature life as far as one's emotions are concerned. This is emotional intelligence in action and it enables one to perform better and more effectively at work and in one's social life and to be a happier person. It may be noted here also that studies have shown that there is little connection between one's IQ level and one's level of EI, i.e. between the degree of one's academic intelligence or 'brains' and one's level of emotional

---

14. Goleman, EI, 43 and chapter 5; Goleman, WWEI, chapter 5; Goleman, TNL, 45-48, 254-255; Cosgrave, 46; Yeung, EI, 41-68.

well being or maturity. The brainiest person around may be emotionally out of control, while the less academically gifted may display a high degree of EI in relation to managing their emotions. So, even an Einstein may be emotionally challenged in this area, while one like the Curé of Ars, who, we are told, was no intellectual luminary, may excel in emotional self-awareness.

Goleman illustrates one aspect of managing one's emotions when he tells the story of the 'marshmallow test'.[15] This test was given to a group of four year olds. These children were told that they could have one marshmallow immediately as part of a test but that, if they waited and didn't eat it till the person conducting the test ran an errand and came back in about fifteen minutes, they could each have two marshmallows. While about one third of the group grabbed the one marshmallow and gobbled it up on the spot, and the rest succeeded in restraining themselves for the fifteen minutes, the really important point was that, when these children were followed up and tested again as adolescents, it was found that those who had resisted impulse and not eaten the first marshmallow immediately were now as adolescents more socially competent, personally effective, self-assertive and better able to cope with the frustrations of life. They could manage stress better and meet challenges more competently, were more confident, trustworthy, capable of taking initiatives and still able to delay gratification in pursuit of their goals. More surprising than this even was the finding that these children were far superior *as students* to those who had acted on whim. In other words, their ability to resist impulse and restrain themselves helped them academically; the ability to delay gratification contributed powerfully to their use of their intellectual potential quite apart from IQ itself.

The basic point here is that resisting impulse is the root of emotional self-control and there is no psychological skill more fundamental than the ability to delay gratification. Restraining one's emotions and delaying one's response to impulse are, then, two of the most essential emotional skills there are and they make a major contribution to one's success in life and to how well one can use one's mental and other capacities.

---

15. EI, 80-83; WWEI, 79-80.

Also presented as elements of emotional self-management are transparency, flexibility, the drive to improve and an optimistic outlook. Transparency refers to being open to others about one's feelings, beliefs and actions. This again is an emotional or psychological ability or skill that is rooted in self-awareness and is guided and kept appropriate by one's competence in managing one's emotions. Flexibility is a psychological ability that is related to the openness just mentioned. It involves openness to change and variable circumstances and facilitates one in overcoming obstacles that one encounters. People who have positive emotions tend to be more flexible in their thinking, in working towards their goals and in their co-operation with others in joint tasks. Such flexibility tends to create a good climate in a group, especially if it is practised by the leader. Rigidity creates stress and damages morale.[16]

The drive to improve and to grow as a person, as a worker, team member or leader is an emotional competence that is essential for any worthwhile achievement. It pushes people to meet their objectives and standards, to set challenging goals and take calculated risks, to find ways to do better and learn how to improve their performance. This drive to achieve is basic to success and is the single most important competence that sets the star apart from the average performer in any area of life. It includes the emotional competence of motivating oneself to undertake the tasks and challenges that one is presented with over time and to deal with the struggles and setbacks that life throws up. This applies in academic matters, in sport, in business and even in prayer.[17]

Finally, in managing one's emotions having an optimistic outlook is a significant help. This too is an emotional skill or competence that will enable one to do better than a person who tends to be pessimistic or negative in her/his outlook. So hope and optimism help people to be successful and to achieve better results in every area of life. An example will help confirm this assertion. A study of insurance salesmen in the US was commissioned to find out why so many of them quit their job and in

16. Goleman, TNL, 83-88; Goleman WWEI, 95-101.
17. Goleman, WWEI, 113-118; Goleman, TNL, 39; Cosgrave, 47-48; Yeung, 7147-8; Yeung, 71-84.

such a short time. The psychologist conducting the study recommended that the company hire people with an optimistic attitude rather than those who had a high IQ as had been the policy. The result was that the optimists sold 37% more insurance in their first two years than the regular salesmen and they quit their job at half the rate of the others. Even those who were lower in IQ than the regulars outsold them by 21% in the first year and by 57% in the second. It is clear then that optimism and hopefulness are emotionally intelligent attitudes that help one significantly in managing one's emotions positively and in a way that brings more success and better results.[18]

Awareness of others

The two elements of EI so far considered are personal to each of us, being concerned with one's self-awareness and one's self-management. Now we move on to consider what EI requires of us if we are to relate to others in a way that is emotionally and hence fully intelligent or rational. As would seem obvious, this emotional skill is, simply, awareness of others. This is the third element of EI that is necessary, if one is to relate well to others and conduct one's relationships in a truly intelligent manner. At the centre of this awareness of others as understood here is empathy. This is the fundamental 'people skill', as Goleman says,[19] meaning that it is the basic virtue or competence that is needed in order for one to make and keep good relationships with other people. Essentially, empathy means being attuned or sensitive to the feelings of others and so being able to read how others are feeling in whatever situation you are in. Of course how empathic one is depends on how much one is in touch with one's own emotions. The more open and attuned one is to what one is feeling, the more skilled one will be in sensing how others are feeling. And the converse, not surprisingly, holds too: the more out of touch one is with one's own feelings, the less empathic one will or can be. And as we have seen, such deafness to the feelings of others is a major lack or deficit in the EI that is our concern here.[20]

---

18. Goleman, EI, 87-90; Goleman, WWEI, 124-9; Cosgrave, 48.
19. Goleman, EI, 43.
20. Goleman, EI, 96.

Given the nature of empathy as here outlined, it is not difficult to understand that possessing empathy in any reasonable degree provides one with the foundation for being a caring person. Empathy is the root of caring. The degree to which one can empathise with another or others is the degree to which one can care for that person or persons. And if you lack empathy, you won't be able to care for the other at all. The extreme example of this lack of empathy is the psychopath (or sociopath). (S)he is not lacking in knowledge or intellectual ability. What (s)he does lack, however, is empathy and as a result (s)he will be insensitive to the feelings and viewpoints of others. Because of this emotional deficit, such a person can inflict pain or hurt on another without being at all aware of or caring about doing so. (S)he can act cruelly or even brutally in relation to another and yet feel no revulsion or twinge of conscience, since (s)he is emotionally quite deaf to the impact of his/her actions on the other person or persons.[21]

There are many less extreme instances of lack of empathy that could be mentioned. One could imagine a preacher who regularly gives homilies or sermons but is so much out of touch with his/her own inner feelings that he/she fails to connect with the interests, concerns and difficulties of his/her congregation as they struggle to remain strong in their faith in an increasingly secular society. Or a lecturer who is so much out of touch with his/her own emotional life and hence with that of the audience that (s)he speaks continually in a bookish, theoretical, abstract manner that does not resonate at all with where his/her listeners are at and so fails to provide them with any intellectual nourishment or stimulation, even though the lecturer may have given a learned discourse based on extensive research. (I am reminded here of the oft repeated statement, almost a mantra, of the late Fr J. G. McGarry, founder of *The Furrow*, in our pastoral theology class in Maynooth in the 1960s: to get them where you want them you must reach them where they are.) Or again one can think of a husband who is so caught up with advancing his career and other external things to the neglect of his inner feelings that he fails notably to tune into the concerns, distress and

---

21. Cosgrave, 48; Goleman, EI, 106-110; Goleman, *Social Intelligence: The New Science of Human Relationships* (Hutchinson, London, 2006), 127-129; henceforth referred to as Goleman, SI.

even anger of his wife who is exhausted from the ceaseless demands of being wife, mother and homemaker alongside her job in the workplace.

It may be noted that in our western society at least women generally are better than men at the empathy being discussed here. They would seem to be better listeners and also better at sharing their own deeper feelings than their male counterparts. As a result they will likely develop more nourishing personal relationships and friendships, may well enjoy a more vibrant and extensive social life and be emotionally healthier people.

It has been mentioned that empathy is the root of caring for another; it is the emotional competence or skill that enables one to recognise the feelings and needs of others and to take steps to respond to them. This point leads to another very important insight. Caring for others is basic in the moral life of all of us. The more we care for others the more moral we will be. Indeed caring for others is the essence of being moral just as not caring is what makes one really immoral. It follows then that empathy is essential to truly moral living. The more empathic one is and hence the more caring one is, the more moral one is likely to be, while of course the converse holds also. Clearly, then, this element of EI plays a big part in the kind of moral life one leads, i.e. in the sort of man or woman one has become and is as a person. Thus one must say that the foundation of good moral living is to be found in empathy.

Here we find a clear link between one's emotional life and one's moral life: the more emotionally skilled or mature one is in this area, the more moral one is likely to be and vice versa. One's level of emotional growth will have a direct impact on one's level of moral maturity. This will be particularly true in regard to caring for others, justice, fairness and providing for the most needy in society.

It follows also that being emotionally literate and mature will be necessary elements in intelligent human living. To be truly intelligent requires more than high academic abilities. One must also be intelligent or adult in relation to one's emotions. This is intelligence in the full sense, intellectual and emotional. Then one will possess EI and be rational or have rationality to the degree necessary to live human life as it should be lived.

Managing relationships well[22]

The three elements of EI that have been discussed in the previous pages come together in or provide the necessary foundation for this final element. Without some real ability in these three elements it is highly unlikely that one will be successful in managing one's relationships well. In fact it will be very probable that one will perform poorly. But if we manage these relationships well that will yield notable benefits: it will improve their quality and enrich our social life and that of others and bring one fuller happiness. So, assuming one has some reasonable ability in each of the first three elements of EI, we may move on to discuss this fourth and final element.

Goleman says that managing relationships skilfully boils down to handling other people's emotions.[23] This is the fine art of relationships and as experience teaches, it is one of the most important arts or skills in human life but also one of the most difficult to practise consistently. The person who is a star in this art will have many warm and nourishing relationships and will very likely be a mature and happy person. Incompetence in this art will probably result in some real degree of social isolation and even unhappiness.

i) Authenticity

The first requirement of this social skill is emotional authenticity or integrity.[24] This means acting and speaking from one's genuine feelings or, as Shakespeare put it, it is imperative that you 'to thine own self be true'. In other words, one must act and speak in accord with one's real and deep feelings and values. This will require you to avoid doing or saying what is designed merely to get people to like you. To do that would be emotionally dishonest and involve sacrificing one's personal integrity to the desire to impress.[25] That way lies inauthenticity and very likely failure in the art of relationship.

---

22. Goleman, EI, 43-44, and chapter 8; SI, 84, 91-100; Goleman, TNL, 51-52
23. Goleman, TNL, 51; Goleman, EI, 112.
24. Goleman, TNL, 51-52; Goleman, EI, 119-120.
25. Goleman, EI, 119-20.

ii) Listening

Essential also to the art of good relationship is the ability to listen well to another so as to hear what is being said and what is not being said, to pay attention to ideas and attitudes but also and especially to the feelings being expressed or implied. Most of us know the importance of attentive listening, though great numbers of us, especially men, are often far from good at practising it at whatever level it is required or appropriate in a particular relationship. Basic to the art of listening is the ability to read accurately and respond appropriately to the non-verbal cues that are part of every interaction with another person. This will occur instinctively – if one has this emotional skill – and will ensure a smooth and harmonious relationship as one synchronises one's responses with the other person's expressions of attitudes, values and feelings. The responses in question here are such things as smiling, nodding, inclining oneself towards the other and various verbal expressions that indicate that one is attuned to what the other is saying and feeling. If one is doing this successfully, one will feel the dialogue is going well and the other will feel you are on his/her wavelength emotionally. This is emotional rapport and it reflects the depth of engagement between the persons involved. If, however, synchrony is not achieved here, there will be emotional dissonance and the interaction will not go smoothly, even if one who lacks the emotional skill in question here fails to notice this.[26]

iii) Concern

Another element essential in managing relationships well is the extension of empathy into action or concrete assistance. This may be referred to as concern. Concerned people are those most willing to take time and make the effort to help out someone who needs that help. Not everyone who is concerned actually does something to help but such concern provides a strong incentive to care for the other in concrete ways.[27]

iv) Assertiveness

It will be important also in relationships to exercise the emotional skill often referred to nowadays as assertiveness. This

26. Goleman, SI, 91-2; Goleman, EI, 114-117.
27. Goleman, SI, 96-97.

combines empathy, self-control and an awareness of what is emotionally appropriate in the situation. Hence, it calls one to avoid aggressiveness, on the one hand, and excessive reticence to express oneself emotionally and make one's point, on the other. Employing this skill artfully enables one to exert maximum influence on the interaction taking place with the other person. People who can exhibit this ability to be assertive are usually viewed by others as confident and at the same time likeable. In general, the appropriately assertive person makes a favourable and usually an influential impression.[28]

EMOTIONAL INTELLIGENCE IN PARTICULAR AREAS OF LIFE

One can easily see that EI as described above will and should have deep and extensive effects in and on our daily lives. And, of course, so will its absence. It will be helpful and instructive to look now at some particular areas of our daily lives to see how emotionally intelligent living would impact on them and what changes it would require us to make so as to ensure the insights of EI are put into practice in these areas. Five areas will be looked at and an attempt made to spell out what emotionally intelligent living in each area would look like and involve.

Emotional intelligence and health[29]

It is now clear from various studies that strong distressing emotions and especially anger, anxiety and depression can have serious negative effects on one's medical condition or state of health. Like smoking or high cholesterol these emotions can pose a major threat to health. Anger is an emotion that, above all others, can do serious damage to one's heart. Since being angry increases one's heart rate and blood pressure, a lot of damage can be done to one's heart when such increases are repeated over and over again by a person who is frequently or even habitually angry. Anger is particularly lethal in those who already have heart disease and if anger becomes chronic, then it is at its most dangerous. Luckily one can reduce one's levels of anger and so lessen the damage to one's heart. Stress or anxiety is another emotion that is toxic for one's health. It can weaken one's

28. Goleman, SI, 94-96.
29. See Cosgrave, 51-52.

immune system, i.e. lower one's resistance to infection, and so increase one's chances of getting a variety of diseases, e.g. colds, flu, asthma, ulcers, diabetes, etc. The stress or strain that goes with high powered jobs and high pressure performance in the workplace is included here, so that one's job can take its toll on one's health. Depression, it is becoming clear, can also inflict damage on one's health, because it tends to make one's sickness worse and one's recovery more difficult.

Toxic, ie. negative or emotionally distressing, relationships are a major risk factor for disease and death; when such relationships continue over many years, they can speed the onset of disease or worsen its symptoms.[30] Also studies show that people in lower positions in an organisation are four times more likely to develop cardiovascular disease than those on the top rungs, because of the whims of those very top rung people. Unfair criticism by the boss is very stressful too and can increase one's chances of heart disease.[31] Of all the sorts of stress the worst by far is when someone is the target of harsh criticism and is helpless to do anything about it.[32]

Another example of one's emotions damaging one's health is when one is hurt and enraged by some offence one has suffered like an insult or a physical assault but one holds on to one's feelings of anger, rage, bitterness and even buries them. Such buried feelings retain their energy and power and can give rise to physical symptoms like skin disease, fever, ulcers, heart problems or even cancer. It has been found, especially in the Charismatic Movement, that letting go of these deep feelings often causes the physical symptoms to disappear and one is then cured. This is understandable, since holding on to the strong feelings was what caused the symptoms in the first place.[33]

The other side of this medical coin is that positive emotions can improve one's state of health at least to some degree, e.g. an optimistic outlook, hope for recovery, having friends to share one's deep feelings with and to support one in an illness can all have a positive influence on one's health. Goleman says that,

---

30. Goleman, SI, 224, 226.
31. Goleman, SI, 227.
32. Goleman, SI, 230; See SI, chapters 16-18.
33. Cosgrave, 'To Repent and Forgive', The Furrow, February 2005, 90; also below, chapter 10.

the feeling that the people in one's life are emotionally supportive has a positive health impact; socially integrated people – those who are married, have close family and friends – belong to social and religious groups, and participate widely in these networks – recover more quickly from disease and live longer.[34]

In short then attending to emotional needs is medically very beneficial and medical care that neglects how people feel is no longer adequate.[35] Medical care must be given with compassion.[36]

Emotional Intelligence in the workplace
While EI as applied to any area of life is relatively new, some might say that to imagine that it could be applied with benefit to the workplace would be a recipe for chaos and likely to have an adverse impact on worker effectiveness, management-worker relationships, decision-making, production and the financial welfare of the company or firm.

This has not, however, been borne out in the places, mostly in the US, where an EI approach has been adopted and put into practice in particular companies. On the contrary, it has become clear that the most effective workers in the workplace and especially the stars are those who are highest, not in IQ or technical expertise, but in the EI competencies that are relevant to and important on the job. Of course IQ and expertise are necessary and of great value but EI and its skills play a bigger part in achieving success at work. 'IQ takes second position to emotional intelligence in determining outstanding job performance', says Goleman and he adds, 'It is the emotional intelligence abilities that matter more for superior performance'.[37] As noted earlier, IQ alone explains surprisingly little of achievement at work or in life. The highest estimate of how much difference IQ accounts for is about 25% and it may be much lower.[38]

The question then is: what are the EI competencies that are so

---

34. SI, 247.
35. Goleman, EI, 164-285.
36. See Goleman, SI, 254.
37. WWEI, 5 and 19.
38. Goleman, WWEI, 19.

important and indeed decisive for success in the workplace? Most of them have been mentioned already in our discussion of EI itself and its elements: self-awareness, managing one's emotions, empathy and managing relationships. Some specific skills in the EI area that have particular relevance on the job may be adverted to here.[39]

i) Dedication to customer service[40]

This is fairly obvious but it involves more in an EI understanding of it that might appear at first sight. One must not have the attitude that the one and only thing (s)he is there for is to make sales at every available opportunity, in other words, to make as much money for the company as possible. This approach is company-orientated, not customer-centred and is likely to lead more often than not to customers feeling that their real needs were not adequately met, since they may well have felt pushed to purchase something that wasn't fully right for them. The emotionally intelligent attitude to one's customers is to seek to identify their real needs and to do all one can to meet them, even if this means not making a sale. Then the salesperson functions as the customer's or client's advocate or advisor. Sometimes this might even involve recommending the products of a rival as more suitable for the specific needs of the particular customer at this precise time. Thus the salesperson takes the long term view, seeks to please the customer and so, to preserve the relationship into the future. Such a service-oriented approach will normally be conducted in a tone that is emotionally friendly and this will very likely result in the customer feeling good, not just about the service but also about the company or store.

ii) Building good working relationships

What has been said earlier about managing relationships is, of course, relevant here but a few other points need to be added. Relationships are the key to doing business, says Goleman, and the building and maintenance of networks are crucial for success.[41] This applies within a firm or company, since such

---

39. See Goleman, WWEI, chapters 7-9; EI, chapter 10; Yeung, EI, 147-160.
40. Goleman, WWEI, 151-154.
41. WWEI, 207; see also EI, 159-163.

relationships and networks provide the worker with support and information. In addition, networking, especially with key figures, will help build up a reservoir of goodwill and trust, and so can be valuable in relation to difficult choices or negotiations and even one's promotion prospects. The same holds in regard to inter-company collaboration, since it too can produce concrete benefits for both companies.[42]

iii) Managing conflict

Disagreements leading to tension and potentially explosive situations occur in the workplace with some regularity. 'Those who can resolve conflict and head off trouble are the kind of peacemakers vital in any organisation.'[43] In such situations one has to negotiate the conflict so as to resolve it. This will require a move away from aggression and threats to an effort to preserve the relationship between the individuals or groups or even companies. Here EI competencies are necessary. Being a person who is emotionally intelligent can be a great help in spotting the brewing storm and taking steps to diffuse it. Here good listening and empathising along with tact are what are needed. Goleman summarises the steps that must be taken to achieve a successful negotiation:

- calm down, tune into your feelings and express them;
- show a willingness to work things out by talking over the issue rather than escalating it with more aggression;
- state your point of view in neutral language rather than an argumentative tone;
- try to find equitable ways to resolve the dispute working together to find a resolution both sides can embrace.

This indicates that what is needed to resolve conflict is empathy along with an assertive attitude that faces the issue but also listens and seeks to achieve a mutually acceptable compromise. This is, of course, far from easy and requires other EI competencies or skills like self-awareness, self-confidence and self-control.[44]

---

42. Goleman, WWEI, 210-211.
43. Goleman, WWEI, 180.
44. Goleman, WWEI, 182-183; also EI, 263-269.

Emotional Intelligence and leadership[45]

It will come as no surprise that the level of one's emotional competence or integration will be of great significance in relation to how successful those in leadership positions will or can be. Since one's emotional maturity is vital for making and managing human relationships of all sorts, one who is deficient in this area will have a very uphill job indeed in the task of being a good leader, whether that is in business, in government, in sport, in the Christian ministry or any other area of life.

We have often heard it said that leadership demands one's head not one's heart. Studies in recent years have shown, however, that this view is outmoded and indeed counter-productive. In this area too intelligence needs to be understood in its wider sense and, hence, a leader needs to attend to and be competent in the areas of emotional intelligence already discussed, if he/she is to be successful as a leader. This is easily illustrated. If a leader is given to angry outbursts or is quite insensitive to the feelings of those around him/her, then clearly, those under his/her leadership will be upset, probably fearful and distracted and will function much less well than they otherwise would. If a leader is unpredictable and given to mood swings, then too those around him/her suffer and so will his/her effectiveness as a leader. Even if such a leader sees leadership as domination and getting his/her own way, it is unlikely that that way will always be very balanced or that the decisions he/she makes will be the best for the enterprise in question even most of the time. In addition, this leader's staff and co-workers will suffer great stress and will probably function very ineffectively. In other areas of leadership too how one deals as leader with the people around will be crucial. The giving and receiving of criticism is one such area. If criticism is delivered in a harsh or angry or sarcastic manner and as almost a personal attack on the one to whom it is directed, then that will have serious effects on motivation, energy, confidence and cooperation and great damage will have been done not just to the one criticised but to the relationship with the leader and so to the part the one criticised will in future play in the enterprise or group. Inept criticism is the

---

45. See Cosgrave, 50-1.

number one cause of conflict in the workplace, says Goleman *et al.*[46] Bias or discrimination by the leader on any grounds will also tend to have profoundly negative effects.

Such dissonant leaders tend to be out of touch with the feelings of those under their leadership. This tends to give rise to feelings from frustration to resentment, from rancour to rage. This will very likely affect the atmosphere or climate of the whole firm or group, since studies have found that 50% to 70% of how employees perceive their organisation's climate can be traced to the leader.[47]

On the positive side the leader's main function is to generate excitement, optimism and passion for the job ahead as well as to create an atmosphere of co-operation and trust. EI is clearly needed to accomplish these tasks and in particular the four core elements of it that were discussed earlier.[48]

While the EI skills needed for good leadership can be learned in and by a demanding process of formation and growth (see Goleman, TNL, chapters 6 through 8), leaders are often not helped by the absence of constructive feedback about their performance as leaders. This arises from the natural instinct to please the boss and it often results in a widespread tendency to give positive feedback and withhold the negative.[49]

Emotional Intelligence and personal morality[50]
There is a negative and positive side to the ways in which one's level of emotional well being can affect one's morality.

If one is emotionally immature or unintelligent, then the level of that person's moral maturity will be affected in a negative way. For example, one who is prone to angry outbursts or fits of jealousy will very likely not have a great deal of self-control in these areas and so may well get into conflict and damage his/her relationships with others by selfish and aggressive behaviour. One who is deficient in empathy will tend to be insensitive to the needs and difficulties of others and so will probably be limited and even at fault in regard to care, compassion and

---

46. *TNL*, 22.
47. Goleman, *TNL*, 18.
48. See Goleman, *TNL*, chapter 3.
49. Goleman, *TNL*, 92-6.
50. See Cosgrave, 52-53.

altruism. A person who has poor impulse control will tend to act to satisfy his/her own needs or wants, ignoring the impact this may have on others. Thus he/she may act selfishly. It can be seen, then, that emotional immaturity is closely linked to and may well be the cause of moral immaturity.

On the positive side a similar close link between the emotional and the moral can be seen. As has been noted, one's level of empathy has a strong connection with one's level of caring, compassion and altruism, so that, the more empathic one is, the more one displays these morally positive attitudes towards others. Similarly, if one has learned to manage one's anger well, he/she will be a person who practises the virtue of meekness to a high degree. And if one has acquired the ability to make and manage personal relationships maturely or intelligently, then he/she will be one who loves others maturely and competently. It will be obvious too that being able to motivate oneself will be vitally important in regard to fulfilling one's duties, especially those one finds it hard to warm to, and in persisting in one's efforts despite failure and difficulties. Delaying gratification and disciplining oneself also have major moral implications in relation to our moral choices, behaviour, character building and moral development.

Vacek confirms and deepens this close connection between our moral life and our emotional life. He says,

> Emotions are necessary both in grounding ethics and in making moral decisions; without our emotions we would not experience objects to have any value, e.g. the value of persons ... they are essential for morally discerning what we should do and how we should be ... emotions are needed in order to 'know' the values at stake in any particular moral decision.[51]

A brief quotation from the previous chapter will bring out another point about the vital role our emotions play in what we do morally.

> One of the most important things about our emotions is that they enable us to commit ourselves to value and

---

51. Vacek, 72, 74, 81.

especially to persons, and to reject or refuse commitment to what we perceive as disvalues or evils in relation to persons. If we had no feelings, we'd be unable to commit ourselves to anyone or anything. We would be quite incapable of caring, empathising, loving – or hating, for that matter. In a word, commitments and especially moral commitments are a matter of the heart.[52]

In short then, it can be safely stated that being emotionally intelligent has great significance for one's moral life and one's level of moral intelligence or maturity, so much so in fact that it is obvious that we have a real duty to do all possible to reach emotional maturity, in order that we may then live a morally mature or intelligent life, whether we are Christians or not.[53]

Emotional Intelligence and social and global morality
Critics have commented that recent writing on EI confines itself to issues concerning the individual person and his / her personal development and to that person in one-to-one relationships or at most in small groups like the workplace, the school or the family. There is no reference, the critics say, to wider issues in society, much less global matters that are today the concern of citizens everywhere. Hence, it is said, that EI is presented in an individualistic manner, focusing on the micro-world of the individual to the neglect of the macro-world of particular societies and cultures and the wider international and global scenes.

It has to be admitted that there is validity in this criticism and efforts need to be made to fill this important gap. Here in relation to this very undeveloped area of EI some pointers are all that can be given as to how EI considerations might illuminate and enrich particular areas of life in individual societies and in the global village to which we all now belong.

i) Social and international justice
One of the main concerns of EI is to improve the relationships between people in various settings and situations. This is

---

52. Chapter I, 14.
53. See Goleman, EI, 104, 285-286; William Spohn SJ, 'Principles and Passions', *Theological Studies*, USA, March 1991, 69, 87; G. Simon Harak SJ, *Virtuous Passions: The Foundation of Christian Character* (New York, Paulist Press, 1993), chapters 4-6.

obvious from all that has been written in the previous sections of this study. It needs no great insight to understand that, if the abilities or skills of EI that have been shown to be vital to personal relationships, in the workplace and in leadership were to be acquired by those involved in political, economic or cultural conflicts and negotiations and were put to use in those circumstances, then there would be many more satisfactorily resolved disagreements and peaceful resolutions of potentially damaging and even explosive situations at regional, national and international levels. In other words, EI competencies are, as has been noted, very necessary and valuable in the work of resolving conflicts of all kinds and so in making peace in society and internationally. Thus EI can contribute significantly to the task of promoting justice and peace between ethnic groups and nations by providing instruments or tools that have the potential to improve relationships, facilitate negotiations and thus smooth the path to greater mutual respect and harmonious living.

ii) Option for the Poor

The Catholic Church, borrowing from liberation theology, teaches that all Catholics are called to make and live out the preferential option or love for the poor.[54] It is not too hard to see that, if one has true empathy and concern, then one will be likely to look sympathetically on those who are poor and contribute at least to charity for them or even undertake some work of justice that will result in bettering the situation of those living in poverty, whether at home or abroad. This will be more likely to happen, if one has developed the EI abilities of self-confidence, the drive to achieve one's goals and a commitment to be of service to others in whatever ways they need.

iii) Environmental issues

Here too one can see ways in which EI competencies can contribute to a commitment to care for the earth and protect and even enhance the environment. For all of us and especially the Christian it is again empathy and the call to care that urge us to become friends of the earth. Christians have an added incentive in that church teaching

---

54. Pontifical Council for Justice and Peace, *Compendium of Social Doctrine of the Catholic Church* (Libreria Vaticana, 2004), n 182.
55. Ibid., 461-467.

reminds us that we have the capacity to transform and in a sense create or at least co-create the world through our work and also a responsibility to promote a sound and healthy environment for the benefit of all. In these ways we show respect for the common good.[55]

The EI skills referred to just now in regard to the option for the poor will be relevant here too as will be the EI relationship skills that enable one to elicit desirable responses in and from others, namely, being able to influence and persuade, good communication, initiating change, inspiring and guiding others, nurturing good working relationships, promoting good collaboration and teamwork.[56]

CONCLUSION

Over the course of this chapter our rather lengthy discussion of EI, its central elements and its impact on a variety of particular areas in our daily lives will have alerted the reader to the fundamental meaning and significance of EI in and for our lives as human beings and as Christians. Though reflection on EI is relatively new and unfamiliar to many, it is clearly of basic importance for our own personal development, the quality of our relationships with others, our participation in small groups and even our role in society itself. The fundamental point being made in our study is that, unlike what many of us learned earlier in our lives, our emotions have an indispensable role to play in the above mentioned aspects of human living. It is true to say, as noted earlier, that, when maturely integrated and wisely exercised, they have real wisdom and they guide our thinking, our valuing and our decision-making. As Vacek says,[57] they are indispensable apprehensions of moral reality, ie. they are essential for us in order that we recognise and appreciate the moral dimension of our lives and actions. In consequence our emotions make an essential and basic contribution to truly intelligent human and moral living. Hence, we must constantly educate and cultivate our emotional life.[58] EI is thus an element of human rationality that in many ways and areas of life matters very significantly and often even more that IQ.

55. Ibid., 461-467.
56. Goleman, WWEI, 27 and chapters 8-9.
57. Vacek, 68.
58. Vacek, 94.

Understanding and Managing Anger

From what has been said in the two previous chapters it will be clear that we now understand the psychology of our emotional life much better than in the past. In addition, the renewal of moral theology, especially since Vatican II (1962-5), has provided significant new insights into the moral life and, in particular, into moral responsibility. In the light of all this renewal and development one may now venture to present a renewed understanding of anger, outline how best to manage it and how it should be assessed morally. This is what the present chapter endeavours to do.

A look at the past

In the past our thinking in relation to the emotions generally and anger in particular tended to be negative and dualistic. It was based largely on the idea that reason and the emotions or passions, as they were called, were at war and the task of the Christian was to subject the passions to the control of reason. This dualism led to a negative view of the emotions as a threat to one's moral and spiritual life and also to anti-body and anti-feminine attitudes and practices. As a result there developed what may be called an ascetical or penitential approach to the emotions and the body, namely, rigid control with stern mortification of the senses and unremitting self-denial, especially in regard to sexual feelings and fantasies.[1]

In this context anger was seen as one of the seven capital (or deadly) sins, a vice that could give rise to a variety of sins. Anger, more than any other passion, blinds one's reason, it was said, and leads to grave moral disorders. So, one is obliged to repress the passionate impulse of anger, if it is inordinate, or moderate it, if it is too impetuous. But anger can be righteous as in the case of Jesus (John 2:13). Meekness (in the sense of modest or moderate) is the virtue contrary to anger. It permits anger only

---

1. Cosgrave, William, *Christian Living Today: Essays in Moral and Pastoral Theology*, Columba Press, Dublin, 2001, 42.

to the extent necessary and proper, e.g. to resist the invasion of people's rights or to defend cherished objects. This is based on the scriptural injunction: 'Be angry and sin not' (Eph 4:26).[2]

Understanding the emotions today[3]

An emotion, as the word indicates, is a feeling that tends to move one out of oneself. It is an impulse to act and usually brings bodily changes with it like the release of adrenaline, etc. So, our emotions are powerful forces within us providing us with psychic energy for action. They can ignite our best behaviours, eg. love, courage, hope, but also impel us to our worst excesses, eg. violence, abuse, guilt.[4]

Eugene Kennedy says:

> If a man wants to understand himself … his emotions tell him … the kind of person he is … Beneath his feelings lies the real man or woman with all the facades and pretences stripped away.[5]

One can, however, repress or deny one's emotions, that is, one buries their energy within. But that only leads to that energy surfacing later in a variety of forms that will likely be unhealthy, emotionally and/or physically, as will be noted later.

Note too that there are no 'mere' feelings. One's feelings contain a cognitive element that gives one insight into a situation, making one aware of some threat or injustice or joy. They also provide one with an initial assessment of each situation, perhaps by generating guilt or anger or peace. Reason then comes in to confirm or modify or reject this moral judgment. Clearly, then, emotion and reason are not opposed to each other. In fact when one is emotionally mature, one's emotions provide one with a

---

2. Davis, Henry SJ, *Moral and Pastoral Theology*, vol 1, Sheed and Ward, London, 1938, 236, 142-3, 268; Palazzini, Pietro, Editor, *Dictionary of Moral Theology*, compiled under the direction of HE Cardinal Roberti, Prefect of the Supreme Tribunal of the Apostlic Signatura, London, Burns and Oates, 1962, 72, 776.
3. See chapter 1 above for a fuller account of the emotions.
4. Whitehead, James and Whitehead, Evelyn Eaton, *Shadows of the Heart: Spirituality and the Painful Emotions*, A Crossroad Book, Crossroad, NY, 1996, 3.
5. Kennedy, Eugene, The Pain of Being Human, Image Books, Doubleday, NY, 1974, 47.

wisdom that will guide one's thinking, valuing and decision-making. One's emotions also enable one to appreciate values, moral and non-moral, and supply one with the energy and motivation to pursue those values and realise them in one's daily life.

It can be seen, then, that if one's life is to be fruitful and happy, one must come to grips with one's emotions, befriend them even,[6] and promote all possible emotional growth. This will give one the foundation for moral growth as one struggles to attain moral maturity. This more positive view of our emotions will here shape our approach to and understanding of anger and, in particular, its moral dimension.

A contemporary understanding of anger

Everyone knows from experience what it is to be angry. Anger is one of the most commonly experienced emotions there is but at the same time it is likely the most poorly handled emotion in our experience both personally and socially. Part of this difficulty in handling anger would seem to derive from our poor understanding of it and its dynamics.[7] This lack tends to give rise to problems in our relationships, in our dealings with others in society and, perhaps most importantly of all, in our own emotional and moral lives. All this has led to anger getting an undeserved negative reputation at both the emotional and moral levels.

In the light of the more positive understanding of the emotions generally that has been summarised above and with the help of a more enlightened view of anger itself in contemporary thinking, a more psychologically healthy and a more adequate moral picture of the emotion of anger may here be attempted.

(a) Anger: energy for action

If we reflect on our experience of anger, it will quickly be apparent that, when one is angry, one is aroused emotionally and even physically. One is energised by one's anger and ready to go into action to address the issue that is making one angry. Thus anger provides us with energy to do something about the situation we find ourselves in.

---

6. Whitehead and Whitehead, chapter 2.
7. Sofield, Br Loughlan ST, Juliano, Sr Carroll, SHGT, and Hammett, Sr Rosine, CSC, *Design for Wholeness: Dealing with Anger, Learning to Forgive, Building Self Esteem* (Ave Maria, Indiana, 1990), 17-18.

(b) Triggers for anger

Experts tell us that there are four main triggers or stimuli that can lead to one getting angry. These are the following:

i) Frustration of a need or a want, e.g. missing a bus or a train, being blocked in completing some project or task that one is absorbed in.

ii) Suffering some injustice or noticing others being unjustly treated, e.g. being passed over for promotion, having precious property stolen, seeing the weak being exploited by the powerful.

iii) Experiencing a threat to one's self-esteem, e.g. being insulted, being considered a failure, having one's good name impugned.

iv) Being injured physically, e.g. being assaulted, or being injured by a drunken driver.[8]

It is important to note, however, that in a real sense anger is in the eye or mind of the beholder, that is, the one who is angry. Situations or triggers themselves don't cause one to be angry. It is how one sees the situation that may lead one person to fly into a rage, while another may remain quite calm or be only mildly annoyed. So, it is one's beliefs about anger and about oneself and others too that help explain such different responses to the one situation. For example, if one believes that one should not be angry with one's parent or teacher or church leader, one may suppress one's anger, while others may be fuming in the same set of circumstances; if one is low in self-esteem, one may perceive an insult or put down where others see a sensible comment or even a joke; if one is not interested in the poverty of the Third World, one may not even notice an injustice perpetrated by the rich West on the poor in Africa, while others will be filled with anger over the exploitation involved. Hence, it is one's perceptions of situations and circumstances that cause one to be angry and these perceptions are influenced profoundly by one's beliefs and attitudes. It may, then, be necessary to examine and perhaps change these beliefs and attitudes, if one is to integrate one's anger in a mature way.[9]

8. Solfield, Juliana and Hammett, 25-29.
9. Solfield, Juliana and Hammett, 25-29.

(c) The positive role of anger in life

Most of us are so accustomed to thinking of anger as a problem that we find it hard to imagine it could have a positive purpose or role in our lives. But it has and it can be a source of much good in both our personal and social relationships. If one calls to mind a person who has repressed his/her anger or regularly suppresses it consciously out of fear or whatever, it is likely one will find that such a person is meek and mild, lacks strength and initiative and tends to be passive in most circumstances. He or she will tend to lack energy for action and may appear as generally rather lifeless.

Now this gives us a fair picture of what a personality and lifestyle without the energy of anger might look like. Obviously something important is missing here at the emotional level. As a result the moral quality of this person's life will very likely also be less than vibrant and may be characterised more by an absence of major faults than by the presence of notable virtues and good works.

Anger is absolutely necessary for mature human relationships. It provides energy for initiatives and courageous action in our relationships, especially in defending oneself and one's values, facing difficulties and disagreements and expressing one's viewpoint so as to be open and honest and to clear the air in one's close relationships.[10] Anger comes to our assistance also when we encounter frustration in some project we have embarked on or when some need we have is left unmet because of certain obstacles. Here one's anger will provide a spur to overcome the obstacles or work around them. The energy and power of anger are at work also when one is enraged by social injustice and takes moral action for justice and social change, e.g. in relation to unfair work conditions, to exploitation of the poor and weak or when one is unfairly treated.[11]

It will be clear from these points and examples that anger plays a significant role in many areas of our lives and in a potentially very constructive and indeed necessary way. It can be said, then, that anger conduces to virtuous activity and attitudes

10. Padovani, Martin H., *Healing Wounded Emotions: Overcoming Life's Hurts*, Twenty-Third Publications, Mystic, CT, 1991, 28; Whitehead, 45-6.
11. Whitehead and Whitehead, 49-52.

over wide expanses of our lives and, hence, provides the matter and the energy for our practice of the virtue of meekness (or assertiveness). This is a righteous or responsible use of anger and its power and, when done well, shows an emotional and moral maturity that everyone should desire and work towards.

All this demonstrates that having a capacity for righteous or morally responsible anger is a sign that one is committed to significant values, that one cares about oneself, others and society and that one can be motivated to commit oneself to action for justice, love and other values and virtues in a variety of circumstances. Conversely, if one has little or no capacity for anger of this kind, then, that will probably be an indication that one will have little or no capacity for commitment to issues of love, justice and other values. Without the energy of anger one will find it hard to become motivated to engage in action for any of these values. Hence, the presence of such anger provides an opportunity for virtuous activity, while its absence all but removes that opportunity. As Häring says, 'Anyone who is incapable of anger cannot be dynamic in his love.'[12]

In this context it is appropriate to speak of anger, not as a virtue (or vice), but as providing the energy and power for attitudes and actions that will be virtuous (or vicious). Anger is not, then, a moral reality in itself but the attitudes and actions it prompts will be. It remains in itself an emotion that has no morality but it is conducive to moral attitudes and actions and facilitates them. Hence, it can play a very positive part in human life that we need to appreciate and do our best to realise in practice.

Anger in the lives of men and women
Psychologists report few consistent differences between men and women in relation to anger. Research lends little support to the notion that women are less prone to anger than men. As a group women tend to get angry for the same reasons as men and they show their anger in roughly the same ways. But studies have found that men are more likely to express anger publicly and many women report being moved to tears by their anger. These gender differences are rooted in power differences.

12. Häring, Bernard CSsR, *The Law of Christ: Moral Theology for Priests and Laity*, Vol 1, Mercier Press, 1961, 377.

When a man speaks in anger, it is often seen as expressing passionate commitment to a cause. When a woman does the same, it tends to undermine her credibility. This is because women are still a subordinate group in our society where men are dominant and, so, the social rules for the expression of feminine anger are more restrictive than those for male anger. In fact women tend to internalise these social restrictions and, consequently, inhibit their own expressions of anger lest such anger make men less supportive or even hostile.

Nowadays, however, many women are moving beyond this conventional response to society's restrictions on them and are tending towards an angry rejection of what more and more they see as unjust social structures, practices and attitudes. This is the first step in the process of working towards social change that will recognise and realise women's equality with men more fully in society. Women have lots to be angry about as the realities of sexism and patriarchy continue to oppress them. Many women today realise that they may even have colluded with this male dominated society up to now but for the future they are focusing their anger on the injustices they have become aware of and are doing all they can to bring about their liberation in a society where women's equality with men is not yet fully acknowledged and realised.[13] The same may be said of the Catholic Church and, hence, one finds many Catholic women experiencing anger at the structures of the church which tend to exclude them and also at the leaders of the church who show few signs of taking action to bring about full equality for women in practice in the church.

Promoting growth in relation to anger
What has been said above about the positive role of anger in life represents something of an ideal. The reality of most of our lives is probably quite a bit different. Most of us fall short of this ideal, sometimes by a fairly significant margin and not infrequently with a disturbing regularity.

Many people have the experience of losing their temper and perhaps lashing out at one or more people around, whether in one's family, circle of friends or the work place. These emotional

---

13. Whitehead and Whitehead, chapter 5.

hijacks, as some call them, can often involve one in destructive behaviour, verbal and/or physical, as many know to their cost.

Here one is not managing one's anger well, much less integrating it into one's personality and character for constructive purposes. And if this is a regular pattern in one's life, then one is faced with a major problem that is not susceptible of any quick fix solutions.

To deal with such a personal difficulty it is not adequate to devise some techniques with a list of steps leading, one might hope, to peace and better relationships. Rather what is needed is a whole process of emotional growth, which will enable one consistently to integrate one's anger into one's personality and character so that it contributes positively to one's relationships and one's life generally along the lines sketched out above.

Ways of handling one's anger
When a person experiences anger, (s)he may react in a variety of ways. The most obvious and most common one is to express that anger verbally and/or physically. Such expression of anger may be done in an appropriate or inappropriate manner as will be seen later.

But anger is not always dealt with in this way. It may also be repressed, as has been mentioned above. If this happens, a variety of difficulties may ensue. Repression is a form of denial and can occur in relation to feelings of anger or hostility towards a parent or authority figure like a teacher, priest or bishop, or a celibate may repress sexual or genital feelings, because (s)he assumes they are 'bad'. Engaging in such repression uses up some of one's ordinary resources of psychic energy and makes it more difficult for one to be one's true self in an emotionally mature manner. In addition, the buried energy of one's anger will probably seep out in disguise, as it were, and result in the person becoming, eg. irritable, resentful, moody, frustrated, etc., or even developing physical symptoms of illnesses like colds, fevers, ulcers, skin diseases, asthma, arthritis, high blood pressure, depression or more serious complaints such as heart problems or cancer.[14]

---

14. See Cogley, Jim, *Wood You Believe*, Vol 2, *The Emerging Self: Healing and Self-Awareness, Exploring Spirituality and Psychology through handcrafted wood symbols*, Author House, Bloomington, Indiana, 2005, 12-3 where 29 symptoms of repressed anger are listed, Solfield and Hammett, 29-32.

Anger can also be expressed directly or indirectly. Directly expressed anger is the usual way people react, when angry, as has been mentioned above. Of more interest here is what is usually referred to as indirectly expressed anger, otherwise known as passive aggression.

This is anger in disguise. Outwardly it does not appear as anger and may be done coolly and calmly. In addition, the angry person will usually engage in this kind of activity quite unconsciously, hiding even from him/herself that it is anger which is motivating the action in question. The reason one expresses anger indirectly is that (s)he is afraid to express it directly lest conflict or confrontation might result.

Two examples of indirect anger or passive aggression will clarify the issue in question here. Some people have a tendency to 'forget' things like appointments, promises, anniversaries, etc. over and above the ordinary level of forgetting which is the lot of most of us. This may be called motivated forgetting, where the person 'forgets', because (s)he really doesn't want to remember. And the reason the person unconsciously wants to forget is that this is his/her way of getting her/his own back on the person who triggered the anger in the first place, or when the anger is free-floating, on anyone who happens to be in the wrong place at the wrong time. This 'forgetting' will usually annoy the person on the receiving end of it or cause some inconvenience, embarrassment or frustration. This is precisely what the passive aggressive person wants to achieve and is the payback (s)he unconsciously seeks. Another commonplace example of this passive aggression is when a person is regularly late. This too is motivated or unconsciously deliberate lateness with the same intention as the 'forgetting' just now discussed. Here it could be that one is five minutes late for work on a regular basis or for a date or for class or Mass, etc.[15]

It is no co-incidence that such 'absent-minded' or passive aggressive people are also the 'nicest' people. They are this way because they chronically repress their anger and seldom if ever display anger overtly. Because of this, people who suffer from their passive aggression find it very difficult to get angry with

15. Cosgrave, 56.

them and confront them with their aggravating behaviour. As a result the passive aggression may continue almost indefinitely.[16]

Other expressions of indirect anger are sarcasm, cynicism, resentment and humorous remarks with a sting in the tail.

Anger and morality

As has been noted, anger is viewed in the Catholic moral tradition as one of the capital sins. There is an important truth here as will soon be clear but speaking of anger simply as a sin is at best misleading and at worst inaccurate.

Earlier an exposition of the positive aspect or value of anger was presented. This makes it clear that anger is placed in one's personality for a positive purpose and contributes to our emotional and moral welfare in significant ways. Hence, insofar as one's actions, habits and tendencies that are fuelled and motivated by anger have constructive results for others and for oneself and are expressed assertively rather than aggressively, they will be morally right. Such anger or anger-motivated activity may be said to be righteous or rational and it is important and right to cultivate its use or practice as much as possible. This is the morally responsible way to integrate or manage one's anger and involves the practice of the virtue of meekness. One may express what righteous or morally right anger is in the words of Aristotle. He said:

> Anyone can become angry – that is easy. But to be angry with the right person, to the right degree, at the right time, for the right purpose and in the right way – that is not easy.

But it is the righteous use of anger and is morally what we are called to do.[17]

Unfortunately, many people misuse their anger and behave in aggressive and destructive ways when angry. Here is where moral fault may enter and sin may be committed. In such situations one's anger-fuelled activities will be morally faulty and may be classed as irrational and unrighteous. Sadly, such

---

16. Wicks, Robert J, 'A Threat to Christian Communities: Angry People Acting Passive-Aggressively', *Human Development*, Vol 5, No 4, Winter 1984, USA, 7-12.
17. Cosgrave, 56-57.

activities are quite common in our daily lives, though for the most part in ordinary circumstances they don't tend to be very serious. If one expresses one's anger aggressively and destructively, it is likely that one or more people will be hurt and a relationship or relationships may be damaged or even destroyed. Even one's family or community may suffer harm. In such cases there will likely be moral wrong, whether serious or not will depend on the circumstances and the extent of the damage done.

In relation to sinfulness in such cases that too will depend on the harm done and the circumstances but also on the degree of the agent's appreciation of what (s)he is doing and the degree of her/his freedom in acting. Obviously, it will be very difficult to estimate sinfulness accurately in such cases. Each case will need to be judged on its own merits. The main emphasis should perhaps be on repenting and trying to ensure the same fault does not occur again, rather than agonising over the degree of sinfulness in any particular situation.

It seems right to say that, because repression of anger is done unconsciously and is not free activity, it should not be classed as immoral or sinful, even though it may be emotionally damaging and unhealthy.[18] In regard to indirect anger there may be fault in the anger-motivated behaviour and perhaps some sinfulness, e.g. in being regularly late or forgetful, but it will be difficult to estimate culpability and moral responsibility, since the agent will usually be quite unaware that (s)he is hiding his/her anger and its true motive even from him/herself. It would seem that rarely would serious sin be involved here.

If one asks how, apart from the above examples of immorality, anger proves to be a source of other immoral acts and is thus a vice and a capital sin, one may mention the following. It can give rise to unreasonable indignation at supposed slights, hatred of others, grave contempt, pre-occupation with thoughts of revenge, attacks on others, quarrelling and fighting, wounding and even killing.[19] Or again: 'The daughters of wrath are impatience, indignation, insult and abuse, quarrels and blows, cursing'.[20] These things can occur between individuals but also

18. Cosgrave, 58.
19. Davis, I, 242-3.
20. Häring, 377.

within and between families and neighbourhoods and even at the level of communities, e.g. in Northern Ireland and in the Israeli-Palestinian conflict. They can, then, be very deep-rooted and difficult to eradicate. Though they will usually involve wrongdoing, measuring their immorality will be very difficult and assigning blame generally won't do much to solve such problems.

Anger and forgiveness

A link between anger and forgiveness may not be readily apparent. But if we understand what forgiveness really is and involves, then it will be quite clear. Forgiveness is not simply an intellectual exercise. When one is hurt or offended in a notable way, then one's emotions are stirred up. One will feel anger, resentment and even bitterness and may perhaps entertain thoughts of revenge. Now, forgiveness means and requires letting these feelings go, so as no longer to feel anger, resentment, etc. Experience shows that this is no easy task. It will require time and effort. One will need to be motivated to work towards forgiveness and be in touch with these feelings, so as to be well placed to detach oneself from them. This process may go on for quite a while until at last one has let go one's anger and is able to forgive the offender. Forgiveness will only be complete when one feels able to contemplate the restoration of the damaged relationship with the offender and is ready to do so. In other words, when one can act as if the offence never happened and reconciliation rather than revenge or punishment is in one's mind, then, one will have forgiven. This may be a long term project in some cases and may not be possible at all in others. We are being forcefully and rightly reminded today, however, that, in cases involving such things as sexual abuse of a child or vulnerable adult, forgiveness, though necessary, should not involve restoring or attempting to restore the previous relationship for fear of further abuse by the perpetrator.

Note too that forgetting the offence is no part of forgiveness. In fact at times one will be unable to forget and indeed it may be advantageous and important not to forget, certainly in relation to dealing with future hurts and the call to forgiveness for them.

All this will apply in three other situations distinct from forgiving a particular offender or offenders. These are when one finds it necessary to forgive oneself for one's own faults and failures, when one feels that one has to forgive God whom one blames for some loss or tragedy that one has suffered and when one has gone to confession but still feels angry, resentful or even bitter.[21]

---

21. Cosgrave, 58-59; Solfield, Juliana and Hemmett, chapter 3; Whitehead and Whitehead, 84-86.

CHAPTER FOUR

The Virtue Model of the Christian Moral Life

In recent years there has been significant interest in and valuable and illuminating use of what are called models of the Christian moral life. Here the word model means an approach to or an understanding or image of the moral life that Christians are called to follow. Models are used in this theological context in both an explanatory and an exploratory manner, the former to clarify and illuminate aspects of the moral life, the latter to reveal and highlight further dimensions or elements of it.[1] Moral theologians remind us, however, that no one model or image of the moral life is itself adequate to present the full reality of Christian morality as a whole nor even of any one truth or mystery of the Christian faith. Nevertheless, each model used can throw significant light on the moral life or some aspect of it, even though it will need to be complemented by others which can illuminate further aspects of Christian living and of course some models do this better than others.[2]

The legal model past and present
In the centuries after the Council of Trent (1545-1563) and due in large measure to that Council's new decree on confession, moral theology was dominated by this legal model of the Christian moral life. This means that Christian living was spoken of largely in legal categories and hence in terms of laws to be obeyed. In consequence great prominence was given to the ten commandments and the six commandments of the church.[3]

However, in the years since Vatican II (1962-5) the limitations of this legal model have been highlighted and most moralists in the Catholic tradition have moved away from it and adopted some other model of the moral life. The most commonly used one has been and is today what may be called the relational

---

1. See William Cosgrave, *Christian Living Today: Essays in Moral and Pastoral Theology*, Columba Press, Dublin, 2001, 9-12, esp. 10.
2. Ibid., 10.
3. Ibid., 12-6. See also John Mahoney SJ, *The Making of Moral Theology: A Study of Roman Catholic Teaching*, Clarendon Press, Oxford, 1989, chapters 1 (on confession) and 6 (on law in the moral life).

model, which, as the name indicates, understands the moral life of Christians in terms of relationships, personal, communal and societal. This is a valuable and illuminating way to approach and understand Christian morality and it remains very popular and influential in today's moral theology.[4]

The recovery of the virtues as a model for the moral life
In more recent years this relational model has been complemented by another model of morality generally and of Christian morality also. This may be referred to as the virtue model, or more usually, as simply virtue ethics. While this understanding of the moral life is deeply rooted in the Christian moral tradition, its more recent popularity seems to be due to a strong trend in moral philosophy, which has rediscovered virtue as a category that is illuminating and enriching in understanding morality and moral living[5]

Most influential among the moral philosophers has been the work of Alasdair MacIntyre, in particular his widely quoted volume *After Virtue – A Study in Moral Theory*:[6]

> In it MacIntyre attempts to resurrect Aristotelian thinking about the virtues, those qualities of mind and character that Aristotle believed to be essential to living a happy and ethically justifiable life.[7]

Taking a narrative or historical approach MacIntyre claims that Aristotle offers the most coherent and complete account of the virtues and that one becomes a good person by cultivating the moral virtues through habit and the intellectual virtues (technical skill, scientific knowledge, practical wisdom, intelligence, etc.) by instruction.[8]

---

4. Cosgrave, 16-22.
5. Jean Porter, 'Virtue Ethics', in *The Cambridge Companion to Christian Ethics*, ed Robin Gill, CUP 2001, 106-107.
6 University of Notre Dame, Indiana, 1981 and 1984.
7. Vardy and Grosch, *The Puzzle of Ethics*, Fount 1994, 105.
8. Vardy and Grosch, 110, 12, 43-44. On the virtue ethics generally, see James G. Murphy, 'Virute Ethics and Christian Moral Reflection', in *An Irish Reader in Moral Theology – The Legacy of the Last Fifty Years, Vol 1: Foundations*, edited by Enda McDonagh and Vincent MacNamra (The Columba Press, 2009, 296-315.

Though not the first to refocus on the virtues as a most illuminating and deeply necessary way of approaching and understanding the moral life, MacIntyre's work has been seminal and inspiring and not just in moral philosophy. It has sparked much interest and reflection among moral theologians and also among biblical scholars. So much so in fact that one may speak of the recovery of virtue as a very significant help in Catholic efforts to understand our Christian moral lives today. As we proceed here in our endeavour to understand the importance, meaning and role of virtue in the moral life we will draw on some of the reflections of these scholars. We will be presenting the virtue model as one that needs to take its place beside other models and which will throw significant light on our understanding and living of the Christian moral life. As will be clear in the following pages, a discussion of virtue as a model is closely related to the emphasis some scripture scholars and moralists have more recently put on moral character as an element of our moral living. That, like virtue, has been neglected in the past but has now been recovered and seen to be an important factor in our Christian moral anthropology.

Why the neglect of virtue and character in the past?[9]
It may be stated at once that one of the main reasons, if not the only one, for this neglect was the dominance in the centuries after Trent of the legal model of morality in the Manuals of Moral Theology, a dominance that continued right down to Vatican II itself.[10] This legal way of understanding the moral life is generally seen as being very act-centred. Its main focus and interest is the individual moral actions a person performs. The impression then comes to be given that the whole moral life consists mainly of doing right acts and avoiding wrong ones. Such an approach would seem to have been much encouraged by Trent's decree on confession requiring the penitent to list his/her (serious) sins by number and times. All this placed the emphasis on acts with the consequent neglect of the person, the moral subject and moral agent who is doing those actions or neglecting to do them. In consequence there is little interest in

9. On this see Cosgrave, 23-24.
10. For other reasons especially in moral philosophy see Murphy, 298.

what is happening to the moral agent, the person acting, as he/she performs these actions, moral and/or immoral. In other words, the legal model of the moral life makes minimal reference to the moral subject's growth or failure to grow in goodness and virtue and also to what kind of person he/she has become and is becoming morally speaking, as his/her life history unfolds. In the context of such a theology there is little reference to the moral subject's character as a free human person, that is, to his/her moral character. Involved here, not surprisingly, is a neglect of the virtues and vices, all of which are or can be dimensions or aspects of one's moral character, of what one is as a person from the moral or, simply, the human point of view.

It is true that one can refer to the understanding of the Christian moral life in the legal model as an ethic of virtue. But even a brief look at the Manuals of Moral Theology from the pre-Vatican II era will show that the presentation of the moral life there was, as already indicated, basically act-centred and not person- or character-centred. The reason for this is that in those textbooks the virtues were not seen as constituting the dynamics of the Christian moral life or as the various dimensions, areas and ideals of that life but rather they were reduced largely to sources of obligation for the Christian. Practising the virtues meant doing and being called to do more good actions, and avoiding the vices meant not doing a whole lot of other specific actions. So the potential of what was referred to as an ethic of virtue was not realised and the legal model remained and remains a predominantly act-centred ethic that pays scant attention to moral character or to the virtues properly understood.[11] Here we find another reason why there has been a very widespread move away from the legal model in contemporary moral theology, spirituality and pastoral practice and a consequent search for a better understanding of the Christian life. It may be added here that among the moral philosophers the main reason given for the neglect of virtue ethics is that it was overshadowed by the development of two normative systems of ethics, deontologism and utilitarianism. The former, being a law-based view

---

11. Cosgrave, 24. Also see J. A. Gallagher, *Time Past: An Historical Study of Catholic Moral Theology*, Paulist Press, NY, 1990, 56-62; William C. Spohn SJ, 'The Return of the Virtues, *Theological Studies*, March 1992, 60.

of normative ethics and emphasising our duties in the moral life, can be said to be another way of talking of the legal understanding of the moral life. Utilitarianism/consequentialism uses consequences or results as the decisive factor in deciding the morality of human acts and sees these consequences as alone obligatory. Hence, it too is act-centred but it is also viewed as in other significant ways seriously flawed.[12]

We turn, then, to the virtue model of the Christian moral life, which, as already indicated, can take a valuable and illuminating place beside and even in the context of the relational model as a significant help to our understanding and living of the moral life of a Christian (or indeed of any) person.

Understanding the virtue model

'Virtue ethics is an ethics of character', it 'takes the central question to be, what kind of person do I want to be? What kind of person would be admirable?' 'Virtue ethics places one's own character at the centre of ethical reflection.'[13] Here the task will be to describe what the virtues and moral character are and how they relate to each other. To accomplish this task properly it will be necessary to develop and work with an adequate understanding of the human person. Vatican II in *Gaudium et Spes* states that 'the moral aspect of any procedure (or action) ... must be determined by objective standards. These (must be) based on the nature of the human person and his acts' (n 51). In other words, human activity must be judged morally by reference to the human person integrally and adequately considered. Stated differently again, the human person adequately considered is the criterion or norm by which one is to judge or discover if an act is morally right or wrong, whether that act is performed by an individual person, a group or a community.[14]

Such an understanding of the person or such an anthropology, though essential for arriving at a correct view of the virtues and moral character, will be assumed here, as we keep our more precise focus on the topic under consideration.[15]

---

12. Murphy, 299-301.
13. Murphy, 301, 304.
14. Richard M. Gula, *Reason Informed by Faith: Foundations of Catholic Morality* Paulist Press, 1989, chapter 5, 63-64; quoted henceforth as RIF.
15. See RIF, 64-74 for such an anthropology presented in personalist terms.

The virtues and moral character

In relation to the virtues Hauerwas says that 'there has been no satisfactory, unambiguous moral definition of the virtues'.[16] We can, nevertheless, provide and use what Hauerwas calls the common meaning of 'virtues'. This meaning is as follows: a virtue is a (moral) trait of character like kindness or honesty.[17] Or again, 'that which causes us to fulfil our function as humans'.[18] Or, as Murphy puts it: 'Virtue is the disposition to choose those courses of action which contribute to one's happiness or flourishing; the virtues like prudence or temperance are character traits.'[19] We can say also that virtues are moral habits: 'Virtues (or vices) are stable dispositions that enable us to be (or not to be) all that we can be and to realise (or not) the best kind of life we ought to live.'[20]

In relation to moral character[21] we know from experience that certain people are generally consistent in the way they react to situations. We can rely on them to make a certain kind of response in most circumstances. They are predicable and seem to have certain stable characteristics. This predictability and reliability seem to come from these people's commitment to particular values and from their maintaining certain attitudes and intentions. People often refer to this predictability and stability as the person's character. Others speak of it as integrity.[22]

This character, which manifests itself in and through one's actions and is clearly a moral reality, refers to who one is as a free human being, a moral subject. One's character is one's moral identity as a person, one's moral self. My moral character is who I have made myself and become as a result of my life experiences and in particular as a consequence of my moral choices and actions over my lifetime. Each person's moral character

16. Stanley Hauerwas, *A Community of Character: towards a Constructive Christian Social Ethic* (Note Dame, Indiana, 1981 ans 1986), 111. (Hereafter referred to as *CC*).
17. Stanley Hauerwas, *Vision and Virture: Essays on Christian Ethical Reflection* (Fides, Notre Dame, 1974), 55-54.
18. Hauerwas, 111.
19. Art cit, 302.
20. Richard M. Gula, *Just Ministry: Prefessional Ehtics for Pastoral Ministers*, Paulist Press, 2010), 62.
21. Cosgrave, 25-26.
22. James F. Gustafson, *Christian Ethics and the Community*, Pilgrim Press, Philadelphia, 1971, 166-72.

consists of a very specific and personal configuration or arrangement of virtues and vices, affections, intentions, dispositions, emotions, beliefs, values and priorities. One's character gives one a particular direction or orientation in and to life, so that one acts in a consistent way, either doing good or evil. The character one has built represents the characteristic way one has of determining what is appropriate for one to do in any particular situation. Everyone's moral character is unique, but no one type of character is normative for all.[23]

The issue of character is, then, the basic question for each person in his/her moral life. This is confirmed by experience where we discover that, along with the call to do good deeds, we also experience the call, from the depths of our being as persons and ultimately from God, to become good persons. Hence, our moral lives must be concerned above all about the kind of persons we are, are becoming and ought to become.[24]

Relating the virtues and moral character
If now we ask how the virtues (and vices) and moral character are related to each other, it may be said that one's virtues (and vices) are the moral dispositions or habits or strengths that together combine to make up one's moral character. They move us to particular actions in the different areas of life and provide us with the resources to do easily what some who are less virtuous (or vicious) would find difficult.[25]

So virtues are not simply a matter of being – 'be honest, don't be dishonest.' They imply action – 'do what is honest; don't do what is dishonest' – and they give us an inclination to and a facility in doing these acts of virtue (or vice).[26] Gula adds that 'virtue gives us an intuitive ability to see in the blink of an eye the salient features relevant to deciding what to do' ... and 'the power to act spontaneously and fittingly without having to stop and think about what to do every time we do it.'[27]

23. Stanley Hauerwas, *Character and Christian Life: A Study in Theological Ethics*, Trinity University Press, San Antonio, Texas, 1975, 127.
24. Cosgrave, 25-26.
25. Hauerwas, 115.
26. MacNamara, Vincent, *The Call to be Human: Making Sense of Morality* (Veritas, 2010), 159.
27. JM, 62.

Thus as we acquire the virtues (or vices) we form our character. But of course this is not a quick or easy process. Like acquiring any habit (in sport or in business, etc.) it takes continual repetition of the right choices to develop any virtue and so to form one's character.[28] A virtue like any habit is an attribute one acquires by practice: the more one practises it in one's specific actions the stronger it becomes and of course the less one does this the weaker the virtue becomes.[29] It is clear, then, that the formation of character is directly related to our growth or lack of growth in virtue (or vice) and if one declines so does the other.

We may note also that growth in virtue (or vice) frequently occurs as a result of imitating others. 'To form good character', says Gula (JM, p 70), 'we need to have people of good character in our lives who can model for us what being good looks like'. And at the level of community living it is true to say that the character we acquire is in part the result of internalising the beliefs and values, causes and loyalties of the communities that make up our environment. Thus, it is evident that to form our character well and to grow in the virtues we need people who share our interests, ideals, values and concerns. Such people will support and perhaps challenge us in our practice of the virtues and so by a process of observation and imitation we are aided in the formation of character.[30] For the Christian of course Jesus is the supreme model and the Christian community of the church will be the one that provides the greatest support, guidance and challenge to virtuous Christian living.[31]

Unfortunately, as experience teaches, all this can take place on the negative side too as similar dynamics take effect and bring about a strengthening of our vices, a weakening of our virtues and a deformation of our moral character.

These close links between the virtues and moral character make it possible to speak of a person's good moral character in terms of that person being a virtuous individual. To be virtuous is to have acquired those moral habits, attitudes and beliefs that

---

28. JM, 63, 69.
29. Gula, 70.
30. Gula, 71-72.
31. Ibid., 72-74; William C. Spohn, *Go and Do Likewise: Jesus and Ethics*, Continuum, NY, 29-31.

we call the virtues and to practise them consistently in one's daily life. Practising the virtues leads to genuine human and Christian fulfilment or flourishing for individuals and groups; it makes us good persons and both expresses and builds one's moral character. Hence, when one speaks of a person being virtuous, one is describing that person's moral character and is saying that, as well as being good, that person does good in a consistent, if not perfect, manner in his/her daily living.[32]

Another way of speaking of a person who has good moral character and so does good by practising the virtues is to say that that person has made significant progress towards being fully human. To be good in the fullest sense is to be fully human, that is, to have achieved fulfilment as a person and to have realised one's moral potential as a human being. While none of us achieves this lofty goal in this earthly life, it is obvious here that growing in virtue or forming one's character morally is something that humanises us, makes us more human, better human beings. Practising the virtues and thus building one's moral character enhances our humanity and brings us closer to being the person God wants and calls us to be.[33]

Two points will be clear from these reflections. Firstly, building one's moral character by living a virtuous life and so becoming a more fully human person is a lifelong project that is always a work in progress and is never complete here below. This implies a call to continuous moral growth throughout one's life as one seeks to practise the virtues ever better and build one's moral character to an ever higher level of virtue and goodness. Secondly, this process of living morally by practising the virtues and becoming a better human person is not to be seen as some kind of heavy burden or oppressive duty imposed by some external agent or institution like the church or society or God.[34] Rather the call to be human by being virtuous and of good moral character is what our very nature as human persons-in-relationship-and-in-community inclines and moves us to respond to. As we do so we achieve the goal of human living, our fulfilment as persons. Being virtuous is, then, the human thing

---

32. Cosgrave, 37. 38.
33. Cosgrave, 32.
34. Murphy, 304.

to do; building one's moral character is the very thing that accords most of all with one's deepest human instincts and inclinations as a person. At the same time it has to be said that becoming virtuous and building one's moral character are both gift and task for us in this earthly existence: gift in that one's very nature as a person (and ultimately God) inclines one towards those goals and helps one to realise them; task in the sense that, at the same time, as experience shows, especially in a sinful world, it is regularly a challenge and a struggle to practise the virtues and to make oneself, even with God's grace, a more human and a more virtuous person of good moral character.

Personal factors influencing our virtues and moral character
In discussing the virtue model of the Christian moral life, it will be important to note briefly the factors personal to the moral subject that will influence the actions and omissions that he/she performs, and, hence, that will be significant in relation to practising the virtues and building moral character. Short notes on each of these five factors or elements will suffice here.

i) Knowledge
Here we refer, not to academic or abstract knowledge, but more directly to knowledge of moral values. This is evaluative knowledge or a real appreciation of these values and the corresponding disvalues or evils. Basic here too will be knowledge of oneself. This will involve being aware of one's values, attitudes, dispositions, intentions, feelings, needs, weaknesses, blind spots, limitations, and level of moral maturity. This is a tall order but such self-knowledge is the cornerstone of moral, spiritual and psychological growth.[35]

ii) Freedom
We believe in free will, though we know it is always limited by various factors within and without. This freedom enables us to take responsibility for our actions and omissions and also for what we are, have become and can become as persons. We can increase and deepen our freedom of choice over time and so take greater responsibility for ourselves as persons and moral subjects and for what we do and don't do.[36]

35. Cosgrave, 32.
36. Cosgrave, 32-33.

iii) Emotions[37]

Our emotions have a very powerful and often overlooked role to play in the development of the virtues and one's moral character, and also in influencing how that character impacts on one's moral judgments and choices. A person's morality or moral sense has its roots in his/her feelings and it is from them that that morality gets its nourishment and power to shape character, choice and virtuous living. In other words, the springs of morality are in the heart. Our basic moral experience is that of value, especially the value of persons. This experience contains an emotional element, namely, an appreciation of and care for the human person. Emotion pervades our moral knowledge and contributes notably to our moral choices, our growth (or decline) in virtue and the building of our character. Feelings can guide our perceptions and moral judgements and they give energy and motivation to our commitment to good (and evil) and to becoming a good (or bad) person. Our feelings can also give rise to a deeper insight into the values we appreciate and love and can facilitate us in judging and choosing wisely. Thus are the virtues and moral character influenced and formed in significant ways by our emotions. It follows that emotional maturity is essential for moral maturity. So moral living has to be an alliance of feeling and reasoning, of heart and head.[38]

iv) Intention

One's intention in doing an action is the purpose of one's action; it is what one is pursuing when one acts. It is the intention that gives personal meaning to one's action and as such it is part of the objective act. Different intentions will make different acts.[39] Clearly, then, our intentions in choosing and acting will shape our character. If these intentions are consistently positive and good, they will form a pattern that will establish a virtue or virtues and thus will build moral character in a positive direction. So, for instance, if a person consistently has the intention in acting of being kind or generous or loving, then he/she will in time develop the corresponding virtues or character traits and

---

37. Cosgrave, 33-34; Gula, JM, 50-56; see chapters 1 and 2 above for more detail on this topic.
38. JM, 53-4.
39. Gula, RIF, 187, 265-6.

so become a kind, generous or loving person.[40] Thus will that person's moral character be built up as he/she becomes a virtuous person. All this makes it clear that one's intentions are a major factor in the growth of the moral subject in virtue (or vice) and they contribute significantly to the development of a good moral character (or its opposite). Hence, in choosing and acting we must attend to our intentions with discernment.

v) Imagination[41]

Many of us seem to have the idea that imagination is something that is largely confined to poets, novelists and outstanding artists, scientists or inventors. These people are, of course, brilliantly imaginative. But all of us have imaginative powers and they are at work every day in what we are thinking and doing, including especially our moral thoughts and actions. The imagination has three basic functions:

1. Interpretive function

It is one's imagination which gives one the ability to interpret and come to understand the realities and activities that come into one's experience. The way we interpret the world determines how we relate to it. It is our imagination which enables us to make this interpretation. It goes without saying that this process will impact on one's moral sense and outlook and will be very significant in our practice – or non-practice – of particular virtues and, hence, in how our moral character is formed. For example, the Good Samaritan saw the wounded man on the side of the road as another human being in need of help and so he stopped to assist the injured man. The priest and Levite, however, interpreted the situation quite differently. They viewed the victim of the robbers as a source of legal defilement and so they passed by on the other side.[42]

2. Empathic function

It is our imaginative abilities that enable us to empathise in some degree at least with other people and so to understand

---

40. Gula, JM, 49-50.
41. Ibid., 56-60; Also Philip S. Keane, *Christian Ethics and Imagination*, Paulist Press, NY, 1984, chapters 4 and 5.
42. JM, 57.

their situation and feel for and with them. This aspect of our imagination is closely related to our emotional capacity; in fact it has its roots in our emotions. If we are emotionally open and mature, then the empathic dimension of our imagination will work well and enable us to empathise with others. It is a short step, then, to caring for them. Such caring and compassion is at the heart of morality. When we empathise, then, we are on the way to practising virtue and building our moral character.

3. Creative function

All of us in different degrees have a creative dimension to our imaginative powers. This creativity enables us to ask at every level and at the moral one too: 'How can I do better?'; 'What new ways can I devise to help me grow morally, to practise the virtues better?'; 'How can I change my moral life so as to relate more caringly to others, do more good and become a better person?' It will be important for one's moral life, then, to cultivate this creative role of one's imagination so as to ensure a more mature practice of the virtues.

The range of the virtues

The virtues one will give priority to will depend on one's understanding or interpretation of the human person, society itself and Christian teaching. It is true, as MacNamara says,[43] that societies through the ages have a somewhat different vision of the human being and of what makes for a flourishing society. Still, there will be a fair amount of agreement on a widely recognised range of virtues (and vices). In the Christian moral tradition the moral virtues that have been given priority are called the cardinal (or hinge) virtues. These four were originally grouped together and given priority by Plato (427-348 BC) and were accorded the title cardinal virtues by St Ambrose (340-397 AD).[44] Though there has been no universal agreement on what are the primary virtues, in slightly revised form this quartet of virtues has long been listed as follows: prudence, justice, fortitude (or

43. p 160.
44. Vardy and Grosch, 110-11; John Langan SJ, 'Cardinal Virtues', in *A New Dictionary of Christian Ethics*, ed. John Macquarrie and James Childress, SCM Press, London, 1987, 76-7; Henceforth quoted as DCE; Porter, 99.

courage) and temperance. To them in the Christian dispensation are added the three theological virtues, faith, hope and charity (or love). Many writers see the virtuous action as the one that finds the middle way between the extremes of too much and too little, excess and deficiency, e.g. generosity stands between the extremes of prodigality and miserliness.[45]

Some modern writers feel that this list of the most important virtues needs some further revision, so as to get our priorities fully right in this area. Thus, for example, James Keenan designates the following as the cardinal virtues: justice, fidelity, self-care and prudence.[46]

The need to complement the virtue model

It is generally agreed that no one model of the Christian moral life is fully adequate to present the total reality of how Christians should live as disciples of Jesus. In consequence of this it will be important to point out two ways in which the virtue model needs to be complemented so as to be more adequate in its representation of the moral life of Christians.

i) Using the relational model

It can be said that the virtue model may tend to focus a person on him/herself and on the moral life and its development that one desires and seeks in his/her own life. Because of this temptation, it will be important to ensure that we consider the virtue model or approach in the context of, or, rather along with the relational model. This will remind us that the Christian life is a network of relationships, personal, communal and societal, and that it is in and through these relationships and not otherwise that one is called to grow in virtue and build one's moral character. In other words, only by loving God and one's neighbour (and oneself) as we relate to others in our communities can one grow in the various virtues and so become a more virtuous, a more human and a more holy person. Only by such giving can we receive.[47]

---

45. Vardy and Grosch, 45-6; Hauerwas, 'Virtues', DCE, 649.
46. James Keenan, 'Virtue Ethics' in Bernard Hoose, ed, *Christian Ethics, An Introduction,* Cassell, London, 1998), 84-94 at 91-93.
47. Cosgrave, 16-22.

ii) Ethical methods for resolving moral dilemmas

The virtue model of Christian moral living is valuable in making clear that our moral living is not to be seen as a burden to be carried nor a never-ending series of moral problems or dilemmas that we have to grapple with day in and day out. But moral difficulties and uncertainties about a variety of actions do crop up from time to time. It has been suggested that the virtue model can provide guidance in relation to resolving these moral doubts or problems, if one is uncertain about the judgment to be made in a particular case. So, for example, one could ask the question in relation to a proposed action: is this action one which I consider to be admirable or which other adults would judge to be so? What would I say of this behaviour if my son or daughter did it? Or would I want either of them to know I did it?[48] This is helpful, as far as it goes and would provide a fitting moral judgement, even if largely intuitive, on many situations.

But more perplexing moral dilemmas do occur. Examples are the following: the question of the use of IVF by a childless couple to achieve a pregnancy, the issue of the use of embryonic stem cells in the search for a cure for diseases like Parkinsons, or whether withdrawal of nutrition and hydration in the case of a person in a permanent vegetative state is morally acceptable.[49] It would seem that one would need to complement the virtue model with a system of ethical decision-making that would enable one to address these and similar moral problems in a systematic manner. Such systems might be the traditional Catholic one which is usually referred to as the Principle of Double Effect[50] or perhaps what many Catholic moral theologians have developed in recent times, namely, the system called Proportionalism[51]

48. Murphy, 307.
49. see Pádraig Corkery, *Bioethics and Catholic Moral Tradition*, Veritas, Dublin, chapters 2 to 5.
50. See Richard McCormick SJ, *How Brave a New World?, Dilemmas in Bioethics*, SCM Press, London, 1981, 413-429; William J. Conway, 'The Act of Two Effects', in *An Irish Reader in Moral Theology: The Legacy of the last Fifty Years, Vol I: Foundations*, edited by Enda McDonagh and Vincent MacNamara, Columba Press, 2009, 387-398.
51. Hoose, Bernard, Proportionalism - The American Debate and its European Roots, Georgetown University Press, USA, 1987.

or the Basic Goods Theory that is proposed by another school of thought within Catholic moral theology.[52]

Practical implications for our christian lives[53]

i) This virtue model of the Christian moral life places the emphasis on the person, the moral subject, and what he/she has become and is becoming morally speaking. This is important so as to avoid an act-centred view of the moral life and to ensure we focus on personal progress at the moral level.

ii) This virtue model emphasises growth and possible decline in the moral life; both will go on over time and require continual effort to promote the growth and reverse the decline.

iii) We are reminded in the virtue model that one's moral character and the virtues (and vices) one practises impact significantly on what one does and does not do but also that the actions we perform or omit develop or damage that character and those virtues (and vices) and do so, as it were, automatically, that is, by the very nature of those actions.

iv) The more we practise the virtues and build our moral character the more we strengthen our inclination to do good and avoid sin. Hence, the virtuous person can be at peace and without anxiety about regular or serious sinning, since his/her whole being is turned away from this reality. However, it is always possible to act out of character and so we need to be alert to the temptations that will inevitably come our way.

v) One will need to have an open but critical attitude to the messages and influences of the various groups and communities to which one belongs, including especially present-day western society and culture. In this the guidance of the church's teaching and one's own mature Christian instinct will provide both direction and directions.

vi) In assessing oneself as a Christian, that is, in examining one's conscience, it will be helpful to focus more attentively on the various virtues and vices rather than simply take an act-centred

---

52. Todd A. Salzmann, *What Are They Saying About Catholic Ethical Method?* (Paulist Press, New York, 2003), chapter 1.
53. Cosgrave, 38-40.

approach. The quality of one's relationships and one's contribution to them should also figure prominently in one's reflections.

vii) Finally, one should remember that perfection is for heaven and is not attainable in this life. However well one practises the virtues and has built one's moral character, here below imperfections will remain. So, aim always for growth morally speaking and hope that as a result one's moral efforts and God's grace will finally bring one to perfection with the Father in the heavenly kingdom.

Assessing the virtue model of the christian moral life
Positive points
In addition to what has already been said about the advantages of this virtue model of the Christian moral life we may list briefly the following points.

i) It presents a positive understanding of the Christian life and avoids any preoccupation with sin and vice, though these are not neglected and do find their appropriate place.

ii) It focuses on the moral subject and the deeper levels of moral living: habits, commitments, emotions and intentions, in a word, on the 'heart'. It points up how this shapes one's actions and also how those actions impact on the moral agent. Thus it reminds us that our basic call or responsibility in life is to become the best person one can be.

iii) It emphasises the growth process of the moral subject over time and the process of maturation that is inherent in the moral life with its accompanying moral psychology.[54]

iv) It sees the moral life, not as a long series of duties and a list of rules to be obeyed that can make Christian living appear burdensome. Rather it presents moral living as a call to fulfilment, to become the person you should be. That is experienced as humanising and pleasurable. Duty is only part of what the good life requires.[55]

---

54. Spohn, 28.
55. Murphy, 304.

v) It offers the most promising avenue to appreciate the role of Jesus in the NT and facilitates our understanding of how the life of Jesus forms the basic norm of Christian ethics.[56]

Alleged weaknesses

i) As already noted, this approach to Christian living can become self-centred as the moral subject focuses on his/her inner life in terms of character building and personal growth. This, of course, can be avoided and is not inevitable.

ii) Some question whether this model is really practical in moral matters and especially in regard to moral decision-making. We have noted this earlier. Its advocates, however, stress that this model can improve our ability to know and do what is right and that in making us better persons it facilitates us in making better and wiser moral judgments.[57]

iii) It is said by critics that virtues are very much influenced and shaped by the different cultures in which people live. As a consequence, particular virtues can mean different things in different societies and at different times and can experience varying degrees of prominence as cultures vary. So, some say, there is no such thing as justice-as-such but only justice-as-understood-in-Athens, justice-as-understood-in-Thebes and justice-as-understood-in-Sparta. Thus, it is said, there is a relativism about the virtues that raises important difficulties.[58] Those who advocate virtue ethics accept that there is a cultural shaping of the virtues but deny that this gives rise to a relativism that renders it impossible to develop and live by a virtue ethics.[59]

iv) Some claim that particular virtues can clash and be in conflict in certain situations. This refers especially to love and justice and it is alleged that a conflict between an ethics of justice and an ethics of care can arise with the former being more characteristically adopted by men and the latter by women.[60] This view has, however, been challenged and seen as seriously flawed.

56. Spohn, 29; Murphy, 309-10.
57. Keenan, 90.
58. MacIntuyre, 139; Vardy and Grosch, 117; Spohn, 61.
59. MacIntyre, 277; Vardy and Grosch, 117.
60. Spohn, art cit, 67-8.

Thus, it is asserted that 'charity may surpass justice but cannot substitute for it. On the other hand, justice specifies the duties that flow from the order of love,[61] and the theory about men and women differing in this context has been rejected as sexist in that it reinforces the tendency to confine women to the domestic sphere and to promote men as alone suitable for the public realm of institutions and power.[62]

v) Some are of the opinion that this model of the moral life either neglects principles and duty or gives them insufficient attention or is even in conflict with them. This is denied by the defenders of virtues ethics. Gula says[63] that principles can help us notice aspects of a situation which we might otherwise miss and they can point us in the direction we ought to go. Virtue makes it possible to fulfil one's duty as a true expression of one's self. Without virtue duty is empty. We would simply go through the motions because we have been told to do so or because some authority figure is watching. Acting out of a virtuous disposition entails a difference in kind and quality from acting out of duty and principles. For the virtuous, living morally is more than doing one's duty or following a rule or principle. It is striving for excellence.[64]

---

61. Ibid., 74.
62. Ibid., 68.
63. JM, 67.
64. Ibid, 67.

Men and Women are Equal:
But how do they complement each other?

The Catholic church teaches and western society in general agrees that men and women are equal as persons and, in Christian terms, as children of God. This is a major advance from the deplorable historical record in both secular society and in the church, where over many centuries women have been held to be inferior to men and treated accordingly.[1] But even today the equality of men and women is not fully recognised in practice either in society or in the church. In relation to the church it is not just a question of priestly ordination being denied to women but the problem is much wider than that, extending to the whole issue of an exclusively male hierarchy and the fact that all positions of authority and jurisdiction are in the hands of a male clerical elite, while women and indeed the laity in general are confined to merely advisory roles and positions where they are always subject to male clerical control.

This chapter will treat of one specific issue. This is the issue of the complementarity of men and women and how even today it would seem to be interpreted in a way that continues the practice of treating women as inferior despite the official church teaching that they are equal to men.

Hence, the present chapter will begin with an outline of this interpretation of complementarity. Then in its second section we present contemporary criticisms of and reservations about this view. Finally, in the third section what is widely considered an acceptable understanding of complementarity that preserves the equality of men and women in practice as well as in theory is set forth.

---

1. Margaret A. Farley, *A Framework for Christian Sexual Ethics*, Continuum, New York & London, 2006, 2008, 138-40.

Distinguishing sex and gender

Sex refers to the biologically distinct designs of the male and female bodies, that is, to the physical and physiological differences between men and women that are of basic significance in reproduction and which have remained essentially the same throughout time, except in our day by surgical intervention.[3] There are, then, two sexes, men and women, a fact that is obvious to all.

Gender is rather different, though it assumes the above distinction of the sexes and has its ultimate source in that distinction. Gender may be said to refer to the social differences between men and women. In the patriarchal view gender is about the differentiation, usually on the basis of sex, between social roles and functions labelled in society as masculine and feminine.[4] It concerns how men and women as sexual persons should act, what qualities of personality and character each should develop and have and what social roles they should be assigned in society.[5] In this context there is frequent reference to masculine and feminine sexuality. These are labels given to the qualities or traits of personality and character that men and women, respectively, have in any particular society and culture. Because of these personality qualities, particular social roles or tasks in society are judged to be appropriate and natural for men and others for women. Implied here is the social norm or arrangement that men are excluded from some roles in society and, more importantly from our viewpoint here, women are likewise excluded from other such roles or responsibilities.

Based upon an essentialist view of gender this patriarchal vision of man-woman relations ascribes to women and men two

---

2. See Rosemary Radford Ruether, *Sexism and God-Talk – Towards a Feminist Theology*, SCM Press, London, 1983, 94-9; Anne E. Carr, *Transforming Grace – Christian Tradition and Women's Experience*, Harper & Row Publishers, San Francisco, 1990, 123-5.

3. Elizabeth A. Johnson, *Truly Our Sister – A Theology of Mary in the Communion of Saints*, Continuum, New York & London 2006, 20.

4. Sandra Cullen, *Religion and Gender*. Into the Classroom – Religious Education in the Leaving Certificate. Series Editors: Eóin G. Cassidy and Patrick M. Devitt. Veritas, Dublin 2005, 22; Carr, 76-7.

5. Johnson, 20-1.

virtually separate kinds of human nature, each gifted with its own characteristics, a position commonly described as dualistic anthropology or an anthropology of complementarity.[6]

Masculine and feminine qualities

The personality traits in question here are quite familiar to us all, so familiar indeed that we take them for granted and count them quite natural to men and women. The main ones may be listed as follows. The masculine qualities or traits that we associate with men in our society are chiefly these: Being unemotional and cool, logical and rational, detached and emotionally uncommunicative, competitive and aggressive, strong and dominant, good at taking initiatives, making decisions and giving leadership, career oriented and focused on work and the possibilities of promotion. A corresponding set of traits are spoken of as feminine or as characteristic of and natural to women: emotional and intuitive, warm and tender, affectionate and caring, talkative and good at personal relationships, sensitive and self-sacrificing, passive and submissive, moody and emotionally changeable.[7]

These qualities of men and women are considered to be complementary and hence form the basis of and in fact constitute the complementarity of the sexes with which we are here concerned. In the past and up to recently they have been taken to be natural to men and women in the sense that they were the way things between the sexes had been arranged by God and the way they should be. Thus masculine sexuality has been considered as innate in men and feminine sexuality as innate in women. Some have spoken of this innateness or naturalness as ontological, that is, belonging to the very being or nature of men and women. Hence, Pope John Paul II and others speak of the ontological complementarity between men and women.[8]

---

6. Johnson, 47.
7. Johnson, 48-9, Cullen, 30; Gareth Moore, O.P., *The Body in Context – Sex and Catholicism*, Continuum, London & New York, 1992, 2001, 121; William Cosgrave, *Christian Living Today – Essays in Moral and Pastoral Theology*, The Columba Press, Dublin, 2001, 118.
8. John Paul II, *Letter to Women*, Catholic Truth Society, London, 1995, n.7. See Kevin T. Kelly, *New Directions in Sexual Ethics – Moral Theology and the Challenge of AIDS*. Geoffrey Chapman, London & Washington, 1998, 50-4 for a critique of the Pope's viewpoint.

Complementarity and social roles

The above understanding of gender and the complementarity of men and women that derives from it have important consequences in the lives of men and women in society and in the church also. Because of the natural personality traits of the two sexes, it would seem obvious that men are suitable for some particular tasks or responsibilities in society and the church, while other tasks fit the personality and character of women much better. The usual examples are again quite familiar. Leadership roles in the family, in society and the church are considered to be by nature the domain of men. Hence, men have long been judged to be superior to and more suited by nature than women for taking responsibility in these social roles.[9] In relation to social roles suitable for women the consensus in society pointed to the domestic area of life. So, in addition to childbearing, women were assigned the responsibilities or roles of supporting and providing for their husbands and family by good and consistent housekeeping and as mothers caring for and nurturing the children in the family. Other social roles deemed suitable for women, especially in recent times, are nursing, education, social service work, counselling and in the church spiritual direction.[10]

In this connection the Pope has important statements about women in his Apostolic Letter, *On the Dignity and Vocation of Women*, 1988, and the Letter already quoted. He speaks frequently of the 'genius of women' exercised in the areas of life just mentioned and he sees their work in these roles as a 'specific part of God's plan for women' (Letter to Women, n.10). He states also that 'in giving themselves to others each day women fulfil their deepest vocation' (ibid., n.12).

As already noted, John Paul calls the complementarity between men and women ontological and goes so far as to say that men and women are incomplete unless they come together in union. This idea would seem to be based on Gen. 1.27 and is not at all easy to interpret. Men and women need their 'other half', who is different from them but will complete them'.[11] It is through the duality of the 'masculine' and the 'feminine' that

---

9. Farley, 134-5.
10. See John Paul II, *Letter to Women*, n. 9.
11. Farley, 141-2.

the 'human' finds its full realisation (*Letter to Women*, n. 7.). 'Masculinity' and 'femininity' complete and explain each other.[12]

It is important to highlight the fact that those who hold the understanding of gender and complementarity that has just been outlined – and this includes the Pope – readily admit that women have been seriously discriminated against and dominated by men and society, even to the extent of violence, in the past and in some places even today (*Letter to Women*, n.3-6). The Pope even apologises for this discrimination (ibid., n.3). He also states that the 'masculinisation' of women must be avoided and women must not appropriate to themselves male characteristics contrary to their own feminine originality.[13]

Despite these latter statements, however, it would appear that this interpretation of gender with its central element, the complementarity between the sexes, forms at least part of the reasoning behind the Catholic church's exclusion of women from any significant leadership or authoritative roles in the church today as in the past. This would seem to be the case, even though such a link is not officially made in the contemporary church's official documents or teaching, and despite the fact that a Vatican Letter in 2004 stated the following: 'women play a role of maximum importance in the Church's life' and 'the reservation of priestly ordination solely to men does not hamper in any way women's access to the heart of Christian life'.[14] (A 1976 document from the Congregation for the Doctrine of the Faith stated that the 'natural resemblance' between Christ and the minister of the Eucharist would be difficult to see if the role of Christ were not taken by a man.[15] But this statement was not repeated

---

12. John Paul II, The Apostolic Letter, *Mulieris Dignitatem* [The Dignity and Vocation of Women] of Pope John Paul II, 1988, Veritas, Dublin, n. 25.
13. Ibid., n. 10.
14. Congregation of the Doctrine of the Faith, 'Letter to the Bishops of the Catholic Church on the Collaboration of Men and Women in the Church and in the World', The Vatican, 31 May 2004, No. 16. Henceforward referred to as CDF Letter 2004.
15. See 'Declaration on the Admission of Women to the Ministerial Priesthood' in *Vatican Council II: More Post-Conciliar Documents*. Austin Flannery, O.P., General Editor, Fowler Wright Books Ltd., Leominster, Herefords, England, 1982, No. 5.

by later Vatican documents including the authoritative letter of John Paul II on the ordination of women in May 1994.)[16]

Discrimination against and inferiority of women
Assuming that the division of personality traits into masculine and feminine was and is natural and so to be understood as the providential plan of God for men and women, then it is also natural and God-ordained that the social roles mentioned just now are to be divided as already indicated, and restricted to men and women in the way that has been set out. Now given all this, it is no surprise that women came to be viewed both in society and in the church as inferior to men, unfit for responsible roles in the public and political arenas and so rightly subject to men, who were in the positions of leadership. This superiority was not confined to politics and public life but came to be exercised also in the family and indeed in all areas of life. Thus developed male domination of women both in society and in the church, a domination that was seen as justified both by nature and by God and, therefore, to be maintained and promoted for the welfare of both women and men and the common good of society and the church. And of course it was men who both justified and imposed this domination and who still maintain it in various societies around the world and to some extent in western society even today. And in the eyes of many it has not disappeared from the Catholic church's practice despite the official and universally held teaching that women and men are equal as persons and as children of God.

It will be clear from what has been said here that the superiority of men over women and the consequent domination of women by men have their roots and justification in the understanding of gender and the complementarity of the sexes that has been outlined in the preceding pages, and that is still deeply rooted in society and the church.

Today, however, this domination and discrimination in western society and in the church are widely criticised and rejected. The equally widespread assertion of the principle of the equality of men and women as persons is very much welcomed

16. See George Weigel, *Witness to Hope – The Biography of John Paul II*, Cliff Street Books, An Imprint of HarperCollins, London 1999 and 2001, 728-30.

and significant progress has been made in society and in the church in making that equality a reality in daily life in church and state. Still, much remains to be achieved before full equality in practice is realised.

Since our interest here is in the understanding or theory of complementarity already elaborated, we will now examine it in the light of recent suggestions and criticisms. In our third section we will endeavour to present a revised view that will, it is hoped, provide the theoretical grounds for and the intellectual justification of the full equality of men and women both in theory and in practice.

COMPLEMENTARITY CRITIQUED: TOWARDS AN EGALITARIAN VIEW[17]

The above interpretation of the complementarity of men and women is now perceived by many as in effect colluding with androcentrism and patriarchy[18] in producing a male dominated society and church.[19] There has been significant progress in recent years in pointing out the weaknesses and inadequacies of this approach to gender complementarity. Biblical, theological and feminist studies have played a major part in this process along with the sciences of biology, anthropology, psychology and sociology. Here we will draw on some of this research to help in detailing the criticisms that are brought forward and the changes in society that call this view of the complementarity between men and women into question. This will serve as the first step towards a more egalitarian anthropology that will favour

---

17. Ruether, 99-115; Carr, 125-6.
18. Androcentricism means literally 'centred on men' and implies that men are superior and the norm for what is human. Patriarchy means literally 'the rule of the fathers', of the male and so involves male domination. See Carr, 84-5, 135-8; Claire Colette Murphy, *An Introduction to Christian Feminism*. Dominican Publications, Dublin 1994, 10 and chapter 6; Sandra M. Schneiders, *Beyond Patching – Faith and Feminism in the Catholic Church*, Paulist Press, New York, 1991, 18-27.
19. Sandra M. Schneiders, 33-4 says : [Women] 'began to realise that their exclusion, marginalisation and oppression were not incidental but structural and systemic. They identified the church as a deeply patriarchal structure, owned and operated by men for their own benefit and firmly committed to the domination of women Catholics by men in general and male clerics in particular'.

and ground a true partnership of the sexes and their equality in practice as well as in theory.[20]

i) Forming personal identity

When one reflects on the common elements of humanity shared by women and men (as will be done in our third and last section), it becomes clear that an individual's personal identity is forged not only by sex and gender but also by race, class, family dynamics, ethnic heritage, social location in place and time and by political, cultural and ecological environments, all in interaction with the way each person uniquely appropriates these factors or influences. And because this is the case, it does happen that the range of differences among women themselves can be just as great, if not greater, than the differences that exist between some women and some men.[21] Clearly, then, we may not attribute all the differences between men and women to sex and gender, just as we must not think that all the similarities between women and between men have their foundation or explanation in sex and/or gender. Gender is not, then, the sole determinant of the personality and character of any person, male or female, though obviously it is of basic importance, as experience makes abundantly clear and as will be pointed out later.[22]

ii) Changes in gender roles recently

It is important to take note of the fact that in the last couple of centuries, especially since women began to enter the work force and became economically independent of men, notable changes in the gender roles of women especially but also of men have taken place.[23] Serious efforts have been and are being made by women but by some men too to eliminate women's inferior position in society and with some success. Female demands for equal pay, equal opportunity, family-friendly work practices, good child-care facilities and better education have been met to some extent at least in some places. All this and

---

20. Johnson, 50.
21. Johnson, 52.
22. Cullen, 26.
23. Cullen, 32; See Schneiders, 13–14; Lisa Sowle Cahill, 'Gender and Christian Ethics', in *Cambridge Companion to Christian Ethics*, Edited by Robin Gill, Cambridge University Press, 2001, 120-1.

related developments have made it possible for some women to rise to very high levels of achievement in many areas of life, e.g., in politics, academia, business and finance, commerce, economics, the arts, the military, etc. It still remains true, however, that the majority of women continue to face a life of poverty and inequality.[24] These developments have occasioned corresponding changes in the gender roles of men, e.g., in regard to child care and active involvement in the domestic life of the family, in working with women in roles unknown in the past and at times under the authority of women, in the encouragement given to men to develop their emotional life and express it more fully, in not being the sole bread winner or even not filling that role at all, in being less career oriented or even leaving concern for career development to his female partner.

All this makes it clear that the traditional division of personal qualities into the two clear-cut categories of masculine and feminine does not fit the reality in the lives of some men and women at least in western society today. Some women have acquired some of the psychological and emotional qualities or traits that have traditionally been spoken of as masculine and some men have developed the so-called feminine dimension of their personalities. Hence, the changes in their social roles. On the other hand, it seems to be a fact that some men don't possess at least some of the so-called masculine qualities and some women lack some of the feminine traits. In consequence one cannot now make universal claims about the personal characteristics of men and women, and so the traditional understanding of complementarity begins to break down.[25]

iii) Human rather than masculine and feminine qualities
This suggests a further point and question. Why should the so-called masculine qualities be confined or restricted to men only? And why should the feminine ones be the exclusive possession of women? Such restriction seems quite unwarranted and is now recognised as a result of male domination, where the men ensured that they possessed the qualities of personality required for leadership and dominance in society, and in consequence

---

24. Cullen, 32.
25. Moore, 124-5; Murphy, 12.

women had to occupy the space defined and left for them by the men. To fit into this space the so-called feminine qualities were developed by women and hence emerged the two categories of personal qualities that are at the foundation of the complementarity of men and women discussed earlier.[26] But it must be obvious that all the personal qualities in question here are essentially *human* qualities and that a person, whether man or woman, would be a better and more fully developed person, if he/she possessed them all or at least tried to do so. Men are improved by cultivating the qualities we associate with women, and women are better women by endeavouring to acquire the so-called masculine qualities. In other words, it seems right to say that men should develop their feminine side and women their masculine side, so as to become more mature and balanced people.[27] So, for example, if it has usually been maintained that emotional sensitivity is a quality of women, we may now think it would be well if everybody had such a quality. Similarly, if in the past we considered it a male characteristic to have a tendency to think logically, we may now think that it would be well if women too possessed this ability. Conversely, we regard insensitivity and irrationality as defects wherever we meet them regardless of sex.[28]

Now it becomes clear that the further this process advances and the more women and men develop all the human qualities that have for long been split into masculine and feminine, so the more does complementarity as usually understood weaken and tend to disappear. Hence, as Moore says (p 126), we have the somewhat paradoxical conclusion that what is desirable is the reduction and ultimately the elimination of complementarity between men and women. An example may help at this point. Suppose a very active and outgoing man, who lacks receptive, passive qualities, marries a woman who is a more passive person. It may, then, happen that this man begins to appreciate the more passive qualities of his spouse and takes steps to develop them himself. Suppose too that his wife is impressed by her husband's active, outgoing qualities and works to become a more

---

26. Moore, 123.
27. Ibid., 125-6; Cullen 30.
28. Moore, 125; Cullen, 30; Johnson, 53; Ruether, 111-2.

active person. Then the end result will be that the partners are no longer complementary in these qualities and dispositions but, because of that, they will both be better, more mature and more human persons. Thus the complementary relationship, in so far as it is successful, ceases to be complementary and is all the better for that.[29]

We may note here, however, that some scholars, especially some feminists, are at pains to emphasise that this potential sharing of all these human qualities and the equality of the sexes that it can produce will not result in women and men ending up being reduced to a dull and stultifying sameness, because it has been found that women and men tend to perceive and integrate the relational and rational elements of their lives in different ways. This leads to studies of women's moral development and psychology, women's ways of knowing, women's ways of loving and women's ways of living bodily that promote the exercise of autonomy with a care for relationships.[30]

iv) Social conditioning and cultural stereotypes
Another major difficulty about accepting the usual understanding of the complementarity of men and women arises from the generally accepted fact nowadays that gender or the so-called masculine and feminine qualities we have been reflecting on are the result of social and cultural conditioning, if not totally at least largely. This has been implied in our earlier reflections. In other words, the so-called masculine and feminine qualities are cultural stereotypes formed in and resulting from a patriarchal society, serving to facilitate and maintain male superiority and dominance.[31] As one author says, '… many of our perceptions of what belongs to the male and what to the female are socially determined and culturally relative, a product of education and socialisation in a particular time and place.'[32] These stereotypes are largely the work of men as the dominant group in society. They are, then, not accidental but created and imposed by the dominant class because that suits them and their position in

29. Moore, 126.
30. Johnson, 53.
31. Cosgrave, 118; Murphy, 10; Farley, 134-5; Moore, 32-3, 123-4; Johnson, 47-50.
32. Moore, 122.

society.[33] It cannot be said, then, that these stereotypes of male and female personality are natural, the work of nature itself and so of God. Rather, they are in great part a human production in the service of inequality between the sexes and the continued subordination of women. As such they are unacceptable morally. Hence, arises the moral duty for all to work towards the dissolution of the complementarity involved in and resulting from these stereotypes, and, positively, to promote the growth of men and women generally as fully human persons sharing all the personal qualities involved in the stereotypes.

This point about social conditioning and cultural relativism becomes obvious when one looks at the variety of cultures in our world and notes the very different social roles that are assigned to men and women in these cultures. In this context the gender-assigned roles that obtain in our western society tend to look quite arbitrary.[34] And it becomes virtually impossible to speak of the complementarity of the sexes that we are discussing as in any real sense ontological, that is, belonging to the very being or nature of human beings in all times and places and, hence, essential and at least basically unchanged and unchangeable. It has in fact already been noted that in our western society the social roles of men and women have changed significantly in recent centuries and this points to real change in the stereotypes we are discussing. The social conditioning and cultural relativism in question here may be illustrated by a minor and slightly amusing example from Africa. In one African tribe women are expected to milk the cows. But in another tribe this is the men's job. However, if a woman from the former tribe were to milk the cows in the latter tribe, even if it were her husband's tribe, she could be cursed, shunned and exiled.[35]

In the light of this important insight about social conditioning and cultural relativism the following points require to be noted. If, as sociobiologists claim, there are some gender differences between men and women as a result of evolution, that is, by nature, it remains true that a large proportion of the psychological and emotional differences are the result of social

33. Moore, 123-4.
34. Farley, 137.
35. Ibid., 137.

conditioning. If, then, men and women are complementary, it is only to a very limited extent that they are naturally so. One who wishes to claim that natural complementarity exists must, then, bear the burden of proof in its regard.[36] But even if one can show that it does exist, that gives no grounds for claiming that one set of skills or qualities is superior to another. They are just different. If some still regard one set as superior to another set, that too is due to cultural conditioning.[37] Another point is that to appeal to the complementarity of the sexes in order to establish a guide for sexual behaviour is ineffective and contributes nothing, firstly, because due to social conditioning and cultural relativism, it cannot provide a universal ethic, and, secondly, because such guidelines gain credibility only if we already accept them as flowing logically from the complementarity.[38]

v) Complementarity as dualistic

Another criticism of the understanding of complementarity under discussion here is that it is dualistic, that is, it splits human psychological and emotional traits into two separate groups and then elevates sexual difference to an ontological principle that cleaves the human race into two radically different types of person, men who have a masculine nature and women who have a feminine nature.[39] This dualistic vision results in a world where men function as the normative human beings fit to exercise authority in the public realm, while women are destined for the private domain. Even in this domain the man should ultimately rule, because his innate ability to reason and make decisions provides for smooth ordering of the household. As Thomas Aquinas writes, 'woman is naturally subject to man, because in man the discretion of reason predominates'.[40] This elevation of men to be the norm of humanity is today spoken of as androcentrism and is rejected as false and discriminatory against women.[41]

---

36. See Cullen, 23-5, and Moore, 122-3.
37. Cullen, 24.
38. Moore, 127.
39. Johnson, 48.
40. Ibid., 48-9.
41. Murphy, 10; Ruether, 20; Carr, 136-7.

vi) Men and women incomplete?

It was mentioned earlier that John Paul II speaks of men and women being incomplete unless they come together in union. This idea deserves some reflection. Its meaning is by no means clear. One could wonder whether it owes something to Plato who wrote of 'the myth that humans in the beginning were not single individuals. Each person was two selves in one. Then they became separated; consequently you spend your life looking for your other half'.[42] In papal teaching it would seem that it is in marriage that one overcomes this lack and achieves completeness. But then one has to wonder about single people and especially those bound to celibacy in the priesthood and religious life. Do they deliberately choose this incompleteness that is to be lifelong and if so, how is such a choice justified? This is an obvious but troubling question, particularly given that papal teaching tends to see friendships between the sexes as dangerous threats to celibacy both for priests and single laity, because of the presumed power of the sex drive.[43]

To us this idea of incompleteness is unacceptable, since no one will now claim that any person, man or woman, is incomplete either physically, mentally or spiritually in his or herself. No essential part of them is missing and a member of one sex can't be said to be a part of a member of the other sex, so that he or she is incomplete, if the other moves away or is no longer in relationship. More positively, when people lack other people, it is not their wholeness that is in question so much as their needs. When a man loses his wife, he may feel incomplete, because now his need for her is unfulfilled. Now, not he, but his life is incomplete. So, if a man and a woman have a close relationship in or outside marriage, it is not so much that they complete each other as that they go well together, they form a satisfying unit, enhancing and enriching each other. One may say they are complementary but this complementarity would seem to have

---

42. John O'Donohue, *Anam Cara. Spiritual Wisdom from the Celtic World*, Bantam Press, London & New York, 1997, 46.
43. Christine E. Gudorf, 'Encountering the Other: The Modern Papacy on Women' in *Readings in Moral Theology, No. 9: Feminist Ethics and the Catholic Moral Tradition*. Edited by Charles Curran, Margaret A. Farley and Richard A. McCormick, S.J. Paulist Press, New York, 1996, 75-6.

an implicit reference to having children and in this regard men and women are plainly complementary, and need to be to achieve reproduction. This is physical and physiological complementarity; it is obviously a fact in human life and a necessary and basic one, as we will see in our next section. But accepting this form of complementarity does not call into question the criticisms of the so-called psychological and emotional complementarity that we have discussed earlier. One can have the former without the latter.[44]

It may be noted here too that the CDF Letter of 2004 speaks, not just of physical complementarity, but also of psychological and ontological complementarity (No. 8). It would seem likely that one should interpret this text to mean that this psychological complementarity is to be understood as also ontological, thus following the teaching of John Paul II in his *Letter to Women*, 1995, No 7, as outlined and discussed earlier. But if this is the case, then this understanding is open to the same criticisms that have been outlined earlier in this section and so must be considered patriarchal and so as denying the equality of women in practice.

This CDF Letter of 2004 does, however, seem to use the word 'ontological' in two contexts where it would seem to be warranted and to have an acceptable meaning in the context of the discussion of the nature and relationships of men and women.

Section 6 of the Letter seems to indicate that it is the relational capacity or reality of human beings, men and women, that belongs to their very nature and so has an ontological character. Later in Section 12 it is asserted that male and female belong ontologically to creation. The meaning of this would seem to be that the division of human beings into two sexes is part of the very being or nature of humanity as God has created the human race and so may be said to be ontological.[45]

Since it is now clear that the psychological and emotional complementarity that has been under discussion here is in large measure a creation of men, the dominant class in society over

44. Moore, 118-20.
45. However, see Ethna Regan, 'Women, Theology and the Church: Whose Expertise?', *Doctrine and Life*, September 2011, 4-17 at 12-13 for a somewhat different interpretation of these two texts.

the centuries, with the purpose of preserving their dominance and the subordination of women, one has to find it morally unacceptable and quite unchristian. If, then, complementarity is to be acceptable in any sense, it has to be rethought and presented in a way that is realistic and yet ensures the equality of women and men, not just in theory but in daily living also. That will be attempted in our final section.

RETHINKING COMPLEMENTARITY: AN EGALITARIAN VIEW

In the previous two sections we have explained, criticised and rejected the understanding of complementarity that has long been accepted. This, however, does not mean that there is no form of complementarity between men and women. There is and it is quite extensive. In this final section we will focus on this complementarity and its particular forms and expressions. The reader will notice that here there will be no division of personal qualities into masculine and feminine and so no basis for postulating any inferiority of women, but rather good reasons for affirming the equality of the sexes in practice as well as in theory.

In contrast to the usual tendency to begin with the differences between women and men our starting point here will focus on the elements or aspects of our humanity that women and men share and have in common. This is intended to put the difference of gender in context and in perspective and help to ensure that this difference is neither exaggerated nor diminished in its many dimensions or in its significance in the day to day lives of men and women in society and in the church.

The shared humanity of men and women
What we are highlighting here may best be expressed by a quotation from a contemporary author.[46] 'Most basically, all human persons share in being embodied spirits in the world, who are conceived ... when egg and sperm unite to produce a growing organism that is ultimately delivered from a woman's body. Through the body all human beings are connected to the earth in an ecological community that includes all other living creatures in mutual interdependence on the life-supporting systems of the planet. To stay alive all human beings have common needs for breathable air, drinkable water, nourishment and

46. Johnson, 51-2.

sleep ... All persons, furthermore, starting in the first minutes of life are connected to significant other persons and develop personality in and through these intimate relationships. All interact with political, economic and social structures, for better or for worse. All are shaped by their culture, geography and the historical time in which they live. And all are destined to die... You die from the same bodily breakdown whether male or female, of African, European or Asian descent, old or young, employed in a skilled or unskilled job.'

In addition, all human persons who are considered normal are moral beings, that is, they distinguish right from wrong in regard to human actions, attitudes and situations, and good from evil in relation to persons and what makes for human flourishing or wholeness.[47] They make moral judgments as well as experiencing moral obligations. They all have a morality and build or fail to build moral character. All this presupposes that all normal human beings have real freedom of will that enables them to choose freely to do or not to do particular actions, to choose specific values, attitudes and priorities and to cultivate various virtues. Also all human persons are spiritual beings. They have a spirituality in and through which they find meaning in life and have ideals, values, virtues and goals by which they live, shape their character, their activities, their relationships and their world. This is true whether this spirituality is open to the transcendent or not, and so whether God, the Supreme Reality, is the focus of their lives or not.

And of course, as has been emphasised earlier, all human beings, men and women, have equal dignity as persons and as children of God.

From what has been outlined here it can be concluded that we humans, men and women, have more in common than what divides us, more similarities than differences.

We turn now to a consideration of the forms of complementarity between men and women that do not involve or arise from gender difference.

---

47. Vincent MacNamara, *The Call To Be Human – Making Sense of Morality*, Veritas, Dublin, 2010, 16-7.

Complementarity apart from gender difference
Experience would seem to indicate that for some people it is qualities that are the same as their own which form for them their true complement. To a large extent in our lives similarity is desirable. People need to have shared interests and tastes, if their relationship is to work and to blossom. And sharing qualities of personality can help too. So it is important in friendship that the friends have things they can do together, e.g. go to the cinema or theatre, take walks, go on holidays, enjoy sports, dining out, or listening to music. Having similar political and religious beliefs may also be important to the smooth working of a relationship as can a true concern for justice and charity. Hence, in these cases similarity not difference provides a basis for complementarity, though of course in other cases it may be a source of tension and difficulty.[48] It can also happen that difference of interest and taste may be a source of strength and enjoyment in a relationship and help it to work better. This may be because the friends or spouses then have time for themselves and time in which to develop other nourishing relationships and interests. Sharing their different experiences arising from these individual interests and tastes can, thus, be something that proves valuable and a contribution to complementarity. Obviously, such differences can be a source of problems but they are not necessarily so.

It will be clear here that the forms of complementarity discussed just now are not concerned with personal qualities or dispositions as was the case earlier. That theory put too much emphasis on such qualities as the basis of complementarity between men and women and neglected the forms of it that have now been highlighted and those that will be discussed in what follows.[49]

Experience teaches that what makes relationships in general and those between the sexes flourish and go well is not so much the personal qualities of the partners but rather their commitment to make the relationship work. If the friends or partners have the will to stay in relationship, then they will take the steps necessary to achieve this. This will require that the partners get to know each other well, that they take account of the other's

48. Moore, 128.
49. Ibid., 128.

likes and dislikes and interests, and that there is give and take in the relationship. Then they will be able to arrive at an arrangement that will suit them both and that they can both be happy to continue. In this situation each friend or partner will do things because they please the other and avoid things because the other dislikes them. Here we have a true form of complementarity, one that is not so much given and a result of the partners' natural qualities, but rather one that can be and is worked at and developed, so that the partners or friends get on better together, deepen their relationship and grow as persons. One could say that this form of complementarity is an expression of the moral qualities of the friends or partners, the virtues that they practise precisely to enable them to complement each other and so for the relationship to flourish.[50]

There is another way in which people can complement each other that does not involve gender differences. This too is very much part of our daily experience and occurs in what may be called non-sexual relationships between two men or two women. Many people like to have and even prefer close friends of their own sex and these relationships can be very deep, very enriching for the friends and so very important in their lives. These friends complement each other but it is usually common interests and tastes and their commitment to each other and their relationship that make these friendships work and prosper.

Complementarity in sexual relationships
We know from experience that there is no call for the reduction or elimination of complementarity or gender difference in some areas of the relations of the sexes. These areas are dress, deportment and sexual behaviour. People do not want or call for men to dress as women and carry themselves like women and vice versa. Nor do people want men to act like women or to seek sexual relations with other men. Similarly for women.[51] So boys are socialised to behave in certain ways towards girls and to find them sexually attractive. The same holds for girls in relation to boys. This is what society regards as normal; to act contrary to this process of socialisation is viewed as abnormal, even

50. Moore, 128-9.
51. Ibid., 126-7.

unnatural. Hence, the negative attitudes to homosexual people and hermaphrodites.[52]

One element of this sexual behaviour which all accept as normal in sexual relationships between the sexes is sexual intercourse. But this too has been understood in a way that reflects the dominant role of men in society and the submissive or passive role of women. Hence, men are said to be active and women passive in sexual intercourse. But this is often not the case; both are active in different ways. The activity of the supposedly 'passive' partner has officially been completely overlooked in the interest of making sexual relations symbolic of social relations, of seeing the woman as subordinate to the man. This is another instance of where the complementarity of the sexes has been used to place women in a subordinate position. It is, however, unacceptable and it is happening less and less as the equality of men and women is more and more recognised and made a reality.

Though today in western society, as already noted, some of the so-called masculine psychological and emotional qualities are to some degree shared by some women, and some of the feminine ones are similarly to be found in some men, there are many other differences or expressions of complementarity between men and women that are fully accepted and are quite common in society generally. Some of these differences appear in the following matters: names, hair styles, clothes, bodily adornment, particular interests, kinds of work and recreation, who one associates with, places where one may go, the responsibilities one takes on as a man or woman, the school one may go to and the subjects studied, whether one is a dominant or submissive person, etc. These differences between men and women are largely social conventions but are treated as 'natural'. To transgress them leads to one being regarded as abnormal, because they are held in society to be extremely important. And of course different societies have different conventions in these matters.[53]

In regard to sexual relationships, then, gender does matter and in a basic way. But what matters is not the so-called complementary qualities or similarities but rather the simple fact that

52. Ibid., 32-3.
53. Ibid., 31-2.

the other person is a man or a woman. So what attracts a heterosexual man to a woman is not what psychological or emotional qualities she may have but her femaleness, the fact that she is a woman. Similarly in the case of a heterosexual woman; she is attracted by the man's maleness, the fact that he is a man. It must be added, of course, that there are different kinds of femaleness and maleness, different kinds of men and women and this will matter to those who are sexually attracted to them. So, for example, a fat or thin person may hold a special attraction for some people and so may a person who is older or younger, strong or vulnerable, fair or dark, reserved or outgoing.[54]

It seems, then, that what is the source of sexual attraction in the case of heterosexual persons is not whether the other person has differences or indeed similarities psychologically or emotionally that may be complementary, but rather the fact that the other person is of the other sex and of a particular type of femaleness or maleness that is found attractive. At the same time experience shows that the so-called complementary traits can increase or decrease the attraction between the man and the woman, though it is clear that it is not these traits that the other person loves but rather the person of the other sex who possesses them. So, for example, a man may find a woman who is emotionally very open and sensitive to be particularly attractive, while he may be put off somewhat if a woman is very talkative or rather overpowering. The same can happen from a woman's point of view, if the man she is attracted to turns out to be very warm and caring, on the one hand, or domineering or insensitive, on the other.

It will be clear from all these observations that it is not the so-called complementary traits of men or women that are the source of the sexual attraction between a heterosexual man and woman. This is confirmed when one adverts to the fact that it could happen that this complementarity of traits might be reduced or even disappear as one or both of the partners grows and acquires the traits of the other. If, then, this complementarity were the source of sexual attraction, the whole relationship would weaken and probably disappear. Neither does this complementarity provide a criterion by which to judge the rightness

54. Moore, 130-1; See Farley, 158.

or wrongness of a particular sexual relationship or action. If it did, then it could be possible that a man could acquire the right complementary qualities so as to become a possible sexual partner for another man. That would spell the end of the church's defence against homosexual activity.[55]

It follows also that this complementarity cannot provide a reason for judging women inferior to men or for any subordination of women to men in social or ecclesial life. This is so because all these psychological and emotional qualities are human qualities to be acquired as fully as possible by both women and men, and hence, are not to be divided into two groups and assigned by men to the two sexes in a way that serves male domination. Consequently, the lack of any of these qualities cannot be a reason for regarding women as unequal to men in theory or in practice and conversely, the possession of a particular group of them, what has been called the masculine traits, cannot provide a basis for regarding men as superior to women in life in society or in the church.

On the positive side, our rethinking of complementarity shows that, while there is true complementarity between women and men in sexual relationships and otherwise, this in no way involves or implies any inferiority of women to men. Rather it suggests and supports the equality of the sexes in theory and in practice. This equality is, then, a basic principle that binds everyone and especially us Christians in all our relationships and institutions, at the personal, social and ecclesial levels.

CONCLUSION

We have endeavoured in this chapter to develop what has been called an egalitarian anthropology, in other words, an understanding of men and women that preserves and promotes their equality in practice as well as in theory. This anthropology envisions a redeemed humanity with relationships between men and women marked by mutual partnership. In this context sexual and gender differences between the sexes assume their rightful proportion and do not translate into a strictly genderised division of human characteristics or of social roles.[56]

---

55. Moore, 131.
56. Johnson, 54.

Nevertheless, it is clear that society makes the biological or sex difference between men and women the basis of a fundamental social difference. While being male or female may be a biological fact about people, being a man or a woman is a matter of belonging to a social category, having a particular social identity. God's creation of human beings as male and female is the foundation of a basic division of adult human beings into two great social classes, a division that runs through the entire structure of societies.[57] 'Sex serves, therefore, to divide the human species in utterly important ways'.[58]

It has been argued that this egalitarian or single anthropology needs to be complemented by an emphasis on transforming the social and cultural structures of society that are the inseparable context in which the patriarchal vision of man-woman relationships is found and has long flourished. Without this social or public emphasis even an egalitarian vision of man-woman relationships can become individualistic and in fact ineffective. Such a transformative vision may seem utopian but it is necessary and in line with the Christian understanding of the reign of God.[59]

---

57. Ibid., 29-31.
58. Farley, 153.
59. Carr, 127-8.

The Christian Life:
Relating its Spiritual and Moral Dimensions

Every human being, whether religious or not, lives a life that has both a spiritual and a moral dimension, two aspects of life that are deeply and inextricably intertwined and interdependent. Both are essential elements of human living. We wouldn't be truly human without either. Together they contribute vitally to making us the meaning-seeking, value-pursuing, good-doing, virtue-practising persons that we are.

If we had no spirituality, we would have no vision of what human life is about. Life would have no meaning for us; we'd be committed to nothing; nothing would have value for us, because we'd have no basis on which to discern or choose values. Our experiences would be superficial and disjointed with nothing to give them depth or unity; they would yield us no meaning as we'd have no understanding of life in terms of which we could evaluate and make sense of them. As a result truly spiritual and human living would prove impossible.

Without morality and a moral sense one would be unaware of the difference between right and wrong, incapable of distinguishing one from the other and so unable to do the good and avoid the evil. One would feel no sense of moral obligation and would be indifferent in regard to acquiring and practising the virtues, building a good moral character or promoting the welfare of others and the common good. In a word, we'd be amoral and no doubt immoral but without knowing about either. We'd not be human in the sense in which we know people are human and should be.

These largely negative statements show how essential it is for human living that one have a spirituality and a morality. But we need to clarify in positive terms what is involved here. It is necessary to provide a fuller explanation of what both spirituality and morality are and in particular what is the precise relationship between them. Such explanations will contribute to a better understanding of both these dimensions of human living and may help us achieve some growth in both our spiritual and moral lives or, more accurately, in our spiritual-moral life as human beings and as Christians.

The legacy of history: the split

Despite the assertion in the preceding paragraphs of the profound interlinking of the spiritual and the moral in human – and Christian – life, they have been presented as quite separate in the theology and spirituality of recent centuries in the Church. It is not necessary here to elaborate on how this split in church thinking came about.[1]

But the result of it was that morality came to be presented in the books of moral theology in a legal way, that is, as a series of principles, rules and laws, especially the ten commandments, that Catholics were to obey. This tended to focus on the minimum requirements of the Christian life, what one was obliged to do to avoid sin. This area of the Christian life was then taken to be what moral theology was to study and expound and what the ministers of the Church were to teach and preach.

Side by side with but quite separate from this went a corresponding understanding of spirituality. Spirituality and the sciences that studied it, namely, ascetical and mystical theology, came to focus on the ideals and goals of the Christian life, since moral theology was already dealing with the minimum demands of Christian living. Hence, spirituality concerned itself with the so-called counsels as distinct from the ten commandments, with prayer, contemplation, meditation, mysticism and asceticism, and the higher paths to union with God.

Thus developed a two-track understanding of the Christian life, where morality and spirituality were treated as separate areas of that life and were studied separately in books that were quite distinct in their subject matter, their method of approach and their aims. Hence, there emerged also a two-tier understanding of the Christian life, the lower level, directed to people living 'in the world' and focused on keeping the commandments, while the higher level of spirituality was concerned with the counsels and the more exalted reaches of the Christian life,

---

1. See Richard M. Gula, S.S., *The Call to Holiness – Embracing a Fully Christian Life*, Paulist Press, New York, 2003, chapter 2. Henceforth referred to as *Holiness*.

which only those in religious life were likely to rise to and practise.

Today writers on the spiritual and the moral life of Christians are conscious of this faulty and inadequate understanding of both that has been inherited from the centuries prior to Vatican II. In consequence, significant efforts are being made today in Catholic - and other - writing on spirituality and morality to correct the faults of the past and to develop an understanding of both that is more biblical, more informed by the best theological insights of recent scholarship and that seeks to highlight the deep unity between the spiritual and moral dimensions of the Christian life. One author says:

> moral theology has before it the task of uniting the moral and the spiritual life into an integrated whole. The call to holiness and the call to decision-making cannot be seen as separate entities; they are interactive parts of one process. Classic Catholic thought was aware of this theme, especially in terms of St Thomas's stress on the life of virtue. But for much of twentieth-century Catholicism, prayer and the spiritual life became something for the chapel, and action became something for the marketplace, with little interaction between the life of prayer and the life of the marketplace ... there is much unfinished business in terms of the integration of moral and spiritual theology.[2]

In the remainder of this chapter an attempt will be made to develop an understanding of the Christian life that will highlight and explain its spiritual and moral dimensions and in particular endeavour to show how they are related and together constitute the core or essence of what it means to live as a Christian in the Church and world of today.

Understanding spirituality today
The word spirituality is widely used nowadays even outside religious circles but it is generally accepted that there is no agreed definition or even description of it. One book lists twenty-three

---

2. Philip S. Keane, 'Catholic Moral Theology from 1960 to 2040: Accomplishments and Challenges for the Future', in Dermot A. Lane, Editor, *Catholic Theology Facing the Future - Historical Perspectives*, The Columba Press, Dublin, 2003, 84.

different definitions.[3] We need to be mindful also that one's understanding of spirituality must allow for and facilitate a significant relationship of spirituality with morality, since, as has been stated, they are in practice two deeply intertwined dimensions of human and Christian life. It seems appropriate, then, to take spirituality in a broad sense that makes it relevant to and influential in all aspects of one's way of life. This seems correct when one takes account of the fact that it is generally agreed that every person, whether he/she is religious or not, has a spirituality and cannot avoid having one, if (s)he is to make sense of life and experience and live in a meaningful and rational manner.[4]

One's spirituality, then, consists in the vision of life and the values and attitudes within that vision which, integrated together, make one's life meaningful and by which one lives and acts. It is made up of the most basic and deeply held values, ideals, attitudes and commitments one has and it brings these into a unified understanding that enables one to live life rationally and energises one to act purposefully and to commit oneself to various goals and activities in different areas of life. One's spirituality will, then, express itself in one's attitudes, convictions, emotions and actions, in one's whole lifestyle and way of coping, in what one values and does not value.[5] So one's spirituality extends to and manifests itself in the various moral, political and religious activities one engages in as one endeavours to answer the call to become the best person one can be.[6] This will be spelled out in more practical terms later.

Christian spirituality
This spirituality is focused on and inspired by the Christian Church's belief in the God of Jesus Christ, who is Father, Son and Holy Spirit. It is life in God's Spirit.[7] Central here will be the religious and moral ideals and values which Jesus practised and taught and which we his disciples are to make our own and by

---

3. See Gula, *Holiness*, 17.
4. Gula, *Holiness*, 18.
5. Gula, *Holiness*, 19.
6. Donal Dorr, *Spirituality – Our Deepest Heart's Desire*, The Columba Press, Dublin, 2008, 7-8. Henceforth referred to as *Spirituality*.
7. Gula, *Holiness*, 20.

which we are to shape our characters and lives.[8] So Christian spirituality gives rise to our Christian way of life which is both religious and moral. As we live that life we respond to God's love in Christ by a variety of religious practices and by doing all possible to love the people in the relationships we have. Hence, Christian spirituality can be described as the way of life of the Christian, based on and inspired by one's understanding of and commitment to the Christian vision of life with its religious and moral ideals and values. It is centred on the God of Jesus Christ and lived in the Holy Spirit and in the community of the Church.[9] One may also express it as follows: Christian spirituality integrates life around the personal experience that God, our ultimate value, values us.[10]

Morality, secular and Christian

Most people feel that they are much clearer on what morality is about than they are on what spirituality deals with. In this they are correct. What they may not be so clear about, though, is the relationship between the spiritual, as already described, and the moral. This relationship will be the main focus of the considerations in the following pages. But to begin with a few brief words on what morality is all about will be helpful.

Morality is concerned with how we conduct ourselves in our relationships with other individuals, groups and communities. In particular it concerns how we discern the needs of others and respond to them so as to promote the welfare of the persons involved. Actions that make for human flourishing are designated as right and those that do the opposite are called wrong. In addition, morality is about a person acquiring those virtues and doing those actions that promote the full flourishing of human life in community and in harmony with the environment.[11] So the moral life of any person and of the Christian too concerns doing what is right and avoiding what is wrong but also making oneself a good virtuous person and helping others to grow as persons through acquiring the virtues and so developing their

8. *William Cosgrave, Christian Living Today – Essays in Moral and Pastoral Theology*, The Columba Press, Dublin, 2001, 235.
9. Cosgrave, 235.
10. Gula, *Holiness*, 23.
11. Gula, *Holiness*, 24.

moral character. From this it will be clear that the moral life has personal, social and environmental dimensions and our moral responsibility extends to working for progress in all three aspects of human living. To be a moral person, therefore, means that we are searching for ways to live together that will enable everyone to flourish.[12] Clearly, then, morality is a human reality that is an essential and basic aspect of everyone's life, whether one is religious or not.

For the Christian all this holds true. But for him/her the moral life has as its context or horizon the love of God in Christ. All the Christian's actions will, then, be understood as responses to this love as it enters one's experience in and through one's relationships with Christ, with the Church, the people in one's life and the world in which we all live. In a word, the Christian moral life is about responding to God's love by loving the people in one's relationships, personal and social and by caring for the earth as a steward of God's creation. As Gula says (*Holiness*, p 30), we should love God directly, we should love our neighbour as an overflow of our love for God, and we should love God in and through loving our neighbour and the world God has created.

We may quote here the 2008 document of the Pontifical Biblical Commission on *The Bible and Morality* (paragraph 0.3.1., p 14):

> morality is secondary to God's founding initiative, which we express theologically in terms of gift. In the biblical perspective morality is rooted in the prior gift of life, of intellect and of free will (creation), and above all in the entirely unmerited offer of a privileged, intimate relationship between human beings and God (covenant). Morality is not primarily the human response but a revelation of God's purpose and of the divine gift. In other words, for the Bible, morality is the consequence of the experience of God ... The Law itself, an intimate part of the covenant process, is seen to be a gift from God ... which the Bible itself aptly expresses with the term 'way' ... a way to follow.[13]

---

12. Gula *Holiness*, 27.
13. Libreria Editrice Vaticana, The Vatican.

The spiritual in Christian living

Here the aim is to reflect on the spiritual dimension of our Christian lives a little more and develop some further perspectives that pertain to it.

i) God in the spiritual: For the Christian the basic or transcendent reality in one's vision of life is God or God's love for us in Christ. This is the foundation or core of our Christian spirituality. On this basis we can and should integrate and unify our values and the whole meaning or vision of life that is ours. So for us Christians life is about God loving us in Christ and we responding to that love in and through our attitudes, virtues, relationships and activities, moral and religious. So one's spirituality will and must express itself in the religious and moral attitudes, activities and practices that fill one's life.

It is important to stress the point that God's love for us always touches or reaches us in a mediated manner, that is, not in the direct way that we relate to and encounter human beings but, as theologians regularly express it today, in and through the human and created realities with which our experience confronts us, e.g., our own humanity, human relationships, groups and communities and especially the Church, virtues, the good example of others, books, talks, music, the beauties of nature, injustice, poverty, prosperity, sin, etc. As Gula says,

> There is no other way for us who are body-persons to experience the invisible except through that which invades the senses ... any event of history or wonder of nature can mediate God's presence in the Spirit'; ... God comes to us in and through our everyday experiences.[14]

ii) Specific spiritual experiences: For Dorr a spiritual experience is any one that 'can have a significant and often a transforming effect in a person's life, any event which touches us at a very deep level'. He says, further, that 'God is behind and beyond our everyday spiritual experiences and they offer us an opening into an experience of God'.[15] From this it will be clear that many of our experiences can and will be spiritual, that is, in and through them we can discern God's presence in the Spirit and,

14. Gula, *Holiness*, 111, 113, 115.
15. Dorr, *Spirituality*, 16, 21. See also 41-2.

sometimes, God's blessing and/or perhaps God's call inviting us to respond to a particular situation or person(s) by some action, moral or religious.

It will be important at this stage to specify some of the experiences that are in question here, that can be classed as spiritual and that, therefore, can be for us experiences in and through which God can enter our lives and bless, invite or even challenge us in various ways. Dorr gives many good examples,[16] some of which are listed here:

- Falling in love and being loved unconditionally, experiences which usually have profound effects on a person.
- Childbirth and parenthood: for many women especially childbirth is one of the deepest spiritual experiences, and for men and women parenthood will often involve numerous experiences that can transform them as persons.
- Healing, physical, mental or spiritual, can often bring new life and energy to a person, when the recovery is complete.
- Forgiveness and reconciliation: again these can be very significant and even life-changing and deeply spiritual realities, especially when close and important relationships, groups or communities are involved. In them many will experience God gifting them the grace to receive these realities and perhaps in some situations to make them possible.
- Being part of a sharing and caring group or community, where one is appreciated, accepted and enabled to participate in a meaningful way.
- A personal call from God to live a particular way of life, e.g. marriage, priesthood or religious life or a suitable career to which one is deeply attracted.
- The feeling that one is a person of worth and value with dignity, rights and talents, who is happy to be him/herself.
- To marvel and wonder at the beauties of nature and nourish one's spirit on the majesty of God's creation.
- It can be a notable spiritual experience to have one's prayer for a significant good heard and answered by God, so that one experiences a moving surge of gratitude and joy.

16. Dorr, *Spirituality*, 17-30.

These spiritual experiences provide an underpinning or basis for ethical values and virtues and genuine moral commitment. Our commitment to moral values and our growth in the virtues will be fostered, if we appreciate and have in our lives the kind of spiritual experiences described here.[17]

While all Christians will have been formed on Christian teaching with its religious vision of life and its moral values and virtues, individual Christians will choose different priorities and concerns within that vision based on their experiences in life. Hence, it will happen that those Christians will respond differently to the various spiritual experiences they will have and they will experience God's touch more in some than in others, depending on how things have gone in their earlier years. Some will, then, opt for a more contemplative or meditative spirituality, while others devote themselves to a more active, outward-looking spirituality, concerning themselves, perhaps, with important moral and political issues of the world.[18]

Relating the spiritual and moral dimensions of life
Up to this point spirituality and morality have been discussed separately, mostly for the sake of coming to understand each of them somewhat better. At the same time it will have become clear that these two basic dimensions of human and Christian life are inextricably united in our lives as we live them. Now I will attempt to take up this union-in-living and show what it involves and how it works out in practice from day to day.

The basic point to keep in mind is that the spiritual and the moral are not to be found in two separate compartments of our Christian lives as we live them. In fact, they are so closely related and intertwined that they cannot be adequately distinguished in a way that would allow one to list their characteristics or elements in two quite distinct categories. Rather in profound ways the spiritual is the moral and the moral is spiritual or at the very least our spiritual experiences underpin and provide energy for our moral values, virtues and commitments.[19] At the same time our moral experiences express, ratify, deepen and even correct our vision of life with its basic attitudes and

17. Dorr, *Spirituality*, 16, 22.
18. Dorr, *Spirituality*, 33-4; See Gula, *Holiness*, 12-17.
19. Dorr, *Spirituality*, 16, 23.

values, in and through which we live out our love of and commitment to God and our neighbour. [20]

Gula puts it in the following way: 'the moral life and spiritual life converge when we begin to explore the sort of persons we ought to become and the sort of lives we ought to live in order to flourish as authentic human beings'.[21] Again he states: 'Christian spirituality and Christian morality converge in the good life', that is, in the Christian life as we live it every day.[22] Or, as Dorr says, 'morality is a key element in spirituality'.[23] More precisely, it can be stated that the moral life is spiritual at its source and the spiritual life is moral in its manifestations. Spirituality gives rise to morality and pervades all aspects of it.[24] On the other hand, in one's moral life one expresses one's spirituality, grounds it in one's relationships with others and with God and also shapes and confirms it and may even modify it. Through spirituality we pay attention to the depth dimension of human life, while through morality we attend to the public face of that spiritual depth. The roots of one's moral life are in one's spirituality and the fruits of one's spirituality are in the moral life.[25]

The significant spiritual experiences that were discussed earlier make it clear that one's spirituality connects with the depths of one's experience, that is, the inner meaning of life or the deep reasons that motivate a person.[26] For the Christian this is where one may encounter God, who can and often does communicate with us in and through experiences such as these. Thus Christian spirituality integrates all one's life and experiences meaningfully by basing them on what gives ultimate meaning and value to life, namely, God's love for us in Christ and God's call to the Christian to respond to that love by a life of Christian discipleship. Thus the Christian moral life springs from our

---

20. Richard M. Gula, S.S., *The Good Life – Where Morality and Spirituality Converge*. Paulist Press, New York. 1999, 5. Referred to henceforth as *The Good Life*.
21. Gula, *The Good Life*, 5.
22. Gula, *The Good Life*, 3.
23. *Spirituality* , 116.
24. Gula, *Holiness*, 31, 39.
25. Gula, *Holiness*, 62.
26. Gula, *Holiness*, 16.

Christian spirituality and incarnates it in our Christian living. Through living thus the Christian becomes an authentic human being who has acquired the virtues and built a moral character that enables him/her consistently to live and act in a Christ-like manner.

It is clear here that one's spirituality as a Christian will include the central values and principles of Jesus' teaching about human life in its moral dimension: God's love for us in the Spirit, the call for us to respond, the basic attitudes, values and virtues that constitute the core of Christian moral living and a whole style of life that is grounded in one's commitment to God in Christ.[27]

At this point it can easily be seen that Christian spirituality and Christian morality come together in a deep union, so that the moral life is rooted in one's spirituality and the spiritual life expresses itself in our moral living, or, in other words, the love of neighbour and self are ultimately grounded in our love for God.[28] To put it another way, one may say that Christian spirituality is centred on the experience of God loving us in Christ and Christian morality is our response to that love.[29] Thus our spirituality nourishes our moral life at its very roots and our morality arises from and reveals our spirituality. In this understanding, then, one's spirituality is seen to pervade the whole of one's moral life and to shape the morality by which one lives. At the same time, one's moral experience can exercise an influence on one's spirituality and cause one to examine one's motivation, increase one's commitment, for example, to social justice or the care of the earth and even confirm one in one's use of spiritual practices that help one love God and one's neighbour more deeply.[30] It must be said also that one's spirituality needs one to engage in an active and committed moral life, lest that spirituality become detached from everyday Christian living and experience and take on an appearance of a kind of 'pie in the sky' religious lifestyle or set of practices. In relation, then, to both spirituality and morality or the spiritual-moral life of the Christian

---

27. Gula, *The Good Life*, 5.
28. Gula, *Holiness*, 31.
29. Gula, *Holiness*, 37.
30. Gula, *Holiness*, 38-9.

the words of Jesus are very apt: 'by their fruits you shall know them' (Mt 7.20).[31]

A balanced spiritual-moral life[32]
The main areas or aspects of the Christian spirituality we have been describing and whose close relationship with the moral life we have stressed, can be outlined or sketched in the following three steps. Here for the sake of clarity we will discuss the religious and the moral aspects of this spirituality separately, while all the time keeping in mind the fundamental unity that does and must exist between them, if we are to present an authentic and balanced Christian spirituality.

i) God's love for us: our religious response – faith and prayerfulness
As already stated, the central truth of Christian spirituality is that God loves us in Christ and in the Holy Spirit. This love comes to us in and through other people and the sort of spiritual experiences already outlined, so that we believe that God has carved our names on the palm of his/her hand (Is 49.16). This sense of the love and care of God enables us to understand God's providence as a living experience by which we believe that God is acting in our lives, so that we can become fully human and truly children of God in Christ. In all this, of course, Jesus is the model for the Christian. He shows us both what God's love for us involves and also how we are to respond to that love in all areas of our lives. To make this response as it should be made we need a deep religious commitment that will enable us to be aware of God's love for us and inspire us to respond wholeheartedly by means of a vigorous life of prayer, personal and communal, regular reflection and, of course, moral action.[33]

---

31. Gula, *Holiness*, 39.
32. This section is based largely on Donal Dorr, *Spirituality and Justice*, Gill & Macmillan, Dublin. 1984, chapter 1. See also Dorr, *Spirituality*, Part III, Spirituality and Morality; and Dorr, *Time for a Change – A Fresh Look at Spirituality, Sexuality, Globalisation and the Church*, The Columba Press, Dublin, 2004, chapters 1 and 2.
33. See Dorr, *Spirituality*, chapter 11; see also chapter 4, 'A Christian Approach to the Mystery'.

ii) God's love for us: our moral response - loving other people
The second element of Christian spirituality is the moral element, in which spirituality expresses itself in the relationships
and activities of one's daily life. This is about loving our neighbours in the variety of relationships one establishes in the course
of one's life from one's spouse and family in marriage to one's
relatives, friends, neighbours and colleagues in the workplace,
etc. Here a deep moral commitment is required to enable us to
practise all the virtues needed to fulfil our duty to love the
neighbour after the manner of Jesus, e.g. respect, care, listening,
trusting, fidelity, helping, forgiveness, etc. This moral dimension is implied in and required by the first element of our spirituality as just outlined, since, as the Bible says, one cannot love
God if one does not love one's neighbour. In fact the principal
way in which we love God is by loving our neighbour.[34] One
may add here that this moral dimension of Christian spirituality
also demands that one love oneself and practise the various
virtues in relation to oneself also, e.g. appreciation, respect,
trust, care, patience and forgiveness.

iii) God's love for us: our moral response - practising social justice
Here again we have a moral dimension of Christian spirituality,
one in which that spirituality extends its ambit to embrace the
good of society worldwide. Loving our neighbour requires us to
work for a better society, to seek to build a society that is just,
not only in its activities but also and especially in its structures,
institutions and laws. This is expressed nowadays in the Church
by saying that we are called to make an option for the poor, so
that we do all we can to share in and attend to the experience
and the needs of those who are poor and marginalized and so
practise justice in the social and indeed the political arena. This
will involve a deep moral-political commitment so that one is
dedicated to building a just society in all its dimensions, including care for the earth and the environment.[35]

---

34. Dorr, *Spirituality*, 90–7.
35. See Dorr, *Spirituality*, chapters 12 through 18 and *Time for a Change*
chapters 7 and 8, where he spells out in detail what one might call the
macro-moral dimension of Christian spirituality.

Religious practices and the moral life[36]

So far in our discussion of Christian spirituality and the place of the moral life in it the focus has been on coming to understand what this spirituality is, what it entails and how morality fits into it and is related to it. This is, of course, important and basic. But it is not everything about Christian spirituality.

Every Christian knows that one has to practise one's faith; one is expected to be a practising Catholic (or Anglican or whatever). This means, as the word implies, that one has to engage in certain practices, religious and moral, in and through which one expresses one's faith or spirituality and, by expressing it, nourishes and strengthens it. Here we are talking especially about such religious practices as prayer, personal and communal, meditation and contemplation, the sacraments, especially the Eucharist, and sacramentals like the rosary, benediction, blessing of throats, novenas, using holy water, statues and medals, pilgrimages, Bible reading, etc. The question in this context is not about these religious practices in themselves but rather how they impact on the moral life of the Catholic (or other) Christian, how these expressions of one's Christian spirituality matter in and for the Christian morality one endeavours to live by, and also how living the Christian moral life affects or could affect these religious/spiritual practices.

At this point it will be important to state that making a genuine effort to live the Christian moral life in imitation of Jesus and following the teaching of the Church is perhaps the most important way in which one may practise one's faith or spirituality in one's daily life. As St John says, one cannot love God if one does not love one's brother [and sister] (1John 4.20). Taking this as accepted, our concern here will be with the Christian spiritual or religious practices listed above.

We may summarise the answer to the above questions in the words of Gula: 'Spiritual practices should bring us to a heightened sensitivity to our moral responsibilities, and moral living should return us to our spiritual practices, where we focus ourselves on our ultimate dependence on God.'[37] Here again it is clear that love of God and of our neighbour are inseparable and

---

36. This section draws significantly on Gula, *Holiness*, chapter 5.
37. Gula, *Holiness*, 148.

our practice in relation to the one will be important for the other.

It is not hard to see that the spiritual practices in question here are all designed primarily to strengthen our relationship with God, to deepen our religious faith. If they are to do this effectively, it will be necessary that one engage in one's chosen religious practices in a regular way. One will need to have a stable pattern of religious practice in one's life, that is, prayer and prayerful exercises that keep one mindful of God's presence and love in one's life and that, therefore, nourish one's religious faith and help to keep one open to God's love and call in one's life.[38] Implied here is the point that these spiritual or religious practices are not to be reduced to simple means to moral action or personal moral growth.[39] Nevertheless, we can see a relationship between them and our moral life and its moral practices.

Reflecting on and nourishing our relationship with God through prayer, etc. can bring us to view our moral life differently. It can open our eyes to the deficient quality of some practices that we have been engaged in and move us to avoid them in future, or it can prompt us to adopt other moral practices, so that, henceforth, we will respond to God's call more fully. This can come about especially if one is reflecting on the example and teaching of Jesus or if one is engaged in *lectio divina* with its contemplative reading of and pondering on scriptural texts, or as one meditates on the infinite love of God the Father/Mother in sending his/her Son to save us from sin and to share with us here below the divine life. Celebrating the Eucharist can be particularly influential in shaping our moral awareness and schooling our imagination, so that our vision of moral living is enriched and we become open to the attitudes and virtues of Jesus.[40] Such a celebration can bring us to a clearer realisation that we belong to the community of the Church and are blessed by that belonging. But it can also challenge us to make our own in a fuller way the vision and virtues of that community that are reflected and celebrated in the Eucharist.[41]

---

38. Gula, *Holiness*, 152-3.
39. Gula, *Holiness*, 153.
40. Gula, *Holiness*, 178.
41. Gula, *Holiness*, 178.

Now while all this holds true, experience clearly indicates that on many occasions our religious or spiritual practices do not have a notable or indeed any influence on our moral thinking or practices. This may at times be due to circumstances or a poorly celebrated eucharistic liturgy or other religious practice or even to over-familiarity. But often, since our religious practices should not be reduced to mere means to moral improvement or action, one will not advert to the often subtle link between such practices and morality. Hence, they may have no moral impact on the one who prays or worships. This would seem to be how things work out in the great majority of cases in our daily lives as Christians, as the experience of many bears witness. As Gula says: 'There is no guarantee that if we do the practices, then we will acquire a certain character or behave in a certain way ... we cannot expect spiritual practices to ensure a certain kind of moral character and behaviour.'[42] One reason for this is that the connections between spiritual practices and the moral life are complex, not simple. 'While loving God can incline us to love others, there is no easy and sure connection between loving God, loving our neighbour and loving ourselves. Nevertheless, spiritual practices carry a rich potential for changing our moral life when we engage in them with the right intention and with deep commitment.[43]

CONCLUSION

The main purpose of this chapter has been to move beyond the split, so common in the past, between the spiritual and moral aspects of the Christian life. The attempt has been made to show the close relationship between these dimensions of our Christian living and how they interlink and impact on each other. They can be treated separately for the sake of better understanding but in practice they come together in the truly Christian personality and character and the Christian lifestyle that we should be living.[44] We have seen that spirituality gives rise to morality and permeates all aspects of the moral life, while morality expresses one's spirituality, grounds it in our relationships with other

---

42. Gula, *Holiness*, 1.
43. Gula, *Holiness*, 156-7.
44. Gula, *The Good Life*, 5.

people, with society, with creation and with God and can shape it in a more Christian manner. Relating the spiritual and the moral dimensions of the Christian life in this way enables us to develop a balanced Christian spirituality with its three elements or aspects, namely, love of God, love of the neighbour and the extension of these into the social, ecological and political areas of life. Finally, we discussed the role of religious or spiritual practices like prayer, Bible reading and sacramental worship in relation to their possible impact on how we understand and live the moral dimension of the Christian life.

CHAPTER SEVEN

Happiness: Challenge and Blessing

'People have never been as preoccupied, never been as ob-
sessed, …with happiness as they are right now.' But 'many of us
have a lousy understanding of just what will make us happy…'
'Finding out what makes us happy is a difficult thing.'[1]

It is quite clear from our experience, however, that everyone
wants to be happy, and if one is not happy, we instinctively feel
there is something missing, something wrong. This desire for
happiness is not, it seems clear, a superficial 'want' like desiring
a better car or designer clothes or a rise in one's wage packet or a
promotion. It is rather a fundamental desire or wish of the
human person, a deep longing for personal peace and contentment, for human flourishing at the most personal level. This desire to be happy in the true sense is natural and right for us
human beings and perhaps the most fundamental desire any of
us can have.[2] A person can say, 'I got a great new job recently' or
'I won the lottery last week' or 'I was awarded my Ph.D. before
Christmas', and no doubt these things have importance and are
usually sources of delight and pleasure and rightly so. But one
can still ask the deeper question: 'Are you happy?' and the answer could be 'not really' or even 'no'.

Significant truths about happiness

Here perhaps one can see emerging a significant truth about
true happiness. This is that merely external things that we can
get and/or use do not by themselves make us happy. For example, take wealth and material plenty. One writer says simply:
'once a person moves beyond the poverty level a larger income
contributes almost nothing to happiness.'[3] Another puts it this
way: 'researchers have found that beyond a certain income
level, more money will not buy more happiness.'[4] Similarly in

---

1. Andrew Santella, *Notre Dame Magazine*, Winter 2009, 33.
2. John Powell, *Happiness is an Inside Job*, Tabor Publishing, Allen, Texas,
USA, 1.
3. Anthony Clare, *On Men – Masculinity in Crisis*, Arrow Books,
London, 2001, 100.
4. Santella, *Notre Dame*, 33.

regard to fame, success, promotion, associating with the great or merely famous. This holds true also in relation to one's personal talents and skills: having a high IQ, being highly talented in business, management or leadership, sport, teaching or writing. It may be added that our pursuit of happiness will not be successful either if we expect other people to make us happy.[5] In all these cases we are looking for happiness in the wrong places and failure to find it is the inevitable result.

Another truth about happiness and our search for it is that, if we set out to seek happiness *directly*, in other words, if we do something *in order* to become happy, then we are again setting ourselves up for failure. Happiness is not the kind of thing that one can achieve by direct and explicit effort to attain it. Rather experience tells us that happiness is a reality that comes to us indirectly, that is, as the result of things that develop or enrich our humanity and so make one a better person and promote one's flourishing as a human being. In a word, happiness is a by-product of activities of this sort and hence, if one wants to be happy, one must focus on doing what makes for human flourishing with the hope or expectation that, if one does this well, the reward or result will be the attainment of an increase in real happiness. As Eugene Kennedy says, happiness 'is more a by-product of doing something worthwhile than a commodity that can be directly sought'.[6] Or as Santella puts it, '… Doesn't happiness usually catch us when we are busy pursuing something else'.[7]

From all that has been said here it is legitimate to draw the conclusion that, as John Powell says in the title of his book already referred to, Happiness is an Inside Job. In other words, we make ourselves happy or unhappy. Our happiness comes from within, from ourselves and in particular from how we perform or engage in the activities that enhance our humanity and enable us to grow as persons and, along with that, how we avoid those things that damage us as persons and make us less mature, less good, less human. In short, happiness arises from our deep needs being truly met.

---

5. Powell, 23.
6. *The Pain of Being Human*, Image Books, New York, 1974, 214. See 20 and 23 also, and Powell, 7.
7. Santella, *Notre Dame*, 35.

Personal essentials for true happiness

In the light of what has just been said about happiness being something that we must do for ourselves, our attention has to focus on our internal world rather than external realities. We may, then, enumerate the main factors that must be present if we are to be truly happy.

i) Having good self-esteem: This means having a positive, accepting and appreciative attitude to and feelings about oneself. It means being happy to be yourself; it is loving yourself as you are. If I am to be a happy person, I must learn to be happy about who I am.[8] This is not at all an easy thing to achieve for some people, because they have been damaged in their youth by negative attitudes and remarks about and to them by significant people in their lives, e.g. parents, teachers or priests. In their case they will likely have a long and difficult struggle to improve their self-awareness and to heal the emotional wounds they suffered in their early years. Doing these things will be vital for attaining good self-esteem and the self-confidence that flows from it. If, then, one esteems oneself appropriately, one will be able to relate to and love others and develop and use one's talents and skills to the full and so realise one's potential in the various areas of one's life and activity.[9]

ii) Being realistic about oneself: This requires good self-awareness, so that one knows oneself well. One has discovered the truth about oneself to at least a reasonable degree, so that one is aware of and accepts the reality that is oneself with one's talents, abilities and potential, one's values, virtues and vices, one's limitations and faults. Realism has to extend also to one's expectations of oneself and of others, so that one avoids unrealistic ambitions, projects and positions for which one is unsuitable, because they are beyond one's capabilities. Without this realistic attitude to oneself, one is likely to bite off more than one can chew in various situations and in different ways, with the result that feelings of failure and stress may well be generated and harm may be done to others and to oneself too.

---

8. Powell, 10.
9. Powell, 10-24; Tony Humphreys, *Self-Esteem – The Key to Your Child's Education*, Gill & Macmillan, Dublin, 1993, 1996, chapter 1; Gael Lindenfield, Self-Esteem, Thorsons, London, 1995, chapters 1 and 2.

iii) Having a positive attitude to life: The person who takes a nega-tive attitude to him/herself, to others and to life and its situa-tions will very likely not be a happy person, because (s)he will tend to focus on the bad, on the faults, mistakes, failures and problems that (s)he and others have or make. Such a person will doubtless find what (s)he is looking for, the negative and the bad and may well exaggerate them beyond what is realistic. This is in line with the old saying, 'two men looked out through prison bars, one saw mud, the other saw stars'. To be truly happy one must be like the one who saw the stars, that is, one must look on the bright or positive side of life and all that goes with that, including especially the positive side of oneself. This is not to ignore the negative but to be, as Powell says, a goodfinder, one who looks for and focuses on the good. The one who looks for the good is the one who usually finds it in oneself, in others and in life generally. Such a person counts his/her blessings, appreciates him/herself and his/her gifts, talents, op-portunities and achievements and in consequence is a person of gratitude who gives thanks for all the good one experiences. This is clearly a necessary attitude to have, if one is to achieve true happiness. As Powell says, 'looking for the good in myself is the only reasonable thing to do, if I want to be happy'(p 92).

iv) Taking responsibility for oneself and one's actions: Some of us are given to blaming others or the system or anything but ourselves for our faults, mistakes and misfortunes and even for our deci-sions and emotions, e.g. anger, depressive feelings. Here we see a shirking of responsibility, a distancing of ourselves from reali-ty and in consequence we refuse and fail to grow as a person. As Powell points out (p 25), 'growth begins where blaming ends, and accepting full responsibility for all our actions... is the de-finitive step towards human maturity'. It enables us to correct our faults, to change our response to others and to life's situa-tions and to become a more mature and better person. This is certainly the pathway to peace and personal happiness.[10] And obviously this is an inside job; only you can do it for yourself.

v) Being a person who loves: As has already been stated, one must, first of all, love oneself, if one wishes to be a loving person who

---

10. Powell, 32.

is good and does good. When one does love oneself appropriately, then one is happy to be oneself and one is well placed to go out to others in attention, care, listening and helpfulness, that is, to love the people in one's life. In other words, it is only a person who loves him/herself who can truly love other people and God too. And when one does that, then one acts in accordance with one's deepest humanity, enriches that humanity and in consequence experiences real happiness, a sense of fulfilment and growth as a person. But for the person who does not love others, there is no real hope for happiness, since, as Powell says (p 67), 'the source of most chronic unhappiness is a failure to love.' In a word, then, to be a truly loving, even if not a perfect, person is essential if one is to be truly happy. And of course this too is an inside job, since only you can do it in your life.

vi) Enjoying the good things of life: One would expect that the person described in the foregoing five points would be one who would appreciate, value and enjoy the blessings of life, the many good things we can experience on our earthly journey. Enjoyment is more a mind-set than a set of circumstances, more an attitude or outlook than a fortunate life situation. And when we can and do enjoy the good things of life, we will then experience more happiness and be happier people. Basic to these good things are friendship and good relationships. Here is where the deeper joys and pleasures of life are to be found and experienced and, hence, here too is the source of much happiness and personal enrichment. Amongst these good things of life must also be counted relaxation, fun and hobbies and activities or exercises that nourish us in body, mind and spirit.[11] Common sense tells us that we should enjoy life and for the Christian it is true to say that 'enjoyment is an art God wants all of us to cultivate'.[12] If you can enjoy these blessings on the journey of life, you will be a happier person. Despite the deep anti-pleasure current in much of Christian tradition, we can make our own the sentiment of ancient Jewish wisdom: 'Everyone will be called to account for all the legitimate pleasures which he or she has failed to enjoy'.[13]

11. Powell, 39-54.
12. Powell, 122.
13. Powell, 121.

vii) Making a real effort to grow as a person and do better: According to Powell (p 84) the average person uses only 10 per cent of his or her potential. This is a shocking statistic and must indicate that many people not merely leave much of their potential for good and creativity unused but as a result must experience frustration and emptiness in significant ways. This surely deprives one of the satisfaction and enjoyment of making full use of one's gifts and talents and growth as a person that follows from successfully meeting new challenges and doing new things. Such a person will be less happy than one who feels free to go beyond his/her comfort zones, develop as a person and enlarge one's world.

So we can say that another necessity for attaining true happiness in life is that one makes a real effort to do better, to stretch oneself personally in a way one has not done before, and so realise one's potential more fully and experience the happiness of becoming a fuller and better person. This may take the form of new thinking, a reordering of one's values and priorities, new and improved relationships or new activities and new hobbies.

Obstacles to true happiness
Some obstacles have already been mentioned or implied in talking about the elements that are essential for happiness. But a few more may be adverted to at this point.

One such obstacle or enemy of happiness is making comparisons of oneself with others. When we do this, it is very likely that we will come out on the wrong side of the comparison and begin to feel less than or inferior to those others. Such feelings usually tend to arise from deeper but perhaps unacknowledged feelings of inferiority and in turn are inclined to generate further negative thoughts and emotions. As a result one's happiness is likely to be lessened.[14]

Another barrier to one's happiness is a tendency to perfectionism. This involves a compulsion to avoid failure at all costs and to judge oneself solely in terms of one's performance. In consequence one has a tendency to go to the opposite extreme and seek to do everything perfectly and to consider oneself in negative terms if one does not achieve this impossible standard.

14. Powell, 6-7.

Thus one sets oneself up for disappointment, discouragement and feelings of failure. Clearly this attitude is the enemy of happiness and one who has it will tend to be less happy than the person who aims at growth or improvement rather than perfection. The former are possible and necessary, the latter is impossible, quite unnecessary and a major obstacle to true happiness.[15]

As already mentioned another frequent obstacle to being happy is having unrealistic expectations of or ambitions for oneself. Some expect too much of themselves and maybe of others too. This can refer to relationships, school or college, one's career, one's daily work, sport, etc. The root of such unrealistic expectations is usually poor self-awareness and perhaps a feeling of inferiority that one has not acknowledged. If one feels inferior without being aware of it, then one may easily begin to build castles in the air for oneself, imagining that one can achieve great things. This tends to drown out the niggling feeling that one is not up to it and to provide one with a sense that one is quite talented and can be a great achiever. The performance, however, will tend to bring one down to earth with a bang and the inevitable result will be disappointment and greater feelings of inferiority and unhappiness.[16]

One will very probably lessen one's happiness also, if one is out of touch with one's emotions, is emotionally immature or represses one's emotions. Our emotions or feelings put us in touch with reality, especially the reality of ourselves and our reactions to what we are experiencing. If, then, one has a healthy emotional life, one will understand and control oneself better, one will relate to others more appropriately and more satisfyingly and so one will be a happier person. If, however, one is emotionally immature or repressed, then life and especially relationships will be less satisfying and one will experience less in the way of happiness.

As implied earlier negative thinking is sure to put a damper on one's happiness, since one will regularly be stressing the negative about oneself, others and life generally. Negative thinking often springs from negative feelings and it will remain one's

15. See Kennedy, 97-9; Powell, 99-108.
16. Kennedy, 45-7.

characteristic pattern of thought as long as one entertains negative feelings and lets them predominate. With such a mental outlook one will have a hard time feeling happy. One's happiness will be lessened appreciably and unhappy feelings may be predominant in one's life.[17] On the other hand, negative feelings can have their origin in a negative cast of mind. So, controlling one's ideas and attitudes tends to make for a positive outlook and a happier personal disposition.

Circumstances matter but not decisively
It is fairly obvious that circumstances can impact on one's state of mind, heart and body and so can affect one's experience of happiness. This holds true especially of significant circumstances one may encounter like serious health or relationship difficulties, major employment or financial problems, a vocation crisis, etc. Such circumstances can give rise to great anxiety, stress and fear, may come to preoccupy one's attention and interest and become the focus of much concentration and energy. This will no doubt jeopardise one's happiness at least for a time. But that is not to say they will make one truly unhappy in a longstanding way, especially if one has attended well to the points made earlier about the personal essentials for true happiness and has achieved a stable state of genuine peace and contentment.

The Christian perspective
All that has been said so far holds true for all human beings and of course for Christians too. For the Christian, however, there is another and deeper dimension to our nature as persons in community. This is our relationship with God in Christ, the divine indwelling in us as graced by God and the hope of eternal life when our earthly journey ends. Our awareness of and faith in God's love for each of us personally is or should be a source of great joy, and our love for God in Christ does or should bring us Christian joy and happiness in a profound manner. Of course, it may not be so in practice for all Christians but it can be. As in the case of other human beings a great deal will depend on the degree to which the Christian has made the essential requirements

---

17. See Tony Humphreys, *The Power of 'Negative' Thinking*, Gill & Macmillan, Dublin, 1996, chapters 1 and 2.

for happiness, that have been outlined earlier, realities in his/her life. If the Christian is notably deficient in one or other or more of these essentials, then his/her relationship with God will not be what it should be and the peace and joy that relationship should bring will leave something to be desired. One could say, putting it in other words, that the holiness of the Christian will be impaired to the degree to which (s)he lacks the wholeness to which we as human persons are called.

Our eternal destiny as Christians is perfect happiness and fulfilment with God at the end of our earthly journey. This is the crowning and perfecting of earthly happiness and was won for us by the death and resurrection of Jesus. It is given to us as God's gift and represents the fulfilment of an earthly pilgrimage that has been characterised by goodness, virtue and Christian faith-love-hope.

CONCLUSION

It will be clear now that happiness is a blessing or gift that we can win for ourselves with the help of others and ultimately with God's grace. It is in fact one of the most important and sought after blessings in human life. However, it is also true to say that happiness is a challenge or task that each of us is called to work at and meet. If one becomes a happy person, it is an achievement of a most personal nature. Only I can make myself happy or indeed unhappy. How this is so has been a major concern of this chapter. Thus we can see how it is true to say that happiness is an inside job. And while the circumstances of one's life can have a big impact on a person, it is not likely that they will make you unhappy or indeed happy, at least in a long term way. As has been outlined, what makes for happiness is working to ensure you have made your own those features or aspects of character that are essential in order that you become a mature and loving person. Happiness is a challenge and a blessing and in each person's case only (s)he can meet that challenge and make the blessing a reality in his/her life. In a word, happiness is an inside job!

A clerical tale

The fact that our happiness depends on ourselves and how we see and react to things, may be illustrated by a tale of three clergymen.

143

A P.P. in a certain part of the country was given a new curate. During their first chat about the parish and its people the C.C. said, 'Father, tell me what kind of people are the parishioners of this parish.' The P.P. answered, 'Father Tom, perhaps, you'd, first, tell me how you found the people in the parish you have just left'. Fr Tom responded with some vigour. 'They were poor enough! No cooperation, no interest in the parish or the church, no desire to work with the priest to improve the parish, no generosity.' The P.P. replied, 'Well, I believe you'll find the people of this parish much the same'!

Some years later another curate was appointed to the same parish and he put the same question to the P.P. Again the P.P. answered. 'Fr Joe, perhaps you'd, first, tell me how you found the people of your previous parish'. Fr Joe spoke with enthusiasm and said, 'They were terrific! Great interest, marvellous enthusiasm for the church and the improvement of the parish, loads of volunteers to work with the priests, great generosity. It was an uplifting experience for me! The P.P. replied, 'Well, I believe you'll find the people of this parish much the same'!

CHAPTER EIGHT

The Mid-Life Transition

We hear a lot of talk nowadays about the mid-life crisis or transition but many of us don't take it all very seriously. This is a pity, because there is here a serious issue, as will be clearly seen in the following pages. It is widely agreed among those who are well informed that to neglect mid-life issues is very unwise. Giving them significant and informed attention is, however, seen as very sensible and beneficial, even if not always very easy. In this chapter we will outline what is in question when the phrase mid-life crisis, or better, mid-life transition, is used.

The stages of the human life cycle
Up to recent times, at least at the popular level, people have spoken of just two stages or phases in human life, youth and adulthood. Youth was regarded as lasting till about twenty and was characterised by growth and change. After that came the long years of adulthood which we tended to see as a kind of plateau or single unit. But in this view there was little awareness that there might be major psychological, emotional or spiritual changes within the many years of adult life, or specific phases of widely varying types involving significant developments that needed personal attention if one were to negotiate them positively and constructively. Today we are better informed and largely as the result of the research work of such notable figures as Carl Jung and Erik Erikson.

Jung (d.1961) was the first to speak of mid-life as an identifiable stage of life. Comparing youth and mid-life to the morning and afternoon of an ordinary day, Jung made the famous remark that, thoroughly unprepared, we take the step into the afternoon of life. But we cannot live the afternoon of life according to the programme of life's morning. For Jung youth is the time for developing one's ego or consciousness, largely in response to the expectations of society. But mid-life has a different purpose and task. It is the time for moving inward as we grow and adapt, psychologically, emotionally and spiritually, to one's changing self and the changed circumstances of one's life. This

is where the mid-life transition finds its place as the whole personality flowers and re-orders its values and priorities in the
light of one's experience of living through youth and young
adulthood. In this phase of life one ideally becomes one's true
self, an integrated and mature person. There will be pain and
tension in this phase of life but also new energy, creativity and
joy. Thus, the mid-life transition, which usually takes place between thirty-five and the early fifties, is essentially a positive reality and the most important of the phases of one's life.

Erikson built on Jung's insights and perceived eight stages in
the human life cycle, each stage involving a specific task or challenge. The first five stages encompass childhood and adolescence. Stage six is young adulthood with its task of acquiring the
capacity for intimacy. Stage seven is mid-life where the challenge is to become a generative (or caring and creative) person.
The final stage is old age and its task is the achievement of personal integrity. Erikson uses the word 'crisis' in relation to each
stage of development but by that word he means, not trouble
and difficulty, as in the ordinary usage of the word, but rather a
turning-point or opportunity in one's personal growth. In relation to mid-life the challenge to be faced and negotiated is called
generativity. This means becoming a truly effective, caring and
concerned person in relation to other people, especially the
young, and also society and the world generally. There will be
pain and struggle in going through one's mid-life transition but
it will, when well negotiated, lead to a deeper, more caring,
more creative and happier life.

The mid-life transition
To begin it may be mentioned that mid-life can commence anywhere from about thirty-five and continue till about fifty-five.
As a general statement we can refer to the forties as the main
time in life in which the mid-life transition occurs. But, of
course, there are no clear and definite dividing lines in anyone's
life between mid-life and the other stages of the human life
cycle. It may be noted too that for some the mid-life transition is
easy and smooth, while for others it may be very difficult. And
given our usual lack, until recent times, of any awareness of the
various stages in one's life, many may fail to notice what we are

referring to as the mid-life transition or may even regard all talk of such a thing as so much empty rhetoric.

The mid-life transition may be described as the passage one makes from young adulthood to middle age. It is the process in and through which a person grows in his/her more personal dimensions and moves on, positively and hopefully, from being a young adult to the stage where one is capable of living as a mid-life adult in a basically mature, creative and happy manner. In the view of many the mid-life transition is the most important development or time of potential growth in a person's life and, hence, its successful completion or the failure to negotiate it successfully are laden with very significant consequences for each of us in the later stages of life. Clearly, then, this transition involves a deep personal challenge and within it we find negative and positive elements. We will look at these in turn.

i) The negative side

In relation to the attitudes and priorities of the mid-life person one is, above all, conscious of one's advancing years. One tends at this stage to count the years one may have left rather than the years from one's birth. One is also acutely aware of one's physical decline and that one's options in life are now quite limited. Promotion in one's job or career will very likely have levelled off and many of one's dreams seem set to remain just that, dreams. With one's parents now probably deceased and one's children grown up and gone, one may begin to experience what is called the empty nest syndrome and part of that may be that one begins to find one's marriage less satisfying, supportive and joyful than one had thought, when the partners were busy with the children. For the single person and the celibate there may be the feeling that job satisfaction is not enough; loneliness and a feeling of isolation may enter one's experience as one faces the now emerging deeper question, is there anyone who really cares for and loves me deeply for myself rather than just for what I can do?[1]

At mid-life some people become anxious and fearful about the ever-nearer approach of death. The unmistakable ebbing of

1. On this latter point see the concluding pages of this chapter on the Priest at fifty and also Brendan Hoban, 'Elephants in the Livingroom', *The Furrow*, December 1996, 659-69.

one's physical powers and attractiveness causes many to worry, and loneliness and a feeling of isolation are not uncommon at mid-life. One may begin to wonder about the value and/or meaningfulness of one's commitments as a vague restlessness and dissatisfaction creeps into one's consciousness. Doubt and uncertainty can make their presence felt as one becomes unsure of values, goals and priorities that were hitherto unquestioned and eagerly pursued. Questions may arise that may give one pause: Where do I go from here? What's left for me now?

This negative and perhaps painful dimension of the mid-life transition need not be what people often refer to as a crisis. Rather it often contains a reminder to adapt, a call to move on, to make the transition to the different level of mid-life, to the maturity that should characterise one in one's middle years. Since, however, as one author has said, most of us by mid-life are accomplished fugitives from ourselves, the mid-life transition will often involve a major element of struggle and require a lot of time and attention to negotiate successfully.

ii) Making the mid-life transition successfully
Our discussion of how one might negotiate the mid-life transition well and respond constructively to the demands of one's middle years may usefully be structured around four basic personal needs that are very prominent in the experience of middle-aged people. These are four areas where significant personal reassessment takes place in mid-life and where as a result, important personal growth may come about. To the degree that it does we speak of the mid-life transition being successfully made. We will examine each of these four needs or areas of life in turn.

1) Being personally effective
In young adulthood, the stage of life before mid-life (usually one's twenties and early thirties) a person chooses a career or vocation, even though, as experience shows, it may not be a final choice. It is sometimes exploratory or provisional, as one tests one's dream or vision for one's life. In addition, in this phase of one's life cycle the young adult develops the capacity, usually in the context of marriage, to make and keep personal relationships, that is, the capacity for intimacy.

In mid-life, however, the person moves on a significant step in these two areas. She/he may now re-evaluate or test the dream of early adulthood and may, in consequence, move to another career or vocation. This is because one feels one can be more personally effective in this new role or job, having now discerned that it is more fully in accord with one's deeper instincts and ambitions and more compatible with the talents and gifts of mind and personality that one now realises more clearly that one possesses. Even if one does not change one's job or vocational choice, the middle-aged person usually seeks to find new ways in which to exercise and use to the full his/her personal strengths and competence and to do so more creatively and productively. Hence, in mid-life one may assume a leadership role and take on some position of authority in the wider society, in the church or in one's community. This is something the person in mid-life often feels he/she needs and wants to do in the search to be more effective and to exercise more personal power and influence. Thus she/he is enabled to be more creative and to contribute more efficaciously to the communities of which she/he is a member.

It will be clear from what has been said here that a lot of personal re-assessment and change is involved in this mid-life transition. As a result, there may well be a good deal of personal and even relational turmoil and heart-searching. This is typical of mid-life and its transition but, if it is understood as a normal ingredient of this stage of life, one will be less inclined to see it as a problem or crisis and thus will have a better chance of viewing it positively as a stage in a growth process in which one must let go some elements of one's past in order to move on to a deeper level of maturity that is appropriate to one's middle years.

2) Caring for others

In mid-life one begins to realise that with this greater exercise of personal initiative and power there goes also greater responsibility. One begins to feel that one is now more accountable for what one is and does and this involves feeling called to pay more attention to and exercise more care towards what one is able to create and produce. In one's middle years one begins to want and need to care for others, whether these are one's own children, younger colleagues in the workplace or clients in one's business. This need may extend also to some project or plan one has in mind or some community or institution of which one is part. At this stage in one's life cycle one is psychologically and emotionally ready to spend oneself in such generous concern for others, thus being creative and caring with the maturity and resources of a mid-life adult. Some speak of this attitude to and involvement with others and one's communities as showing oneself to be a truly generative person. Obviously, this newly acquired capacity for leadership and commitment to the well-being of others would have existed before mid-life but when one reaches one's middle years it attains a new depth, vigour and range that is seldom evident earlier. Such a developed capacity for care and concern is a sure sign of a successful transition into the middle years of life. Hence, in these years one may well involve oneself in a leadership or mentoring role in social matters, in educational or environmental concerns, in politics or sport, etc.

It is important to remember also that in mid-life, as in all phases of the life cycle, one has to accept many things that happen to one, that are given or fixed, what you might call passivities, because of one's earlier choices or the circumstances in which one happens to be. This can refer to health, intelligence, academic and emotional, one's social class, one's culture, one's marriage and family situation, one's career, one's religion, one's single or celibate state, etc. In consequence of all this, many of the responsibilities one will have in mid-life, much of the caring one finds one has to do and many of the roles one is called to fulfil will be things one has to accept without there being any great element of personal choice involved. This should not, however, take from the growth and deeper involvement with others that should mark the transition to mid-life as discussed above.

It is possible, on the other hand, that a person may fail in making this mid-life transition with its call to care more widely and deeply for others and for one's communities and society. One may resist the demands and efforts required by this new social responsibility. To the degree that one does so resist and as a result fail to make the transition to the adult maturity appropriate to mid-life one will stagnate and become self-absorbed and in consequence will lack the psychological, emotional and personal resources that a middle-aged adult should have. Then boredom and a pervading sense of emptiness may characterise one's experience of life and this will have notable knock-on effects in the later stage of one's life.

3) Attending to one's inner world

At mid-life one tends to begin to reflect more on oneself, one's accomplishments, one's strengths and limitations, one's relationships, one's future. One begins to enquire about the meaning of all one has been doing, to question the values and priorities that one has lived by up to now, to wonder about the commitments one has made in the earlier phases of one's life. One now moves from exploring the outer world to exploring one's inner world and all that has been going on there. This inner examination or reflection is related to a number of external and internal developments in one's life at middle age. At mid-life one will have settled into one's career and now one may find that promotion to higher levels becomes unlikely as one's abilities are known and judged most suitable for one's present position. One's children are leaving home and becoming independent. One now becomes acutely aware that one is in the second half of life and time is slipping away. One turns then to assess more fully one's strengths and limitations as one contemplates what one has achieved so far and what one might focus on in the years ahead.

Thus at mid-life it is likely that one will become a more reflective person, raising and facing questions about oneself, one's past and future that previously weren't in one's mind or from which one shied away. This reflection may be disturbing and challenging but it will be essential if one is to advance to the level of maturity appropriate to middle age. It may well involve re-examining the central ideals of one's youth, re-assessing the dreams one followed or failed to follow in earlier years, and working towards a fuller integration of the various dimensions of oneself as a person, so that the process of individuation, that is, becoming a unique individual person, one's own man or woman, may advance as it should.

d) Having significant relationships

In mid-life there usually emerges a deep personal need that may well not have been clearly adverted to or experienced earlier.

This is the need to be personally significant to at least one other person, to be appreciated and loved for what one is as a person rather than for what one has done or can do, to experience real intimacy in a deeply personal and enduring manner. For married people many will have experienced this intimacy in their marriage relationship, though at mid-life there may well be questions about its quality and depth, especially as the empty nest syndrome becomes a reality. It is in this context that marital intimacy may deepen and grow or problems in the marital relationship may become apparent. The search for deeper intimacy and love may, then, take significant and sometimes unexpected turns.

For the celibate this need to feel personally loved may become very powerfully present in mid-life, especially if one has not had significant relationships in one's earlier years. Some celibates react by getting married; others find the resources in mid-life to develop deep friendships of a celibate nature with men and/or women, despite these being officially considered to be dangerous and even inappropriate. Then they are enabled to meet their mid-life need for personal appreciation and love in a mature, enriching and celibate manner. Still others committed to the celibate way of life and especially male celibates may attempt to fill the void caused by the absence of real intimacy in their lives at mid-life by taking refuge in one or more of a variety of compensations. Examples are plentiful: over-eating, over-drinking, sexual activities and liaisons of various types, whether heterosexual or homosexual, dominating people in different ways, authoritarian attitudes and practices, becoming aggressive and venting one's anger in inappropriate and hurtful ways, focusing on making money or acquiring large quantities of expensive and showy material goods. The likely result of living with this unfulfilled need for friendship and intimacy, whatever the compensations one may have used to fill the gap, will be feelings or states of loneliness, emptiness and even depression, states which clearly indicate that one has not made the mid-life transition at all well.[2]

---

2. See the last section of this chapter for further reflections on the celibate priest at fifty.

Men and the mid-life transition

In relation to the experience of men in regard to the mid-life transition it seems true to say that in our Western society they are culturally disadvantaged in that they seem often to have a more difficult time getting in contact with their emotions and deeper selves than women do. This seems to be how men are socialised in our society. Hence, their awareness of their mid-life transition and what it might involve for them may be less clear and quite a bit later than it seems to be for the average woman. As a result a man's response to this transition may be delayed and may encounter greater problems than would seem to be the case with many women. One element of these male difficulties concerns the problems many men can have in expressing their tender emotions in close relationships, especially in marriage and family life. This will impact on their relationships, especially with women, in notable ways and may lead to those with whom they relate having feelings of being unappreciated and taken for granted. If in mid-life a man begins to realise that this has been a problem for him in his deeper relationships, he may find that his wife or partner has become alienated and that his children have grown up and gone. In addition, in mid-life women are often going in the opposite emotional and psychological direction to men as they grow in self-confidence, seek more independence, take more personal initiatives, and in particular take a position in the workplace where they can use their talents and skills to greater effect. All this can have a negative impact on a man in his middle age, giving rise to confusion, restlessness and perhaps unhelpful efforts to compensate like recourse to alcohol, extra-marital affairs, boredom and states of depression.

In spite of this, however, there is in the middle years real hope that the male mid-life transition can be negotiated in a positive and beneficial manner. Men can then develop their more tender or so-called feminine side and so come to be able to establish worthwhile relationships. Then they will have acquired the ability to love well along with their ability to work well, the signs in Freud's view of the truly mature person.

Women and their mid-life transition[3]

For women too mid-life is inevitably a time of questioning and re-assessment regardless of the choices they may have made in their earlier years. The woman whose family is grown up and independent may find herself wondering what her role now is. This is particularly so in the case of the woman who may have abandoned her career during her child-rearing years. Suddenly she finds herself with time on her hands and little prospect of her getting back into her former career area. Has it been all worthwhile? Who needs her now? What has she to show for her years of self-sacrifice? Does anyone really care? These are some of the troubling questions she is now asking herself.

On the other hand, there is the woman who dedicated herself to her career and who worked hard to reach a high degree of excellence in her profession, bypassing in the process the opportunity to have a family. Now at mid-life she is probably wondering if the cost of success has been too high. Indeed she may be asking herself if she has been successful at all as she wonders, 'Is this all there is?'

Then there is the woman who has spent herself in the rearing of her family, while at the same time keeping on either full-time or part-time work outside the home. For many years she has felt pulled in many directions and may at mid-life feel that she is taken for granted, seeing her life as continuous giving, often with the giving going unnoticed. She now wants to support her partner, who himself is negotiating the malaise and uncertainty of mid-life already described. Somewhere in the midst of all this she can feel that her own identity is submerged and lost.

And what of the religious sister at mid-life? She too is evaluating her life as she searches again for meaning and depth. By now she feels somewhat distanced from her family, particularly if her parents have died. Her brothers and sisters are engrossed in their own family life, and very often have no understanding of what her life is about. The realisation that there is no one person to whom she matters deeply and the realisation that she will never have a family of her own become more deeply felt at this

---

3. I am indebted to Sr Ita Moynihan, Loreto Community, Wexford for the reflections in this section on the female mid-life transition, as originally published in The Furrow, April 1995, 216-8.

stage. The question 'who will be there for me?' may not be bringing forth the positive response one would like and the result can be a feeling of emptiness.

By now you may be wondering if we can only expect negative experiences and developments at this phase of a woman's life, especially given the fact that into this mid-life stage also come the trials and traumas of coping with menopause and the inevitable biological and emotional changes which it will bring. But the picture need not be a bleak or depressing one. There are positive aspects to this phase of life too. By mid-life we should be free of the pressures of measuring up to others' expectations of us or of trying to prove ourselves in the eyes of other people. Having spent most of our adult lives trying to please and support parents, spouse, children or colleagues, perhaps we can now accept the opportunity to give time, space and care to our own inner selves. It is important to accept the fact that we are no longer youthful and that our energy level may have decreased somewhat. Without this acceptance it is unlikely that we will make the necessary adjustments in our life-style and allow for a healthy growth in to this phase of our lives.

Jung stresses the need for reflection in the second half of life. We tend to move our emphasis from the importance of doing to the value of being. There is greater need for individual space and at the same time there is an increased emphasis on the value of depth relationships. Ideally, life partners, freed from some of their other responsibilities, should be able to provide mutual support for each other at this stage, and to deepen their own relationship. As we know, unfortunately, the reality is sometimes far from the ideal, but happily we also see evidence of a new blossoming in the lives and relationships of many couples at this time of life.

For the single and celibate the place of deep friendship is crucial in our lives. As we ask the deep questions that surface at mid-life it is very important to have someone to walk the journey with us, someone with whom we can be truly ourselves. If we are to be fully alive, integrated human beings, we need to be warm and loving and capable of deep friendship with other women and men. In this situation we can hopefully negotiate the mid-life transition successfully and continue our development as happy human beings.

The religious dimension

Since the turmoil of the mid-life transition affects the whole person, it is understandable and to be expected that one's religious faith and practice may well come in for some questioning, doubting and re-assessment at this stage of one's life. One may begin to find one's prayer, both personal and liturgical, unsatisfactory, unhelpful and even boring and empty. One may have second thoughts about one's religious vocation as priest, sister or brother, as many married people may have about their marriage vocation. One may even find oneself raising questions about one's Christian faith itself as one begins to find it, perhaps, less helpful than previously and as giving less meaning to one's life than in earlier years. One's attendance at Mass and other religious practices and even one's membership of the Church may also become problematic for the mid-lifer. One may begin to feel one does not get much out of these things, while one may also become more conscious of the weaknesses and faults of the church leadership and the negative aspects of the institutional church, things which today are given widespread emphasis and severe condemnation not only in the media but by many members of the Church itself.

All this may occasion much soul-searching and even a religious crisis in a person in mid-life. But it may also provide an opportunity and a challenge for growth in faith and commitment to the Christian way of life, and a call to re-insert oneself again into the church community with greater understanding and fervour. The fact that at mid-life one tends to become more reflective and more oriented towards the interior life may well lead one towards new ways of experiencing the God dimension of one's life. Since at mid-life one also moves towards more extensive and deeper caring for others, it may happen at this stage that one wishes to get involved further in the pastoral ministry of the Church community. This may lead one to take on a helping and/or a leadership role at some level in the Church. It is not difficult to see that this latter will be facilitated more by a collegial model of ministry and church organisation. One may hope to experience this in one's local community rather than a hierarchical or authoritarian system that may well work towards the exclusion from ministry of members of the lay faithful.

Concluding these remarks on the mid-life transition
It will be abundantly clear from what has been said in the previous pages that the mid-life transition is a reality of major significance in human life, one that determines how we live our middle years and the quality of life we will then have. This will, of course, have major knock-on effects in relation to one's later years and the happiness or lack of it one will then experience.[4]

The reader will have noticed that we have in this chapter said little enough about how precisely one is to get through one's mid-life transition successfully. We have spoken of problems, possibilities and goals for the mid-life person but not much on detailed prescriptions about how to realise these. The reason for this lack is, of course, that negotiating the mid-life transition depends very much on how we have made the earlier transitions in our lives. In addition, the transition at mid-life involves a growth process that affects the person in all one's dimensions and aspects and is very personal to each one. It is not possible in any substantial or helpful way to detail how this deep process that is unique and multi-faceted for each one is to be worked through in any particular case. This we must do, each for him/herself, according to where one is as a person on entering mid-life, the difficulties one experiences at that time and the possibilities that are open to one then.

It is hoped, nevertheless, that what has been said so far in this chapter will raise the reader's awareness of the phenomenon we call the mid-life transition, will give him/her a better understanding of it and will encourage a positive and hope-filled attitude and approach to this very significant reality by which we move from young adulthood to middle age.

The priest at fifty
In the light of the foregoing reflections on the mid-life transition and in particular what has been said about the celibate person at mid-life, it will be revealing to look at some recent experience in relation to some priests and their mid-life decisions.

We are all aware that a great number of priests have left the active priestly ministry in the last forty or more years, some say

4. On this later stage of life see Catherine McCann, 'Successful Ageing', *The Furrow*, December 1993, 681-5; also her book *Falling in Love with Life – An Understanding of Ageing*, The Columba Press, Dublin 1996.

in excess of 100,000, and the trend is by no means at an end today. It is reported that most of these men left to get married or at least married after their departure. There were, of course, other reasons for some priests leaving but in relation to one age group the reason given proves very interesting and in its own way revealing and, perhaps for the church itself, challenging.

At fifty job satisfaction is not enough[5]

It has been noted in recent years in the U.S.A. especially that priests at about fifty years of age have left the ministry and have subsequently married. On interviewing many of these former ministerial priests, researchers have discovered that these men tell almost the exact same story in regard to the reason for their decision to leave the active ministry. It is as follows.

For many years these priests found their priestly life and work very satisfying and fulfilling. They got their energy from their priestly ministry; it gave them good job satisfaction and made their lives meaningful. They were happy and contented and no doubt effective priests. As these men neared fifty, however, they experienced a change. Despite their priestly work continuing to be worthwhile and personally enriching, they began to experience a sense of emptiness and dissatisfaction. They gradually became aware of a new need within themselves, a yearning not previously noticed. In time they came to be able to name this as the need for meaningful or deep relationships; in other words, for intimacy. Up to this point they had been happy to get their affirmation and sense of fulfilment from their work as priests. Now they discovered that this by itself was no longer adequate. They now experienced the need to be valued, not just for what they did but also for what they were as persons. In a word, they began to feel the need to be loved for themselves and not just for their work and achievements.

Their response to this felt need

These priests typically turned to their brother priests in an effort to have this newly experienced need met. But they found that their colleagues in ministry were either unwilling or unable to

5. The main source of these reflections on the priest at fifty is 'A crisis for Midlife Priests', Loughlin Sofield, S.T., M.A., in *Human Development* (U.S. Jesuit sponsored publication), Summer 1992, 30-3.

respond to what was being asked of them. The result was, predictably, that the needy priests sooner or later discovered a sensitive woman who was able to perceive the individual priest's personal need accurately and caringly and to meet it with a love that said, 'I love you for what you are and not just for what you can do'. These priests, then, tended to leave the ministry in order to get married to the woman who loved them and whom they in turn had come to love. In other cases priests in similar difficulties were able to develop mature and healthy relationships with women (and/or men) at this point in their lives and so they continued on happily in the priestly ministry and in the celibate state.

Understanding this need
Before you begin to think dark thoughts about this whole matter, especially about the decisions of the priests in question to return to the state of the lay faithful and about the priests themselves, thoughts like, 'they should have said their prayers', or 'they never grew up', or 'some women would chase anything in a collar', it will be important and perhaps eye–opening to attend to what the psychologists have to say about this development. In the view of these scholars it is quite normal and psychologically quite healthy and, indeed, a sign of personal growth for these men to experience this need for real intimacy around the age of fifty years. You may call it an element of the mid-life transition – or if you prefer, crisis – or simply a common psychological fact. But it is not an illusion or a form of self-deception by a disappointed man or a rationalisation for what they wanted to do all along. Rather it is a sign that one is growing into another phase of one's life psychologically and emotionally, a phase, as has been mentioned earlier in this chapter, that tends to involve some unrest and re-evaluation of one's attitudes, values, goals and priorities. And this signals a real deepening and maturing of the personality as one advances in mid-life and moves on to a new emotional and psychological level. It is noteworthy too that priests generally tend to experience this need somewhat more acutely than other men, since priests are, typically, compassionate, kind and gentle with a greater need than usual to belong, to be needed and to be loved.

In the light of these insights from psychology it will be imperative to accept the reality and the normality of this need for deep intimacy in many priests as they reach the age of fifty, and to set about doing all possible to meet it sensitively and constructively.

Meeting this need

Here we reach the real problem. And because of our celibate commitment as priests there are special difficulties in meeting it even today, when our understanding of the celibate and the emotional life is much better than it has been up to now.

We have stated that many priests in the fifty-year-old age bracket have been able to meet this human need successfully and happily, while remaining in the celibate priesthood. They have done this and are doing it, because they have developed the ability to relate deeply to others, men and/or women, in healthy and enriching ways. In other words, they have been able to establish meaningful relationships of a celibate nature with good friends in their lives and these relationships or friendships have proved to be precisely what they needed at their time of life. Thus the intimacy needs of these men are met in a warm, constructive and ongoing way and as a result they continue as fulfilled and happy priests. (Intimacy here and in its proper meaning refers to deep personal relationships characterised by mutual openness and sharing but not necessarily by any genital activity.)

How to achieve intimacy

While it is possible to satisfy the intimacy needs of a fifty-year-old celibate priest in an enriching and celibate manner, it is very difficult to explain how someone who is experiencing this mid-life problem should go about overcoming it in his own life, or even in one's own life. It is as difficult as telling people how to make friends or establish warm personal relationships. Everyone must do it for himself and, of course, a great deal will depend on how one has fared in this matter in one's earlier years. Hence, while many may help no one can substitute for your own personal efforts. The following points are regularly put forward by way of suggestion:

1. We need to become aware and accepting of the need of these priests and of anyone similarly placed, even ourselves, when the landmark of fifty years of age arrives.

2. As has been mentioned, a lot will hang on whether one who has reached fifty was in his earlier years able to develop a real capacity for significant relationships and real friendships with men and women. Not just those in which one discusses business or clerical issues, the problems of others or the usual trivia of clerical or social life but the real thing where mutual personal openness and sharing are the order of the day. If such relationships have been part of one's early years, then it is quite likely that the problem we are discussing won't arise at all at 50. If they have not been experienced, then significant difficulties may well present themselves. And, of course, there is no quick fix. Neither having sex nor rushing into a hasty marriage nor more penitential practices nor even prayer on its own can solve the problem, the reason being, of course, that these things miss the real point, namely, one's emotional need and how to satisfy it in one's circumstances. (This is not to say that prayer is of no benefit here. It can and usually will be, since it will involve reflection and a call for God's help. But more will be needed at the human level, as experience shows.)

3. Fifty-year-old priests in need of genuine intimacy may turn rather naturally to their brother priests for help. They may be lucky, as the U.S. priests mentioned at the beginning of this discussion were not. Most of us priests are not emotionally mature enough to be able to provide such deep personal support or to help a troubled colleague to sort out his emotional difficulties. Usually, some kind of confidant will, however, be called for. An understanding counsellor or spiritual director may fill the bill and help to lead one through a time of emotional turbulence.

4. Priests at fifty who are themselves experiencing the need for intimacy should take certain initiatives. They should seek out persons and programmes that affirm, value, support and challenge them as persons and as priests in the celibate state. Difficulties may still be encountered, e.g one may experience great loneliness or fall in love or confide in one who turns out to be unhelpful or even hostile. Nevertheless, since the matter is of

great personal importance, it will be essential to continue one's efforts to make progress in search of support in one's difficulties and towards growth in the emotional dimension of one's life. As Sandra Schneiders has been quoted as saying, 'Bypassing the challenge to intimacy is not a viable alternative. It is a resignation from the human adventure, a self-consignment to perpetual childhood' (*New Wineskins*, p 221).[6]

5. It would be good if parishioners could become aware of this whole dimension of their priest's humanity, so as to be able to reach out to him in positive and helpful ways that nourish him emotionally and psychologically. Priests in turn need to allow themselves to be ministered to in these important areas of their lives.

6. Quoted by Sr Ita Moynihan, Loreto Community, Wexford, in 'A female perspective', *Intercom*, November 1993, 31, a valuable and insightful comment on the original publication of the above reflections on 'The Priest at Fifty' in that journal, October 1993.

CHAPTER NINE

What Theologians Today are saying about Sin

Much new theological thinking has been going on in the Church since Vatican II (1962-5) and much significant illumination has resulted from it, even if also at times some confusion and some disagreement. In consequence we have today a deeper and more balanced understanding of sin (and many other topics). Not everyone has been in a position to keep up to date with all this new thinking and, hence, it may be of value and interest to survey the scene, as it were, and gather together in summary form the essential lineaments of current thinking on this topic.

To begin with, a short outline of the main images or models of sin in the Bible and Christian tradition will make clear how diverse are the ways in which one can begin to approach an understanding of this central teaching of our faith. It will remind us also that many of these models have not been found especially illuminating by the church community over the centuries and so have not been widely used or developed. But our main focus of attention will be the two models or images that have dominated the theology and spirituality of the Church for many centuries, the one now largely laid aside, the other now newly installed as the dominant understanding of sin in our day.

Images or models of sin in the Bible

As one might expect the Bible has no systematic account of sin. Rather it uses many images or metaphors or models to express its teaching, though even together these do not add up to the full theological concept of sin that has been elaborated over the Christian centuries.

Missing the mark: this image is very prominent in the Old Testament especially. It means failing to attain a goal or falling short of God's will for us. It can also have the meaning of breaking or failing in loyalty in an agreement between nations.

Rebellion against God: This is seen as occurring within the covenant context and so it is viewed as a personal offence or revolt against God. It provokes the divine anger and brings punishments on the offender.

Infidelity: In the setting of the God humanity covenant this image is very frequently used. Hence, sin is seen also as adultery or unfaithfulness to God and is the opposite to faith in God.

Iniquity and guilt: Here sin is viewed as a deviation from or a distortion of reality, even of the very inner being of the sinner. It gives rise to guilt and this tends to corrupt the sinner and to be an insupportable burden.

Some special metaphors or images are to be found in the New Testament presentation of sin. While sin is seen as an individual action, it is also viewed as *a state or condition of the sinner*. Thus we find the distinct tendency in the New Testament to shift the focus from individual sinful acts to sin itself. One falls into a state of sin or sinfulness as a result of committing many individual sins. But *sin is a power* in the human community too. It pushes us to commit further sins and so strengthens its power even more. Sin reigns in our world, St Paul says. But most significant of all perhaps, the NT presents *Jesus as the one who conquers sin*. He shows us the Father's love and so sin appears as the refusal of that love.

Other images or models of sin in the Bible are lawlessness, unrighteousness, a state of death, a lie, folly. Note too that in the Pharisaic literature we find sin understood as an offence against or a breach of the law.[1]

Influential images or models of sin in tradition
We may note some other important images or models of sin that are to be found in the Christian theological tradition.

Turning from God to a creature: This was one of St Augustine's 'definitions' of sin and was developed by St Thomas Aquinas. It

---

1. On sin in the Bible see William E. May, 'Sin', in Joseph A. Komonchak, Mary Collins, and Dermot A. Lane (Eds), *The New Dictionary of Theology*, Gill & Macmillan, Dublin 1987, 954-7; John L. McKenzie, S.J., *Dictionary of the Bible*, Geoffrey Chapman, London, 1965, 817-21; James Fischer, C.M., Mary Ann Getty and Robert J. Schreiter, C.PP.S., 'Sin' in Carroll Stuhlmueller, O.P. (General Editor), *The Collegeville Pastoral Dictionary of Biblical Theology*, Liturgical Press, Collegeville, Minnesota, USA 1996, 916-23; William Cosgrave, *Christian Living Today – Essays in Moral and Pastoral Theology*, The Columba Press, Dublin, 2001, chapter 4.

means putting some created good ahead of one's love of God and so turning from God to a creature.[2]

Sin as a stain: This is a quite physical image and sees moral evil or sin as a contamination of the person. It does not succeed well in distinguishing between what is moral and what is non moral or between the voluntary and the non voluntary and so is not very helpful.

Sin as sickness/disease: This model goes back to Jesus himself and links with the image of sin as a state and a power. It suggests healing as a way of understanding reconciliation. It can be helpful, though it may present difficulties in regard to responsibility for sin.

Sin as addiction: Here sin appears as a power that can enslave a person and in a progressive way. Alienation and disintegration can follow. Conversion from such sin will clearly be a process. This can be an illuminating model but has some difficulties, especially in regard to freedom and responsibility. It may not apply equally well to all sins.[3]

Now we are in a position to consider at greater length the two images, models or understandings of sin that have proved most illuminating for the church community over the Christian centuries. These are the legal model, which held sway for hundreds of years down to Vatican II and the relationship model which is the most commonly used one in contemporary moral thinking in the Catholic Church.

The legal understanding of sin[4]
In this understanding sin is viewed as primarily the breaking of a law, human or divine, e.g. one of the ten commandments. Committing a sin is then an act of disobedience. Because laws are usually concerned with specific actions, this legal approach to the moral life tends also to become focused on individual acts, to be, as theologians often say, act centred, to the neglect of the person and what is happening to him/her morally. This act centredness also occasions the neglect of sin in our attitudes,

2. May, 959-60.
3 On these last three images or models see Patrick McCormick, C.M., *Sin as Addiction,* Paulist Press, New York, 1989, chapters 3, 7 and 8.
4. Cosgrave, chapter 1, 12-6 and chapter 4, 62-9.

tendencies, values, goals and priorities. In addition, the legal model of sin tends to give too much attention to the areas of the moral life where there are clear laws to break and to exaggerate the sinfulness of particular actions in those areas. So teachers and preachers often said, 'it's a *mortal* sin to miss Mass on Sunday, to break the fast or to engage in contraception. Neglected then too are sins in our relationships and our community life and so a very individualistic conception of morality emerges that pays little attention to the social dimension of sin. Faulty also is the focus of the legal model of sin on the external act, the matter of the sin, as the primary factor in the sin. This leads to a tendency to see sin where no sin or at most a lesser sin is present. e.g. 'it's a *mortal* sin to commit masturbation, not to go to Mass on Sundays'. In other words, this approach to the moral life tends to collapse the distinction between immorality and sin and so to give the impression that even mortal sins are frequent and indeed easy to commit.

As it developed over the centuries this legal understanding of sin tended, surprisingly, to minimise the seriousness of both mortal and venial sin. It did this in regard to mortal sin by presenting these sins as easy to commit and hence as frequent. It made venial sin appear insignificant in an unjustifiable way. As a result Catholics were given cause for anxiety lest they commit a mortal sin and were regularly in danger of minimalism as they were tempted to go as far as possible while avoiding mortal sin. The impression was, then, given that venial sins were relatively minor and of no great significance morally. Common also in the legal view of sin were legalism and scrupulosity, related distortions of morality which found an easy home under the legal umbrella. Because of the neglect to focus attention on the moral agent in the legal understanding of sin, one's sinfulness tended to be measured in terms of the number of sin acts one had committed. And God was the super accountant totting them all up so as to reach a final verdict on one's eternal destiny.

As you'd expect, the legal concept of punishment for sin was central to the legal model of morality and sin. And God did the punishing. Understandably, the image of God here was forbidding and caused much fear in many a Catholic.

As sinning is easy, so is repentance, according to the legal model. And this holds even for mortal sin. Confession is viewed as a tribunal with its judge and its accused. The medicine of severity was often dispensed here as in secular tribunals or courtrooms and, consequently, many penitents found going to the sacrament to be quite a bit of an ordeal. Relief was the dominant feeling when one emerged from the box.

To sum up, then, the legal model is a valid way of understanding sin but it gives rise to so many distortions and has so many weaknesses that it is surprising that it remained dominant for so long. Only the absence of a clearly superior understanding or model of sin can account for this aided in no little way by the dominance of the legal understanding of the whole Christian life. With the renewal springing from Vatican II such an alternative has become available and has replaced the legal model in moral theology and spirituality generally. To this newer model of sin we now turn.

The relationship understanding of sin[5]
The key word here is relationship or relational. Since our life as human beings consists largely of a network of relationships within which our moral obligations arise and our moral responses are called forth, sin will be found mostly in those relationships and in particular in our responses to other people in those relationships. We may, then, describe sin as any selfish attitude, disposition, tendency, habit or activity that damages or destroys a relationship between individuals or groups. It is unloving or selfish activity (or non activity) or, simply, selfishness in relationship, even one's relationship with oneself. And what damages or destroys one's relationship with others or oneself damages or destroys one's relationship with God.

Sin is a personal reality in that it is the act of a person or persons and affects a person or persons. But it also has a social dimension and that must be given its full weight, as we intend to do later. The roots of our sinful activities are in the attitudes, dispositions, tendencies, habits, intentions, values, goals and priorities referred to above. In a word, they are in the person, the moral subject, and they constitute the sinfulness of that subject. So we can speak of sin as a condition or a state of the person and even as a power pushing one to sin again.

---

5. Cosgrave, 16-22, 69-89.

The relational model sees sin primarily in the choice of the sinner for evil and not in the thing done, the matter. So sin is, above all, a free choice of or commitment to evil, focused, of course, on some object or thing to be done but residing primarily in the heart of the agent. The external deed, then, expresses what the choice of the agent is and means. Here it will be clear that we are not in a good position to judge the sinfulness of other people's actions as distinct from the immorality of those actions. Even in one's own case there can also be uncertainty about that sinfulness. And it will be by no means always evident whether a sin is serious or not serious. However, repentance not categorisation is the sinner's main task. Becoming sinful as a person takes time and effort and will involve a process. Major sin acts will probably have similar characteristics. So serious sin will rarely be instantaneous.

Mortal sin

In the relational model of sin the difficulty of distinguishing in practice between serious and non serious sin is something we have to live with, since it derives from the nature of our choices and commitments. Our deeper choices and commitments are by their nature somewhat obscure. Full clarity is lacking. But we can still describe mortal/serious sin fairly adequately as follows.

Mortal sin is one's deep personal commitment to immorality, one's profound choice of selfishness. It is often referred to today as a fundamental option or basic choice for evil. Such a major choice must come from the heart and obviously cannot happen by accident or on the spur of the moment. It will take effort and time and will usually involve a process of which venial sins may well be a part. It is, then, difficult to commit and, hence, will be rare. And getting out of it will be as hard as getting in to it. It is so significant that it makes one a basically selfish person, who is now oriented towards selfishness and is no longer in the state of grace, i.e. in a loving relationship with God. Such a sin can come about either by a long process of decline into basic sinfulness or by a major choice of an evil like murder or adultery as the culmination of a process of growing selfishness. Clearly in this understanding mortal sin is an adult reality, not something a child is capable of committing.

Should we distinguish mortal from serious sin, as some theologians have been suggesting? Many say yes, because a category called serious sin would seem to be needed and to fit in satisfactorily between the profound choice that is mortal sin and the relatively superficial choice involved in venial sin. However, some theologians in recent years are tending to the view that this triple division does not seem to be very helpful in practice for the individual Christian.

Sin and punishment

It is taken for granted in the legal model that sin is punished and God does the punishing. This language, however, needs to be 'translated', as it were, in the relational model. There talk of punishment really refers to the bad effects of sin on the sinner, namely, he/she becomes less loving and less able to love and his/her relationships with others are weakened or even broken. In addition, speaking in terms of punishment gives the impression that after the sin is over God 'adds on' or applies the punishment like a judge does in a court of law. This is misleading. Sin brings its own bad effects with it; they are intrinsic to the deed, not extrinsic.

Very important to state here also is the fact that the God of Jesus is not a punishing God but a forgiving God (See Lk 15). In the light of this we must picture purgatory and hell, not as punishments for mortal and venial sin respectively, but rather as the natural consequences of these sins in the afterlife. Purgatory is a process of purification or maturing from smaller sins, while hell is the state of total selfishness or lovelessness, bringing with it total isolation and the end of all relationships with other people and with God.

Repentance and confession

The main point about repentance or conversion is that it is often not nearly as easy as the legal model seemed to indicate. It will frequently be a difficult and long process, as we will see later in regard to habits of sin. The new name for confession, the sacrament of reconciliation, points to a renewed understanding. It is best to see it as the place of encounter between the repentant sinner or sinners and the forgiving Church and God with the aim of reconciling the sinner(s) and so restoring the broken relationship with the Church and God. The priest will receive the serious sinner in a Christ like manner and the sinner will come without fear or anxiety to be reconciled. One may speak of confession as a tribunal but it will be one of mercy rather than justice.

Social sin
Today the Church at all levels speaks of social sin. This is a welcome development and a significant effort to overcome the individualism of the past. Such sin can exist at many levels from a small group to the international community and its structures and institutions. The official church position here is that personal sin is sin in the proper sense, while social sin is sin only by analogy. The sins of persons sometimes become embodied in social realities, so that their bad effects continue in the form of damage to persons and relationships. Thus we can speak of sinful social situations or structures or institutions, where injustice in some form has become embedded in the very set up or reality of the group itself. Examples are the structures of patriarchy that discriminate against women in society and in the Church, and the First World economic system which lives off the poor Third World. While this understanding of social sin is criticised as being in the end individualistic, it provides a good starting point for our efforts to develop an adequate theology of social sin.[6]

Evaluation
The brief account of the relationship understanding of sin that we have given here provides us with the essential elements of a theology of sin viewed from this perspective. Some accuse this approach of being vague and fuzzy in comparison to the legal model. While it is less strong on clarity than the legal model (which in some ways gave us a false clarity), this model seems to be more realistic and accurate in relation to our moral experience. Much remains to be done, however, especially in regard to developing an adequate theology of social sin and presenting

6. See John Paul II, Apostolic Exhortation, *Reconciliatio et Paenitentia* (1984), nn. 15-6; Mark O'Keefe, OSB., *What are they saying about social sin?*, New York, Paulist Press, 1990; Thomas F. Schindler, *Ethics: The Social Dimension – Individualism and the Catholic Tradition*, Delaware, USA: Michael Glazier, 1989, 135-149.

our understanding of sin in more strictly religious or theological terms. This latter is far from easy, especially when exact moral analysis is required.[7]

Different kinds of sin, especially habits of sin

In the context of this major renewal of the theology of sin that we have been discussing, there was much discussion about the kinds or types of sin which one can commit and helpful insights into both mortal and venial sin were presented by moral theologians. It is quite easy to see that the distinction between mortal and venial sin is based on the seriousness (or lack of it) of the sins one is considering. In other words, sins are mortal or venial depending on the degree of one's commitment to the evil involved in one's action. This is traditional teaching and is taken for granted here.

It is possible also and, I believe, enlightening to make a division of sin on a different basis, not one that is very new and certainly not one that is at odds with the categories just mentioned. The basis here is not seriousness or non-seriousness. It is rather the ease or difficulty of fully repenting of a sin so as to remove it altogether from one's moral character and Christian life. This way of looking at sinfulness in our lives concerns personal sin only and overlaps with the usual mortal/venial divide, so that the sins in both the categories to be discussed here may be mortal or venial. The labels I propose to use for these categories of sin are: Out of character sins and habits of sin.

Out-of-character sins

This type of sin is quite familiar to most of us and is not hard to understand. As experience shows it may be relatively easy to repent of and remove fully from one's moral life. Examples are ready to hand. A person who is as a rule truthful may on occasion tell a lie, whether major or minor. Or a person who is usually calm and well in control of his/her emotions may in a particular situation lose the cool and give way to an outburst of anger and rage that may be quite hurtful or even destructive. Or again in straitened circumstances a fundamentally honest person in

---

7. On the legal and relational models see McCormick, chapters 4 and 5; also Charles E. Curran, *The Catholic Moral Tradition – A Synthesis*, Georgetown University Press, Washington, D.C., USA, 1999, chapter 3.

financial matters may succumb to temptation and steal or em-
bezzle some cash. Similar out-of-character moral failures can
occur in the areas of sexual or marital morality or in relation to
work practices or the duties of employers, professional people
or members of the clergy.

In relation to this kind of sinful action one may say that the
fall is out of character for the person concerned, even if it happens not just once but maybe two or even three times. It will,
then, be something that the person will be well aware of and
probably feel guilty about. The likelihood in such a case will be
that the person will be disappointed with him/herself, because
of this lapse. Such once- or twice-off sins are, then, very likely to
be repented of in a wholehearted and prompt manner and there
is a strong probability that the sinner will be so motivated as to
ensure that he/she does not commit that sin again in the future.

Most of us will have personal experience of such moral laps-
es in our Christian lives and also of repenting thoroughly and
without significant delay. This latter is the point that is of interest here and it is this factor that distinguishes this category of sin
from the second category that concerns us in this context.

Habits of sin
It is the experience of many people that some of our sins and in
particular some habits of sin are very difficult to uproot. Despite
our best efforts they seem to persist and resist all attempts to
banish them. Examples are plentiful: vulgar language, aggressiveness and badly controlled anger, jealousy, attention seeking,
bullying and bossiness, masturbation and sexual fantasies (in
the past usually referred to as 'bad' thoughts).

This category of sin which bears the label 'habits of sin' is far
from new. It is a traditional designation of a well known group of
vices that affect many people. Our concern here is with the fact
that these sinful habits contrast with the first category of sins just
discussed in being very difficult to get rid of, despite significant
efforts and even repeated resolutions in and outside confession.
These points need not be laboured as they are clear from experience and few would wish to raise questions about them.

It will be of interest, though, to ask the question, why is this
so? Why do these habits of sin present so much difficulty in

regard to complete repentance and conversion from them that most people seem to have relatively little success in uprooting them from their Christian moral lives?

The first point to make in answer to this question is that these sinful practices are habits, that is, they are settled dispositions to act in particular ways and are so stable because the actions they involve have been repeated so that the person has acquired a facility in doing them. That is what habits, especially moral habits, are. Hence, in the right circumstances there develops an inclination to or an ease in doing these evil deeds, so that a consistent pattern is formed in one's moral life that can be called a sinful habit or vice. And the longer the pattern remains in place the more difficult it will be to change it and establish a virtuous pattern or tendency in its place. This accounts for some of the difficulty one may find in relation to being converted from such habits of sin.

But one may now ask, why some of these sinful habits develop at all and in many instances seem to have deep roots that prove largely impervious to most efforts to displace or reverse them?

Emotional roots
Modern psychology provides us with some very helpful insights here. These insights point to the fact that our sins and especially our habits of sin are often, if not always, rooted in or closely related to our emotional lives. All of us have some emotional wounds or hurts which we most likely received in the course of our upbringing, some serious and some minor. These wounds can have a very significant influence on our personality and our manner of relating to ourselves and to others. They can, therefore, have an impact on our free choices, whether these are virtuous or sinful. The reason for this is that our emotional hurts or scars affect the way we feel about ourselves, about other people and about our relationships with them and with God too. This is true even and perhaps especially when we are quite unaware of these emotional factors and their impact on us.

In relation to our sins generally and our habits of sin in particular this emotional influence will be clearer if we look at a few examples. Aggressiveness, with the conflicts and destructive actions that frequently result from it, often has its roots in a lack of self confidence. Because one feels insecure and under threat one is inclined to go on the attack as a means of self defence and so one may become aggressive verbally or in one's attitudes or even physically. The frequent use of vulgar language, which is often done in an angry and even aggressive manner, may also be rooted in this emotional deficit. Jealousy has its roots in a poor self image or low self esteem, a condition that causes one to fear losing a relationship or a position of prominence and in consequence may lead to actions motivated by jealousy. Attitudes of attention seeking and superiority may spring from deep and hidden feelings of inadequacy or inferiority.

The habit of masturbation can be a symptom of problems much more profound like some personality difficulty or some emotional state such as stress, tension, loneliness, anxiety or sexual frustration. In adolescence there is usually an immaturity underlying the habit. So, if one wishes to promote emotional and moral progress, one's concern should be directed more to the causes than to the direct repression of the phenomenon.[8]

As for sexual fantasies psychologists and moralists too recognise that such fantasies can be healthy and are even a necessary part of one's psychosexual maturing process, especially in the adolescent years. But they can be unhealthy too, if, for example, they become pre-occupying. Then it might well be that the fantasies are a symptom of deeper difficulties e.g., emotional or sexual immaturity, isolation from the other sex, feeling under pressure. Sometimes, however, a sexual fantasy can become a kind of planning for some immoral activity and then immorality may enter in. But this is not to be presumed in the ordinary run of things.[9]

Healing

It will be clear from what has been said here that our persistent sins or habits of sin are likely to continue to plague us, if we do not remove the emotional roots from which they very likely spring. We must heal these emotional wounds by some process of therapy, if we are to overcome these sinful habits. This will

8. Sacred Congregation for Catholic Education, 'Educational Guidance in Human Love', Catholic Truth Society, London, 1983, no. 99.
9. Cosgrave, 126-7.

require increased self awareness, perhaps sharing with another person about our emotional scars, a great deal of positive thinking about oneself and others, reading and learning about the emotional dimension of our personality and life so as to understand them better, and perseverance in all this over quite some time. As and when we grow in emotional maturity, as outlined here, we will also grow in moral maturity and the sinful habits we are discussing will gradually fade out of our lives. Without this emotional growth, however, our sinful habits will persist and no amount of other supposed remedies like prayer, penance, purpose of amendment or will power on their own will make any worthwhile difference.[10]

We may add here that in relation to religious or spiritual matters a similar point can be made. Many spiritual difficulties are rooted in psychological or emotional ones and the former will not be resolved unless and until the latter are. For example, strong feelings of anger and/or rejection towards one's father and/or mother that have been buried since childhood may well make relating to God as Father/Mother difficult or even impossible. More positively, the more we are in touch with ourselves and the more mature we are emotionally and personally, the better placed we are to engage in the search for God in the depths of our selves and the more likely we will be to establish a deep and truly personal relationship with God in prayer and in our Christian lives generally.[11]

Social roots
In addition to what has here been said about the personal roots or origins of some of one's sinful habits, one may mention another possible source. This is the influence of one's family of origin and society of origin on one's attitudes, especially one's moral attitudes. In these contexts, especially in one's younger years, one may pick up or be influenced towards particular attitudes or settled viewpoints that can provide the inspiration or basis for immoral and sinful habits or characteristically negative ways of acting and relating to particular people or groups.

---

10. On this area see my articles 'The Roots of Sin ', *Intercom*, May 1994, 12, 14, and 'To Repent and Forgive', *The Furrow*, February, 2003, 85-8.
11. See Tony Baggott, 'Getting the Spiritual Life Together', *The Furrow*, November 1991, 628-35.

Examples here are the following: racist, sexist or class attitudes, prejudices against religious or political viewpoints other than one's own, or against the poor, immigrants, refugees, etc.

Such attitudes and prejudices will very likely give rise to deep-rooted negative reactions and activities that can be so fixed or settled as to amount to immoral and sinful habits.

Conversion

Removing such long-standing and entrenched attitudes will usually require a profound process of education as one seeks to come to a real appreciation of the values and people one has long failed or refused to notice and treat correctly. Or perhaps a deep personal experience may help shatter one's prejudices and re-order one's values and attitudes, so that one is freed from the selfish and immoral habits or viewpoints that lowered the moral quality of one's life over many years. Examples here might be: forming a friendship with a person of another denomination or religion or class that up to now one has avoided and even despised; falling in love with a person of another race or ethnic group which one has long viewed negatively; encountering a member of a hated political group or party who is engaged in notable charity work or in generous and selfless activity for the disadvantaged that brings no political benefit.

CHAPTER TEN

Reconciliation:
The Struggle to Repent and Forgive

Most people are aware that in recent times what we used to call the sacrament of penance or confession has been given a new name. It is now frequently referred to as the sacrament of reconciliation, even though in some quarters one notices a retreat towards the old names again. Now this new name is not used for the sake of novelty or just to appear modern or with it. Rather there are very good reasons of a religious or theological kind that justify the change we are talking about. We don't need to go into these in depth here. Suffice it to say that the rethinking of our understanding of the Christian moral life that has been taking place in the last fifty years or so since the Second Vatican Council and that has been referred to in earlier chapters has resulted in the church moving from the older legal understanding of Christian morality to the more biblical, experiential understanding that some refer to as the relationship or relational approach or understanding or model. Along with significant rethinking in regard to the sacraments generally and the sacrament of penance in particular this shift in understanding has made it clear that what is involved in this latter sacrament is basically reconciliation between the serious sinner and the church and God. It is, then, not primarily about penance or confession, though these are elements of it. As a result of this rethinking or new theology theologians generally and official church documents too have considered it right to speak of the sacrament as the sacrament of reconciliation.

Reconciliation in our experience

Now in this chapter we are not going to talk about the sacrament of reconciliation itself as such. Rather our topic will be reconciliation itself, the reality in human and Christian life about which the sacrament is itself concerned. To understand the sacrament well we need to understand reconciliation well, especially its basic elements, repentance, forgiveness and reconciliation as given in our experience and also in the teaching of the church. So here we will focus on these realities with a view to improving our understanding of them and seeing more clearly the relationship between them. This should be of benefit to us also in our ordinary relationships with the people in our daily lives, family, friends, colleagues and acquaintances, etc. in the sense that it will, hopefully, clarify what we need to do when we fall out with any of these people and want to get back together again. It should also be of value in our relationships in and with the church and with God and enable us to be clearer about what the sacrament of reconciliation aims at and achieves and what our role in it requires.

What has just been said here will make it fairly clear that we will be beginning our reflections from our experience of living, not from the Bible or official church teaching or the theories of some high-powered theologian. This will, one hopes, make understanding what is being said easier to grasp. So, essentially what we will be endeavouring to do in this chapter is analysing our ordinary experience and by doing so seeking to promote a better understanding of reconciliation and a better practice of it outside and inside the sacrament. It won't be difficult to see, then, that what we discover in our experience will be quite in line with what the church teaches, that it will clarify and illuminate that teaching and place its challenging nature more clearly before us.

Reconciliation by other names
The word 'reconciliation' is a rather churchy one and not one we use very often in our daily conversation. But the reality the word refers to is very much part of our ordinary experience, especially in our relationships with the people around us. We do, however, use other words to describe this reality. We speak, for example, of making up, letting bygones be bygones, burying the hatchet, getting back together again, healing wounds, restoring relationships, giving and receiving pardon, etc. While these are more common popular expressions, we will retain the word 'reconciliation' here. The reasons for this are that this word will, on analysis, help us to arrive at a clearer understanding of the elements involved in the reality we are discussing and the relationship between those elements. It will also enable us to clarify

what is required in order to achieve the getting back together after a falling out that is the essence of reconciliation. In addition, it is necessary to use it so as to link up with the sacrament of reconciliation and the frequent use of the word in church teaching and liturgical celebrations. In any case it is a word we are reasonably familiar with and whose meaning we basically know. Our focus, then, will be on personal reconciliation, that is, reconciliation in our personal relationships and reconciliation with God. The much more complex matter of group reconciliation will not be discussed, though the elements of reconciliation we will be reflecting on are essential to that too.

Context of personal reconciliation – our relationships
If we reflect a little on our experience in this area of life it will become clear that reconciliation – or whatever other name we decide to use for it – takes place in the context of our relationships with other people, both as individuals and as groups like one's family or the family next door or some club, etc. Reconciliation makes no sense apart from our personal relationships and wouldn't exist or need to exist without them or apart from them. Clearly then, reconciliation is a reality that finds its place in the context of our relationships with those in our circle. Now and again we are or need to be reconciled with other people, whether one's spouse, one's parent, one's grown son or daughter, one's neighbour, one's friend, one's work mate or whoever. It is obvious that it takes at least two people to be reconciled or to make up as it takes at least two to fall out or have a row.

When is reconciliation needed?
Experience tells us that we need to be reconciled with another when we have fallen out with that person, when some fault or selfish action or word by one party to the relationship has upset, angered or hurt the other and so caused him/her to withdraw partly or wholly from the relationship, e.g., a lie, a broken promise, an aggressive action, an insulting remark.

Strictly speaking, reconciliation or getting back together again is only needed or possible when one's relationship with the other person has been broken, not when it is merely damaged. It is only then that one can or should be reconciled. It will naturally take a serious fault or major form of selfishness to break any worthwhile relationship between two people. Minor things will only disturb it or cause annoyance but will not break it completely. So here, then, we are talking about major faults between the partners like marital infidelity, a big falling out over money or drinking, physical violence, a notable betrayal, rejection, insult, etc.

When a relationship is only damaged by something that is done or said, then we cannot properly speak of reconciliation having to take place. It is a case, rather, of one or both undoing the damage by an apology and by the acceptance of the apology. Thus the relationship is restored to its former depth and strength, but we wouldn't normally speak of this as reconciliation. In practice, however, in moral and spiritual preaching and teaching in the church especially the word reconciliation is used to refer to both kinds of damage to our relationships, the kind that breaks a relationship and the kind that only harms or weakens it. In this chapter we will adopt the strict interpretation of the word reconciliation, though without constantly remaking the point that we are doing so.

To put all this in more religious or theological terms, we are here talking about sin and serious sin at that. It is sin in our relationships that makes reconciliation necessary. It is because we have sinned seriously against another that we need to be reconciled. Much could be and needs to be said about sin itself from the moral and religious points of view.[1] But that is not our concern here. We intend to focus on reconciliation alone as the direct and primary subject of our reflections.

Why is reconciliation needed?
Experience tells us that we feel the need to get back together again, to make up, when a valued relationship or friendship has broken down due to the fault of oneself or the other(s) or both. It is because the relationship is important to you that you feel it is worthwhile trying to restore it. It meets some significant personal, emotional need for one or both parties and, hence, you feel called to attempt to patch up the quarrel and to bury the hatchet. You may or may not be successful but that is a different matter.

---

1. See the previous chapter.

The feeling that one wants to attempt reconciliation is not necessarily present after every break-up of a relationship. Sometimes one or both parties feel that maybe it's as well to let the broken relationship go, whether it is between spouses in marriage or between friends or colleagues or whoever. Somehow the relationship seems no longer to be important or to meet any significant personal need. Perhaps it had been declining anyway and was less satisfying than earlier. The break may appear to one or both to be an appropriate occasion to bring to an end what was, at least in hindsight, an already fading and even burdensome relationship. In such circumstances the best thing to do might seem to be to call it a day, as it were, and not to expend any further effort in trying to achieve reconciliation.

What's needed to achieve reconciliation?
If we reflect a little on our experience here, it will soon be apparent that there are two basic elements that must be present for reconciliation to happen. In other words, two things are essential in order that one person is reconciled with another who has fallen out with him or her. These two requirements are an apology, on the one hand, and being forgiving, on the other. In other words, one person must say 'I'm sorry', while the other says 'I forgive'. Again it may be phrased as the guilty party asks pardon, as the one who has been hurt accepts or grants this pardon. In traditional church or theological terms the sinner must repent and the offended person must forgive. In short, then, what is required for reconciliation to become a reality are repentance on the one side and forgiveness on the other.

We may add here that these two basic dimensions of reconciliation must somehow be expressed so that the two people can become aware that each is taking the step required so that reconciliation may occur. Hence, the sinner must indicate by word or action that he/she is sorry, while the offended person must communicate to the other that h/she forgives. If either one does not convey the appropriate message, then no reconciliation is possible. Even though one party should do her/his part, there will be no getting back together, if the other fails to do what is needed from their side and, of course, vice versa. It is clear, then, that both sorrow and pardon must be present and known by each party to be present in order that the parties can be reconciled. Not infrequently, both parties to the problem will need to express sorrow as both may be at fault. Then too both will be called on to show that they forgive each other. If either fails to do this, then they can't and won't be reconciled.

We now move on to discuss at some length each of the central elements or requirements for reconciliation, repentance and forgiveness.

Understanding our experience of repentance

A popular and widely watched firm some years ago had the catch phrase, 'love means never having to say you're sorry'. Now, while this may be an ideal for all of us, it seems obvious in our experience that the opposite is the case. In fact that experience of daily living makes it abundantly clear that love in practice means having to say you are sorry and having to go on saying it. The reason is, of course, that we continue to be selfish, to speak and act in hurtful ways in our relationships and so there remains a repeated need to apologise and to repent, so that the relationship may remain strong and our selfishness or sinfulness may be undone and left behind with the damage it has caused repaired and the hurt healed. We know from experience also that repentance, especially for a serious fault, is often far from easy. It may well take not a little effort and quite some time and may require courage and humility, which we usually find hard to muster.

As a consequence of this some people find repenting impossible in some circumstances. In addition, it happens that in some situations a person won't admit that what he/she has done was wrong or sinful; or he/she is not aware that their deed was hurtful, selfish and sinful. Then no apology will be forthcoming and no reconciliation will be possible. Thus the process of reconciliation is stopped before it starts, because an essential element, repentance, is missing.

Why repentance can be so difficult

In relation to minor hurts or offences it will usually be relatively easy to say 'I'm sorry', because the thing doesn't affect one very much, e.g. showing some minor discourtesy or making a funny remark that comes out less than funny. But when it is a question of more serious matters, then we feel the effort required to apol-ogise and express sorrow. This is not hard to understand. Saying sorry is not merely an intellectual matter involving the rational mind. Rather it involves also our emotions, and so our deeper self. Because of this, we experience difficulty in making an apology for a significant fault or sin. We may explain this as follows.

When we have sinned or done some selfish deed, one usually feels guilty and perhaps even ashamed. This tends to make one feel small and humble; it may dent one's self-confidence and weaken one's self-esteem. One may, then, feel regret, disap-pointment with oneself and maybe even embarrassment, espe-cially if one has to go to another and offer an apology. All this is personally difficult. If, in addition, your self-esteem is already low, then repentance will be even more difficult. It may happen too that a particular sinful action was motivated in part at least by a desire for revenge or by anger. These will tend to put a brake on one's desire to apologise and repent, as then the motive as well as the deed will be seen to be selfish and self-serving. In such circumstances these motives will have to be dealt with and perhaps communicated to the other, if one is to make one's sor-row fully effective. Here we can see where the difficulty of re-penting arises in the case of a significant offence. Our guilt feel-ings and disappointment with oneself will help to ensure that repenting is no facile process but, rather, is intrinsically difficult. In fact it can be so difficult that a person will be unable to get round to it in the short or even the medium term. It may even be the case that he/she finds it impossible to repent truly at all in the case of a major fault or sin.

While all this is true, it is important to note that it is these same negative feelings of guilt and unease in oneself that can alert one to the fact that one has transgressed one's own moral principles. In this sense they serve a positive purpose; they are in a sense the voice of one's conscience calling one to repentance.

In the light of these reflections it will be plain that in many in-stances when we have committed a notable sin, repentance will be a process that will go on over some time and will take quite a bit of effort. One will have to work at it so as to master one's negative feelings and work up the courage and humility to admit one did wrong and sinned.

From what has been said here it can be seen that the impression often given in the past by preachers, teachers and other official church spokespersons in relation to repentance being relatively easy to accomplish, just as committing sin, even mortal sin, was relatively easy, does not tally very well with our experience. That experience seems to indicate that it is harder both to commit a significant sin and to repent of it than the theology and spirituality of the pre-Vatican II era thought and taught. This is both consoling and challenging and needs to be kept in mind when we reflect on and engage in the business of repenting. It should be added here too that telling a priest in confession about one's sin and repenting there can be easier than going to the offended party and making one's apology in person. But there can be no doubt that going to confession can't function as a substitute for the personal encounter with the offended person(s) and full repentance may well oblige one to face the music, as it were, and go humbly to the person in question and say 'I'm sorry'. It does happen, however, that in some cases, both parties to a fall out somehow agree to let bygones be bygones without any very explicit expressions of sorrow or forgiveness. They implicitly move towards reconciliation and move on from the offence.

In short, then, repentance for any sort of significant fault or sin will tend to be a process taking time and effort. This is something one must reckon with personally and it must be taken fully into account by confessors in the sacrament of reconciliation in relation to what has usually been called the purpose of amendment. And of course, we must not forget the basic point, that, if there is no repentance, then there can be no reconciliation.

Repentance as a process: habits of sin
What has been said here about repentance or conversion from our sinfulness and our sinful actions and attitudes being a process taking time and effort is best illustrated, perhaps, by reflecting on our experience of what have long been referred to as habits of sin.[2]

2. These reflections can be found in the previous chapter under the heading 'Habits of Sin'.

Understanding our experience of forgiveness

Forgiveness is the second essential element of reconciliation. As with repentance or conversion there can be no reconciliation in a damaged or broken relationship without forgiveness. And it must be expressed or communicated in some way to the other person(s). So, even if the guilty party is sorry and repentant, he/she cannot restore the relationship unless the offended party extends forgiveness. And vice versa also, of course. Here we will attempt to analyse our experience of forgiveness, so as to enable us to understand it better and so be better placed actually to forgive those who offend or sin against us. And such an understanding of forgiveness should aid us in asking for that forgiveness, when we ourselves have offended.

The nature of forgiveness

It is far from easy to give a description of forgiveness. Perhaps it will be adequate to say that you have forgiven another person who has hurt or offended you, when you are able to act in your relationship with that person after the offence as if that offence never happened. Resuming the relationship with basically the same attitudes and feelings you had for the other before he/she hurt you will be a clear indication that you have really forgiven that person. If you can do this, you will have forgiven fully. But experience teaches us that, like repentance, forgiving in this sense can be very difficult. In fact one may be unable to do it for some time and, if the hurt were particularly serious, it may take a very long time or even be quite impossible.

If we ask, why is forgiving so difficult in some cases?, the answer is the same as in regard to repenting: our feelings are involved and they can't be simply switched off or on whenever one's mind decides. If we are offended in any sort of significant way, feelings like anger, hurt, resentment and even bitterness will likely be aroused. One can even be seething with rage and indignation and in no mood for entertaining thoughts of forgiving or pardoning. In the light of this it is not very difficult to grasp the point that the key to forgiving is to be found in dealing constructively with these feelings so as to let them go and calm oneself down. Again our main problem is in the emotional area of our lives and not in the intellectual area or in regard to one's will power. But this only means that our difficulty is all the greater and presents us with the problem of finding a way to let go of one's anger and hurt so that we may forgive.

Letting go of anger and hurt

As we may well know from experience there is no easy way to do this nor is there any quick fix one might adopt. The process here is bound to be a painful one that may well take considerable time and effort. One can imagine how very difficult it will be for, say, a wife who has discovered her husband in marital infidelity to let go of her deep feelings of betrayal, hurt and rage. Similarly in cases of grave insult, physical violence, public humiliation, etc. Here letting go of such feelings will demand almost heroic effort and a lot of time. Even then it may turn out to be beyond the person involved.

It can happen too that a particular person may be motivated, perhaps unconsciously, by quite different reasons that result in a refusal to forgive. So one may find it attractive to wallow in self-pity over being so hard done by or he/she could possibly enjoy one's feelings of self-righteousness and moral superiority over the offender. Another might indulge in nursing her/his anger and resentment, so as to get even later or to protect oneself from more painful feelings like sadness, loneliness, emptiness, depression, etc. Or not forgiving could enable one to control the guilty party in ways that would not otherwise be possible. Another possibility is that refusing to pardon could provide an excuse for remaining at a distance from the sinner, because deep down one really fears closeness.

Benefits of forgiving

Experience shows us that our very nature as persons in relationship and in community calls us to forgive those who offend us. The Christian gospel confirms this, when Jesus in many places tells us in word and parable that we are to forgive as often as that is needed. The main reason for this and the big benefit of forgiving is that it helps restore the damaged or broken relationship between the parties involved. If the other person in the situation says sorry, then their relationship will be restored. This is the whole purpose of forgiving and ought to be the chief motive of the one who is called to forgive. There are other motives too that can spur one on to grant pardon. One is the sense of relief and of shedding a burden that forgiving brings with it. When you forgive, it also ends your pre-occupation with the hurt involved and with the person who has injured you, a pre-occupation that not infrequently accompanies the refusal to forgive.

The damage not forgiving may do
If one refuses to extend the hand of forgiveness and continues to nurse one's anger and resentment, then, psychologists tell us, one may be on course to bury those strong negative feelings within oneself. This can lead to the development of a deep sadness within or even to depression as one turns these feelings in on oneself. But one never buries such feelings dead, as it were, since their psychic energy continues in them. Hence, this energy will seek an outlet; they are buried alive, one can say, and their energy and power can do a lot of emotional damage to oneself. And this is what they may well do, if they remain buried for a lengthy period. It is possible that with time these repressed feelings, even though one may have long since forgotten about them, may so damage one emotionally that physical symptoms of bodily ailments may appear in the body. Examples mentioned are: skin diseases, fever, ulcers, heart problems and even cancer. This possibility is confirmed by some people in the Charismatic Movement that was very strong and influential in the years after Vatican II. These say that they find in their healing ministry that a refusal to forgive a significant hurt can block the healing process in relation to such ailments.

The other side of the coin is that there is evidence that letting go one's anger and resentment facilitates the healing in question here. It may be called psycho-somatic healing. Again this is not difficult to understand, given that these physical conditions may well have arisen in the first place, because one had buried one's strong feelings of anger, etc. at some point in the past. Hence, it becomes clear that in such cases forgiving will benefit, not merely the relationship that has been damaged or broken but also the one who has been offended or sinned against. It will, therefore, be in that person's own interest to forgive and let go the deep feelings of hurt, etc. that the offence gave rise to. Here is another incentive to be forgiving that will be present in some cases.

Forgiving oneself

For some people this is more difficult than forgiving others. But it is, nevertheless, very important, because without it one will be less at peace with oneself, more negative towards oneself and will, perhaps, find it harder to forgive others. On occasion a person may be angry at him/herself for some failure or sin and may be disappointed for not fulfilling one's own expectations or living up to one's own moral values and principles. Not forgiving oneself can, then, be a form of self-punishment. It is people who are low in self-esteem who tend to be unforgiving towards themselves, feeling, perhaps, that they do not deserve forgiveness. Hence, it will be important to strive to forgive oneself so as to come to a more positive view of and feeling about oneself and as result to be better placed to extend forgiveness to others.

Forgiving God

Occasionally, one may find it hard to forgive God. One may be angry with God because of some tragedy, illness, loss or injustice suffered by oneself or others and so be inclined to blame God for not averting these destructive developments. At times this feeling will be understandable but it will, nevertheless, be important and necessary that one let go of one's anger and hurt feelings against God and so forgive. This form of forgiveness will also bring greater peace of soul and the feeling that one is again closer to the Father in heaven. Helpful in this endeavour will be a correct understanding or image of God. In the past we Catholics tended to have an image of God as a punishing God, ready and waiting to pay us back for our sins perhaps in this life but certainly in the next. This bred fear and anxiety and sometimes led one to behave in a punishing way towards others after the manner of one's image of God. Today, however, we are clear that the God of Jesus Christ is a forgiving, not a punishing God, one who forgives us totally and always no matter what our transgression. The parable of the prodigal son, which is better characterised as the forgiving Father, illustrates this graphically and memorably. Being clear about this will be no small help in increasing our peace of mind and heart, in moving us to seek forgiveness from our loving and forgiving Father and in inducing us to extend that forgiveness to those who have offended us. We are to be forgiving as our heavenly Father is forgiving.

Should we forgive and forget?
We are all quite familiar with the old saying 'forgive and forget'. It tends to be taken as a piece of ancient wisdom that we should abide by. No doubt it is wise to follow it in some cases but there are other cases when it seems it would be far from helpful, certainly in the long term, to do so. It is important to be clear that forgetting is no part of forgiving and is neither necessary to the process of forgiving nor is it at times possible. In fact there are occasions when it is wrong to forget or even to try to do so. Remembering a particular fault and the difficult process of forgiving may be valuable in the future, when one is called on again perhaps to forgive or to empathise with others who are struggling to forgive either oneself or some other person. So the old saying might be rephrased to read: forgive and remember so as to forgive better in future.'

Reconciliation
Our rather lengthy reflections on repentance/conversion and on forgiveness/pardon will have given us a better insight into what is needed to bring about reconciliation. As already noted, these two are the essential requirements for that reconciliation. When the guilty party can say 'I'm sorry' and the offended person is able to declare 'I forgive', then they can and will be reconciled. Their relationship will be restored. Thus when repentance meets forgiveness the result will be reconciliation. But, as has been said, if either is missing, the broken relationship will remain broken.

Experience makes another point very clear in relation to the process of achieving reconciliation. This process will often be very difficult, taking much effort and perhaps a lot of time, even years. Even then there will be no guarantee that it will be successful, as many know to their cost. However, when the reconciliation process does reach the desired conclusion and the broken relationship is restored, then, the parties involved will feel a great sense of relief, peacefulness and happiness. The point then is that achieving reconciliation is a struggle but reconciliation achieved is a joy and a delight. Experience confirms this, not just in relation to marriages but also in the case of friendships and other close and valued relationships. The prospect of this happy outcome of the struggle for reconciliation can at times be a spur to the parties involved to undertake the difficult tasks of repenting and forgiving. Thus another motive or incentive to work towards reconciliation is provided.

Rituals of reconciliation

In our ordinary daily life there are many well established and familiar gestures or symbols or rituals that people use to mark and indeed celebrate a reconciliation that has been achieved in their lives. These symbols or rituals have been devised or elaborated by our society or culture as ways of expressing outwardly and visibly that reconciliation has been arrived at. They also are intended to confirm and seal the process that has just been completed and to celebrate the joy of being back together again with the fault(s) repented of and forgiven. They declare that the parties are happy to be reconciled. Thus, we can say that these rituals are symbolic celebrations of the reconciliation that has taken place. We make use of them because we sense the importance of what has been achieved and also to impress upon us and rejoice in the restoration of the relationship in question. Examples of these symbols or rituals are ready to hand and are quite familiar: a handshake, an embrace, a kiss, a meal or drink together and probably for the married a resumption of sexual relations.

It may be mentioned in passing that similar rituals of restored relations can be found in and between groups, communities and even countries. There might be visits to each other's homes or community premises, some celebratory gathering, resuming diplomatic relations among states or signing a treaty or agreement, or an official or unofficial visit to the other country.

In this context one could expect that religious bodies like churches and congregations would also have special rituals or ceremonials for purposes similar to those just mentioned in relation to secular groups and communities. This is what is in fact the case. In the Christian churches these rituals are usually referred to as sacraments or rituals of a sacramental nature. Thus in the Catholic church (and in other churches too) there are three main rituals involving reconciliation. For us in the Catholic church the sacrament that is most explicitly concerned with reconciliation is confession, to give it its popular name. But, as we noted at the beginning, this is now officially designated as the sacrament of reconciliation, thus expressing clearly what is involved in this symbolic ritual. So, this sacrament is the church's official ritual or symbolic rite or ceremony for marking, sealing, celebrating and bringing to fruition the reconciliation of its seriously sinning members with the church itself and through that with God. This new name for this sacrament should provide some reassurance for those using it that it is not intended to be an ordeal, as was often the experience in the past, but rather a celebration of the sinner's restored relationship with the church and in and through that with our forgiving Father in heaven.

We may mention too that baptism is a sacrament that forgives sins and then makes one a full member of the church, both in the case of an adult joining the Christian church and of an infant brought by his/her parents to be incorporated into the Body of Christ. The eucharist too can be called the sacrament of reconciliation, because, in both past and present, participating in it fully was and is an explicit symbol of one's full membership of the church both legally and spiritually.

Reconciliation with oneself
This is an idea we don't often think about but there is a reality in question here that we would do well to reflect on, especially in the context of our present discussion. The core point here is that, if you are not reconciled with yourself, then, there will be major difficulties in being reconciled in the full sense with others. To put it in other words, if you are not truly at peace with yourself and do not really love yourself, you will find it very difficult to love others at any significant level and to achieve full reconciliation with them, when that is needed. It will, then be important to understand what it means to say being reconciled to oneself and how one can fail in this.

We may say, first of all, that if one has not repented of some serious offence or sin and is burdened with real guilt, if one has not forgiven another after one has been notably hurt or offended but is holding on to anger and even bitterness, if one has not forgiven oneself for some important sin or failure, then one remains in a notable way unreconciled with oneself. One is morally and perhaps emotionally and spiritually at odds with oneself and so will find it difficult to be reconciled with others.

The lack of self-reconciliation can be seen also in deep feelings of inadequacy, insecurity inferiority and low self-esteem and low self-confidence. If one has a notable sense of failure or negative outlook in relation to one's career, one's marriage and family life or even one's life itself, if one suffers from deep loneliness and feels no one cares, if one experiences a sense of hopelessness, uselessness or meaninglessness in and about one's whole existence, if a sense of sadness and depression pervades one's soul; then, one has to say that you are not at peace with yourself, you haven't a right relationship with yourself, you are not reconciled with yourself and your love for yourself is seriously deficient. And it may even be the case that a person is only poorly aware of these realities in his/her deeper self, in his/her heart and soul. This clearly aggravates the problem and makes the achievement of reconciliation more difficult on all fronts.

Bringing about reconciliation with oneself from any of these situations or positions will clearly be demanding. It will require true awareness of one's difficulty, significant emotional therapy, perhaps with the aid of others, and maybe even professionals in the business. Plenty of effort and time will also be required. One can, however, arrive at true peace of soul and mind, at that real reconciliation with oneself, at genuine love of self, if one has the commitment do so and takes the means necessary to arrive at that goal. If one does this, then reconciliation with others will be deeper and more wholehearted and the same will apply to one's reconciliation with the Ultimate Reality, God.

Reconciliation with God
In the ultimate sense this is, of course, the most important form of reconciliation that there is for the Christian or anyone else. This is what really matters in the long run. But it is important to keep in mind that we can't separate it from the other kinds of reconciliation which we have been discussing up to this point. In fact it is only in and through these other forms that we can achieve reconciliation with God.

The way we offend God is in and through offending some human person or persons. In other words, we sin against God by sinning against people, including oneself. Hence, the way of achieving reconciliation with God is in and through being

reconciled with the person, persons or groups we have offended. If we are not reconciled with these people, then we are not
and cannot be reconciled with God. Thus being reconciled with
another person points to or is the symbol and means of being
reconciled with God. One may say that this human process of
reconciliation is the sacrament of one's reconciliation with God,
that is the visible sign and guarantee that one is reconciled with
God. This implies, of course, that, if you are not reconciled on
the human level, then there can be no reconciliation with God.

This applies to all of us in so far as we have sinned seriously
and need to repent, because then we are guilty and have broken
our relationship with some other human person(s) and so with
God. In this context going to or celebrating the sacrament of reconciliation will be the official church symbol or ritual by which
we endeavour to achieve reconciliation with the offended party,
the church as Body of Christ and so with the Father in heaven, a
goal that is guaranteed to be achieved if and in so far as we are
repentant. In regard to forgiving, it may be said that, if one fails
to do this, then one will have real responsibility for preventing
true reconciliation coming about and one will have a duty to repent for that lack of forgiveness and the absence of reconciliation with the other and so with God.

The Christian Religious Dimension

What has been said so far comes from our ordinary experience
of relationships in daily life. It is not difficult to confirm and
deepen what has here been discovered or realised from the Bible
and the Christian tradition. As in the Old Testament there are
numerous occasions on which Jesus called for repentance, forgiveness and reconciliation with other people and with God.
Similarly in the letters of St Paul and other NT writers. A few examples will make this clear.

In Mark's gospel Jesus begins his public ministry by calling
on all 'to repent and believe the gospel' (1.15 and Matt. 3.2). St
Peter is recorded in Acts 2.38 as also calling all to repent. St Paul
refers to repentance less often but in Rom 2.4-5 he says people
are led to repentance by the goodness of God.[3]

---

3. John L.McKenzie, S.J., *Dictionary of the Bible*. Geoffrey Chapman,
London – Dublin 1965, 728-30.

Similarly in regard to forgiveness, Jesus claimed power to forgive sins (Mt 9.6), and the parable of the prodigal son or, better, the forgiving father, illustrates vividly and profoundly the forgiving nature of God the Father (Luke 15). In the NT forgiveness of sins comes through Christ (Acts 13.38; Eph. 1.7, etc.) and is a free gift of God. Forgiveness is also gained through the prayers of the church (James 5.15-16). Jesus conferred upon the apostles the power to forgive sins (John 20. 21-22).[4]

Reconciliation is also prominent in the Bible and especially in the NT epistles. God is the agent of reconciliation and it is we humans who are reconciled. Christ is the means of reconciliation which is extended to the whole world. God reconciles the world to himself in Christ (2 Cor. 5.18 – 21). See also Rom. 5.10, Col. 1.20-22; Eph. 2.14-16.[5]

This religious understanding of reconciliation and its central elements adds a new dimension and depth to the human experience of reconciliation that has been discussed in the preceding pages. This is the divine or supernatural dimension which is found within the core of our human experiences and which our faith reveals to us as we follow the Christian way. This adds to the importance and significance of repentance, forgiveness and reconciliation in our lives as Christians but also provides us with hope and strength through God's grace in Christ in the struggle to undertake and complete the work of reconciliation with others and with God.

CONCLUSION

Our discussion of the models or images of sin in the Christian tradition will have thrown light on the nature of sin as we experience it. Our fuller account of the legal and relational models will have illuminated and helped us in our understanding of sin and in our efforts to repent and be converted.

It will be clear that there are good grounds for making the distinction of sins into the two categories that we have reflected on in the second part of this chapter.

One can hope that, in relation to habits of sin, the reflections on the deeper layers or roots of these often intractable moral

---

4. McKenzie, 284-5.
5. McKenzie, 722-3.

failures will provide some insights that may make tackling them in an effort to achieve true conversion somewhat easier, at least by way of providing a deeper understanding of the problem and some few hints or guidelines in relation to how to make some progress in uprooting them.

CHAPTER ELEVEN

The Decline of Confessions:
Disaster or Return to Normal?

Some people in the church are of the opinion that the sacrament of penance (or reconciliation) is in a state of crisis. The main reason for this viewpoint is that in the last forty years or so Catholics have been going to confession much less frequently than previously and some are not going now at all. The result is that there has been a sharp and major decline in the use of the sacrament by even good Catholics, not excluding bishops, priests and religious. In the eyes of not a few there is here a real cause for concern, perhaps even a sign of weakening of our sense of sin and maybe a sign of the faith of many Catholics atrophying in an ever more secular world. Others in the church, however, seem not to be overly worried by these developments, since it seems to them that the practice of the preceding decades was not at all representative of the history of penance down the centuries. Our question, then, is: Is there really a crisis here or should we interpret the facts in some other way?

Some statistics
The extent of the drop in the use of the sacrament of penance will become clear if we look at some of the findings of recent surveys covering the forty-five or so years since the Vatican Council down to the present.

One survey in the US showed that between 1964 and 1974 monthly confession declined from 38 to 1 per cent of Catholics. Another poll discovered that 27 per cent never confess, 25 per cent confess once a year and only 6 per cent go to confession monthly or more often. In relation to US priests this same survey found that 8 per cent go weekly, 27 per cent monthly, 47 per cent every few months and 18 per cent once a year.

Surveys in Ireland indicate similar trends. Between 1974 and 1984 there was a drop of 20 per cent in the monthly confession rate, from 46 per cent in 1974 to 26 per cent in 1984. The number of those who never go to the sacrament rose from 3.7 per cent to 7.1 per cent. A more recent survey (1989) shows a continuation of these trends. It found that 11 per cent never confess and only 18 per cent go to the sacrament monthly or more often. This represents a drop of 29 per cent in monthly confession between 1974 and 1989, so that by 1989 monthly confession is the norm for less than one in five Irish Catholics.

Since those surveys were taken over twenty years ago, the situation has continued to move in the direction set back then. The most recent figures make this abundantly clear. In a survey carried out in 2007-8 by Fr Micheál MacGréil, S.J., the following is reported.

> The practice of Sacramental Confession was found to be relatively low, with 27 per cent going to Confession 'several times a year or more frequently' and one-third (33 per cent) giving up the practice altogether. This marks a downward trend from 80 per cent in 1988-89 going to Confession 'several times a year or more often' to the current 27 per cent. It means a drop of 66 per cent in 19 years![1]

A US survey in 2008 found that only 61 per cent of Catholics who attend Mass weekly go to Confession once a year or more frequently. For Catholics who go to Mass less than once a week but at least monthly, the figure is even lower (37 per cent). Only 8 per cent of Catholics who go to Mass infrequently have been to Confession in the past year.

The size and suddenness of this exodus from the sacrament as here documented are emphasised and highlighted by the fact that in these same decades the frequency of Catholics going to communion at Mass has gone dramatically in the opposite direction to that which we have just outlined. Nowadays many more Catholics go to communion and go more frequently than previously. In the US the number of churchgoers receiving communion weekly increased between 1964 and 1974 from one fifth to a half, while in Ireland between 1974 and 1984 there was a 10 per cent increase. By 1989 a dramatic leap upwards was recorded, from 5 to 43 per cent. In more recent times that has increased further, even allowing for the decline in the numbers of Catholics going to Mass weekly in recent decades. MacGréil found that Mass attendance by Roman Catholics was 43 per cent

---

1. http://www.amdg.ie/2009/06/16/cardinal-launches-macgréil-survey

weekly or more often and 55 per cent monthly (or more often it was 79 and 85 per cent respectively in 1988-89). Some 78 per cent of those attending Mass regularly receive Holy Communion. 17 per cent would never receive Holy Communion at present, he stated.

A Bit of History
The significance of this recent decline in the numbers of Catholics going to confession will be clearer if we look back into history and see how things were in earlier centuries.

For nearly all of the church's history going to penance or confession has been a very rare event for Catholics generally. For the first five or six centuries the vast majority of Catholics never went to or celebrated canonical or public penance. In fact they were not allowed to do so, since this penitential rite was a once-in-a-lifetime event and people were forbidden to repeat it. In addition, only the most serious public or social sins involved an obligation to resort to this public penance, usually the three major ones, murder, adultery and apostasy (abandoning the faith). And, because the penances for these sins were so severe and were generally done in public, in the sense that the rest of the community knew one was in the Order of Penitents, most people postponed this form of penance till the end of their lives, often enough till their death-bed. What are now called devotional confessions (where only venial sins are brought to the sacrament) were not allowed back then. In other words, this form of penance was only for the most serious sinners; others were forbidden to approach it. Hence, very few Christians undertook this form of penance or, as we'd say, went to confession in this form in those early centuries. So a person like St Augustine or St Ambrose would never have gone to or celebrated canonical penance at all. Historians of the sacrament say that, because this canonical penance was so severe, especially in regard to the penances imposed, it brought about its own demise. So about the sixth century or so it died out and was no longer used or of use to the Christian faithful who had sinned.

In due course another form or ritual of penance emerged to replace the above one and to help meet the need of sinners to receive the forgiveness of God and the church. This is usually called private or Irish penance. It began to be practised in the Irish or Celtic monasteries about the middle of the sixth century (AD 550). It spread outside the monasteries in time and was private, repeatable and allowed one to confess any and every sin. And in regard to the penances the principle was: let the penance fit the sin. This form of penance is the forerunner of our present ritual of penance or reconciliation. From then on people went to this form of the sacrament less infrequently but still not at all frequently. In fact so infrequently that in 1215 a universal law was made requiring as a minimum that all over the age of discretion (probably fourteen) should go to confession at least once a year (if they had mortal sin). From this time till the Council of Trent (1551) once a year seems to have been the practice and frequency for most people. After Trent, which laid down rules about confessing the number and different kinds of one's sin, there was some increase in the frequency with which Catholics approached the sacrament and also went to communion. But, due to the influence of Jansenism and its rigorist attitudes to sin and sinners, this merely meant for most people little more than the minimum required by the law. Such was the situation up to the twentieth century.

Then came the decree of Pius X in 1910 ordering that first communion should be received at about the age of seven and encouraging all to approach the table of the Lord frequently. Up to that time first communion and first confession had been at eleven, twelve or thirteen. Now, with this new dispensation there went the unwritten law or principle that one had to go to confession before one went to communion. Hence, as going to communion became more common and even frequent, so confession did too. Thus in the twentieth century arose the practice – quite unknown in Christian history – of frequent confession, rising in frequency in mid-century to monthly or even weekly confession, not just for priests and nuns and brothers, but also for the lay faithful, a practice that many older Catholics well remember.

Why so frequent in the twentieth century?
In the light of what has just been said this question naturally arises and has already been partially answered. We may list

what seem to be the main reasons behind the new development:

1. As indicated, the growth of frequent communion would seem to be a main or even the main reason.
2. In the context of a legal understanding of the Christian moral life the belief was that mortal sin was easy to commit and so likely to be frequent in one's Christian life, Hence confession was called for in a regular way.
3. Again, given the legal understanding of morality at the time, the fear induced by understanding God as a law-maker, policeman, judge and punisher was pervasive in Catholic circles. So was the fear of going to hell if one fell into mortal sin. Hence, Catholics saw confession as the necessary means of avoiding God's punishment in hell.
4. The belief that confession gave one the grace of forgiveness almost automatically and so much more surely than other means of forgiveness.
5. Also the recognition through better catechesis that confession can help one grow in holiness as well purifying one from sin.

What then is the ideal situation in regard to the frequency of confession?

In the light of this brief historical overview and of the insights of contemporary theology in relation to the sacraments and confession in particular, it will be clear that the practice of the twentieth century is not necessarily the ideal or the norm, and is not at all free from weaknesses and faulty elements. This will have emerged from the list of reasons given above. Hence, it would seem to be the case that the present-day decline in frequency cannot be understood as wholly negative, much less as a disaster. If we list what seem to be the chief reasons for the decline in our day, we will see that the issue is somewhat complex and that there are both positive and negative factors at work in the flight of Catholics from confession since the 1960s. This, then, makes it quite unclear what in our day is to be considered as the ideal or norm in relation to the frequency with which one should go to confession, that is, celebrate the sacrament of reconciliation or penance.

Why the decline today?

There is no obvious or simple answer to this question and no one single reason explains the current trend. In fact people in the church disagree strongly in their explanations of this contemporary phenomenon and in the reasons they assign for it. We will outline the main reasons that are usually put forward on both sides of the argument.

(i) Disaster?

Those who understand the present decline in confession-going as a wholly negative development tend to highlight the following factors as significant:

1. The loss of the sense of sin, a reason mostly given by bishops, some priests and the popes. Even Pope Pius XII held this in the 1940s! It is hard to be sure what this phrase really means, especially if one considers the weaknesses and exaggerations of the past in regard to (mortal) sin and the emergence of a more lively sense of sin in some areas of life in modern times, e.g., the sanctity of life, the call to care for the earth, the awareness of poverty and deprivation today and the duty to share with those less well off, the demands of social justice and the prevalence of white collar crime, etc.

2. Some people and especially educators and liturgists say that the decline is due to lack of understanding of the sacrament of reconciliation and perhaps to poor celebration.

3. Individualism and secularisation in western society have, some say, blunted our sensitivity to the religious and communal dimensions of both sin and reconciliation.

4. The drift from the church and religious practice is no doubt an element of the problem.

(ii) Return to normal?

Those who are not overly worried about the decline in the numbers going to confession these days mention the following main reasons for what they see as basically a reversion to the way things have been down the centuries, in other words, a return to the nineteen-century-long tradition of infrequent confession:

1. The replacement of the legal understanding of the Christian moral life with its emphasis on laws, obedience and punishment and frequently its legalistic attitudes – its replacement by the relational understanding of Christian morality in which the emphasis is on loving God and our neighbour in the relationships which are central to our lives and where we are called to grow to Christian maturity and take real adult responsibility for our moral lives.

2. The virtual disappearance of the unwritten rule that one must go to confession before going to communion, something that only applies in the case of mortal sin.

3. The decline of the image of God as lawmaker, policeman, judge and punisher and the recovery of the concept of God as forgiving and loving.

4. The growth of the conviction, as contemporary theology teaches, that mortal sin is difficult to commit and is, consequently, rare, especially in the life of one trying to be a good Christian.

5. The realisation that there is no 'automatic' grace to be got in the sacrament. Only to the degree that one is repentant is one graced in confession. Also we now accept the insight that real and full repentance / conversion is usually a process which is far from easy to complete and will likely take a lot of effort and time.

6. The failure of many to experience frequent (or perhaps any) confession as a significant help to conversion and growth in virtue and holiness. This may be indicated by the fact that one finds oneself confessing the same sins over and over with little sign of conversion from them. This is especially the case in regard to habits of sin, as has been spelled out in Chapter Nine on sin above.

7. The realisation that church law and in particular the rule about annual confession requires one to go to the sacrament only if one has mortal sin (See *The Code of Canon Law*, canons 988 & 989).

8. The conflict of conscience many Catholics have experienced since the late 1960s over the morality of contraception. In more recent times it would seem that some

Catholics have abandoned confession (and also Mass going and even church membership), because of the scandals of clerical sexual abuse and their mishandling and even cover-ups by church authorities. Also issues around homosexuality would seem to have raised problems for some in regard to confession (and even commitment to Catholicism itself).

9. Individualism, secularisation and the drift from the church do have an impact on the numbers who approach the sacrament of reconciliation or penance.

10. The desire for quality in one's confession rather than the mere regular enactment of a routine ritual. This is related to number six above.

11. The failure of many bishops and priests to make any real effort to renew the sacrament in line with Vatican II. One may add here that the positive refusal of the Vatican to permit any worthwhile scope for the use of Rite 3 (General Absolution) and, more recently, its virtual abolition have given no encouragement to Catholics – to put it mildly - to approach the sacrament more often.

Appraising the situation

Given the great variety and complexity of the factors at work in the decline of confession-going in recent decades, it seems rather simplistic and inaccurate to speak in terms of a plain disaster or of a simple and straightforward return to the normal pre-twentieth century situation. It is clear that there are positive and negative aspects to the decline, though the positive ones would seem to be significantly more weighty than the negative ones.

In the light of this one feels that it would be an over-reaction to the present situation to rush into a state of panic or of great alarm. Equally, though, there doesn't appear to be any easy or simple way to improve the situation, either as regards the quality or frequency of confessing. (The same would seem to be the case in regard to Mass-going at the present time.)

Renewal of the sacrament

Perhaps, to begin with, one may wonder whether the increase in the number of people going to communion, while confession-going has declined steeply, raises some questions:

1. Do these two simultaneous trends in the church indicate that the *sensus fidelium* recognises that going to Mass and communion is a much more important and significant sign or symbol of one's commitment to Catholicism and Christian living than going to confession?

2. Perhaps going to confession, that is, celebrating the sacrament of reconciliation, should by its very nature be a rather infrequent event in one's Christian life, since, strictly speaking, it is designed to deal with mortal sins only; they are now seen to be rather difficult to commit and so will be relatively rare, especially for people doing their best to live good Christian lives, including especially regular Massgoers?

It would seem, in this context, that a central task for the whole church and for local churches and their parish communities is the undertaking of the work of understanding better the situation we are now in as regards the use of the sacrament of reconciliation and the causes of that situation. This will be an indispensable condition for deeper renewal in regard to theology, liturgy and pastoral practice of this sacrament at all levels of the church, a renewal begun by Vatican II and still a long way from completion and full effectiveness.

If and when this work of renewal has been substantially brought to fruition, we may hope that the use of the sacrament of reconciliation by the faithful, ordained or not, will settle at a level of frequency and, more importantly, of quality that will be appropriate for the church of our time and the need of its members for ecclesial repentance, forgiveness and reconciliation. If this should mean relatively infrequent confession, perhaps one should recall that the church seems to have survived and maintained a high level of spirituality over the many centuries when recourse to the sacrament of penance was either non-existent for the vast majority of church members or at best quite infrequent.

If, however, this process of renewal is not adequately attended to and we continue just to hear plaintive appeals from whatever level of the church for more use of confession, then we can expect the present rapid decline to continue and perhaps to become even more precipitate.

CHAPTER TWELVE

Models of the Priesthood Today

In the last forty-five years or so it has often been said that many of today's priests suffer from an identity crisis: such priests are not sure what a priest is or what exactly he is called to do in the church or how his ministry differs from that of the laity. There would seem to be some truth in this assertion at least in relation to some priests. But even if priests have not experienced such a crisis of identity, it is true to say that many have had to contend with considerable confusion, uncertainty and difficulty about their priestly vocation and role. There are no doubt many causes for this, theological, ecclesial, social, cultural, personal. We cannot here discuss all these. Our purpose is rather to focus on one of these factors, a theological one which is at the heart of priestly identity and ministry. This is the nature or concept or model of priesthood itself, in other words, what being a priest is and means as that was and is understood in the church in the past and in the present.

There has been widespread discussion, questioning and debate about this very issue since the time of the Second Vatican Council (1962-65). The understanding of priesthood that most priests in the higher age brackets were brought up with and which they learned in the seminary has in recent years been called into question. Other understandings or models of priesthood have been proposed and have gained acceptance in many quarters. The result of this is that there is no one universally accepted theology or understanding of the priesthood in the church today. There are rather many theologies of priesthood, theologies which in part agree, in part conflict and are not fully harmonisable. Most of them are not fully worked out but are in the process of being elaborated. This is not something to be surprised at nor should it be seen as a decline from the pre Vatican II situation where there was one dominant theology of priesthood with no rivals. Rather we have here an enrichment which involves a diversity or pluralism of theological understandings of priesthood and we can hope that in time it will lead to a fuller theology of priesthood and a richer spirituality and ministry for those who are priests in the church.

In this chapter I propose to discuss three understandings or models of Christian priesthood. The first is the one we have been used to and which may be called the sacral or medieval model. With a great many theologians and pastors today we judge it to be inadequate. The second model is more in line with the NT and the early church view of priesthood and is now being recovered and reformulated for today's church. It may be referred to as the ministerial model. We see it, as many theologians do, as very valuable and helpful, even if not without its weaknesses. Our third model is of even newer vintage and is in the process of being fully elaborated. It has been called the representational model and would seem helpful as a complement to one or more other models.

A problem of language: priest or presbyter?

We may begin by discussing briefly an issue that has been widely aired, if not resolved, in contemporary theological discussion. This is the issue of whether we should refer to the ordained minister in the church by the term priest or the ordained ministry by the term priesthood. This problem arises immediately, when we look at the New Testament. There no Christian minister is referred to as a priest; in fact there is a conscious effort by the NT writers to avoid the language of priesthood and priest, so as to distinguish the Christian ministry and the Christian minister from the Jewish OT priesthood and OT priests. Only Christ is referred to as a priest and then it is only the heavenly Christ who is given this title in *Hebrews*. The whole Christian community is said to be priestly but there the NT stops.

It would seem that the chief NT word for community leaders and leadership is presbyter and presbyterate. The presbyter was not a priest like the priests of the OT; he was not, in other words, a cultic figure, but rather someone with a certain standing and authority within the Christian church. In the immediate post NT period the presbyter emerged as a member of a group or college of presbyters who were advisers to and helpers of the bishop. In later centuries and especially in medieval times priestly language came to be used about ordained ministers and this tended to lead to an understanding of priest and priesthood that was basically cultic, much as the OT priesthood was. This understanding lasted down to Vatican II.

There are three views on this issue of terminology in recent theological writing.

1. Some have argued that, because it is absent from the NT, priestly language and the theological implications that tend to go with it should be eliminated as a foreign import from pagan or OT sources.
2. Others have taken the opposite view, saying that, since this language came to be used extensively down the Christian centuries, it should be continued today.
3. A third position is that the NT practice at least signals that there are dangers in using priestly language here and, hence, we need to be careful in how we use it in our day.

It will be clear that this is not just an issue of terminology. The terminology reflects and points to a particular understanding of the ordained ministry and the ordained minister and, hence, has major theological significance. It seems best, then, to use both terms, priest and presbyter, as Vatican II does, and endeavour to avoid misunderstanding as best we can.

We proceed now to our discussion of the three models of ordained ministry that we have mentioned briefly above.

The sacral model of priesthood
This is the understanding or model of the presbyterate or priesthood that has been dominant in the church since about the fourth century and that is still very widely held, even if at times unreflectively, in our day. Essentially it sees the presbyter or priest as a sacred person who has been set apart by ordination, not merely from the world but from the rest of the church's members. The priest is a person who, in being thus set aside, has been given special sacred powers, in particular those of celebrating Mass and hearing confessions. In consequence the priest exercises the role of mediator between God and God's people or, more accurately, between God and the laity. The priest fulfils this role after the manner of and in subordination to Christ, the High Priest of the New Covenant. Hence, the priest is rightly called another Christ. Because of his role as mediator, the priest is not merely set apart from the laity; he is in a real sense above them, placed, as it were, between heaven and earth for the sake of the People of God.

This theology of the priestly office brought with it certain very important changes in the lifestyle of the priest and in the way he was perceived and expected to live and behave in the church and in society. In a nutshell we may say that the ordained minister became, not just a priest, but a cleric as well. Being a cleric or being in the clerical state was and is the social accompaniment or the expression in the priest's lifestyle of the sacral model of priesthood. This means that the ordained minister is now given the title of priest, as in the OT, and is socially as well as theologically set apart by having to wear a special uniform (clerical dress). He has no secular employment in society but is full time in spiritual or religious work, thus differing in a very significant way from most other men. Above all, the priest cleric is removed from the very material and morally very risky business of sexual relationships and sexual activity by being obliged to be, in the early centuries continent in marriage and, for many centuries now, celibate, i.e. unmarried for the sake of God's kingdom. In these ways the priest cleric is separated from ordinary life and is confined in his ministry largely to ritual matters, in particular administering the sacraments, especially the Mass and the sacrament of penance. He thus becomes, basically, a cultic figure or a sacristy priest. Hence, it came about that the priest became a man apart, a man on a pedestal, a sacred person, a cleric.

It is obvious from what has been said that a process of sacralisation took place in regard to the ordained ministers of the early and medieval church and, in addition, clericalisation had a very powerful influence. This double process was influenced by theological factors, e.g. the OT idea of the priest as a sacred person performing sacred actions largely of a ritual nature. It was also affected by social and even political developments, especially from the fourth century on, e.g. after the conversion of Constantine in 312 Christianity became the imperially favoured religion and in time the official religion of the Roman empire, a move that led to bishops and priests becoming privileged officials who were civilly honoured and given marks of social distinction in a wholly new way.

One practical consequence of this model of priesthood that emerged later was the designation in church and even state law of the priest as a sacred person. It thus became a sacrilege, a violation of a sacred reality, to lay violent hands on a priest or bishop and, by what was called the privilege of the canon, a person who physically attacked a priest was automatically excommunicated. Only in 1983 in the new Code of Canon Law was this privilege abandoned.

Symbolising this model: the priest's role in the 'old' Mass

We may take as a good symbol or concrete expression of this theology of priesthood the way in which the priest was required to say Mass in medieval times and even down to Vatican II. The rite then used was what we call the Tridentine or pre-Vatican II rite or form of the Mass and of course it was in Latin. He was basically seen as a performer of ritual, an anonymous ritualiser with his back to the congregation, celebrating in Latin, a language completely unintelligible to the people. Who he was personally or what his personal qualities were wasn't really important; so long as he performed the rite accurately according to law and to the rubrics the Mass was valid and grace giving. The priest had the necessary sacred power and so the ritual 'worked', provided the people placed no obstacle in the way. The priest's holiness or lack of it was not important in this matter. In other words, the stress was on the *ex opere operato* effectiveness of the priest's action in saying the Mass, not on the person of the priest. The congregation was, essentially, passive and largely excluded from real participation in the Mass. Thus the Mass was really the priest's business; he was the mediator between God and the people. While this form of celebration of the Mass was experienced by many as deeply mysterious and spiritually enriching, it illustrates well all that was questionable about this Tridentine Mass and also the weaknesses and inadequacies of the sacral model of priesthood which was dominant over those centuries.

Model of priesthood re enforced by model of church

During the centuries in which the sacral model of priesthood was dominant, it was re enforced and supported by the model of church that was in possession at that time. This is what we now refer to as the institutional or pyramid model. In terms of this model the church was viewed as an institution in which the authority structure was very much like a pyramid, not just at the level of the Pope in relation to the bishops, but also at the level of the bishop in relation to his priests in a diocese and again at the level of the priest in relation to his parishioners. This meant that the priest, the sacred person with sacred powers, was invested with almost full power within his parish. In colloquial terms he was the boss; he was seen and he often acted very much as the chief rather than the chairman of the parish community. In consequence the priest's word was law; he alone ran the parish and the laity were rarely consulted or given a voice in the administration of their parish, least of all in regard to the sacramental/ritual aspects of parish life. In this model of church and priesthood the priest was very much at the top of the pyramid and the laity were firmly anchored at the bottom. It is not much of a caricature to say that the priest's role could be summarised as: ritualise, regulate and rule, while the parishioners' role was simply: pay, pray and obey!

Strengths and weaknesses of the sacral model
We may list the strong points of this model or understanding of the priesthood in the following way: a) It was officially approved in many church documents, especially from the fifteenth century on. b) It is a model that highlights the sacramental and especially the eucharistic dimension of the ordained ministry. In other words, it puts the ritual element of the priestly role very much at the centre and gives the priest a clear focus for his ministry. c) Because of the priest's exalted position and status, this model requires in the priest a very high spirituality, befitting one who is 'another Christ'. He has to be holy, because his main task is to handle holy things. d) This model gives the priest a very clear identity with no doubts about what his role and standing in the church are. Hence, priests in this model have a real sense of confidence and security in and about what they are called to be and to do in the church. e) There would seem to be little doubt that, as a result of these four strengths or positive aspects of the sacral model of priesthood, many young men were attracted to the priestly life, and the church for many centuries was blessed with numerous vocations to the ordained ministry.

The weaknesses of this sacral model of priesthood are as

significant as its values. They may be listed as follows: a) It is not found in the NT nor in the early centuries of the church's life. It will, therefore, be important to look closely at the NT and the centuries immediately following it to see what model or models of priesthood or presbyterate was/were operative there. b) The sacral model puts nearly all the emphasis on the sacramental or ritual/cultic role of the priest and has little to say about the ministry of preaching or the pastoral ministry to the parish community. As such this model fosters the idea of the sacristy or sanctuary priest, the ritualiser rather than the leader of the local Christian community. c) This model exalts the priest to a very high level and, by attributing to him significant sacred powers, runs the risk of the priest being seen, at least at the popular level, as a 'man of magic'. d) It separates the priest from the community and tends to place him above it in a position intermediate between it and God. e) It brings with it too the idea of the priest as a cleric, i.e. as different and apart from ordinary life and ordinary people and, hence, as special and as placed on a pedestal.

Because of these weaknesses and despite its strengths, this sacral model of priesthood is today being seriously questioned. A significant number of scripture scholars and theologians as well as pastors and lay people are unhappy with it and judge it to be inadequate as an understanding of the Christian presbyterate. In spite of this there is today a strong trend in the church to return to this model of the priesthood. This trend is an important element in the movement to restore the Tridentine rite of the Mass, the 'old' pre-Vatican II Mass. Some years ago the Pope granted permission for a much wider use of this rite and made such use significantly independent of and outside the power of local bishops. Thus, the Pope and the Vatican are giving powerful support to the re-instatement of the sacral model of priesthood as they promote the Tridentine Mass and other liturgical practices that hark back to the pre-Vatican II era.

However, because of the weaknesses and deficiencies of this sacral model of priesthood, there has emerged in recent years another concept or model of the ordained ministry. This sees itself as more biblical, more theologically adequate and more in tune with contemporary attitudes in the church and in society. To this model we now turn.

The ministerial model of priesthood

In this model the word 'priesthood', which characterises and in a way symbolises the previous model, yields place to the word 'ministry'. This latter word is characteristic of the model we are now discussing and can function as a kind of symbol of it. Priesthood or presbyterate is here understood as a vocation to a form of ministry in and for the Christian community as it lives its life in faith love hope. The presbyter is the ordained minister who is assigned a specific role in the religious life of the parish community. His is one among many ministries but it is special in that it is a ministry of leadership in that community.

Before outlining what form this leadership should take, it is important to highlight the fact that the ministry of the presbyter (and all others too) is seen in this model as a form of service to the community. As the word implies ministry is not dominating but serving God's people and it only exists to promote their Christian welfare. To adapt St Augustine's statement we may say that the presbyter/priest is a Christian with the people and a presbyter for them. Clearly then, the presbyter is not above the church community but within it, and from there he serves it in a particular way. In this context it is difficult to think of the priestly or presbyteral ministry as a form of mediation between God and God's people. Rather, the category that seems most appropriate here is spiritual leadership. The presbyter is the one who provides the service of leadership for the Christian community. It will be important to spell out what is involved in this role of service that the presbyter takes on.

Elements in the presbyteral ministry

The first element in this ministry of the presbyter is his ministry of the word, i.e., his call to preach and teach God's word and all it involves and implies to all God's people and indeed to all others as well in whatever ways are appropriate and necessary. Vatican II makes this the presbyter's most important task, as it was the most important task in the ministry of Jesus and his apostles and of the ordained ministers in the first couple of centuries of the church's existence.

Another central element in the ordained minister's role is his sacramental or ritual ministry. The presbyter is here the leader of or presider over the public worship of the community but his ministry may not be understood in a way that almost excludes other ministries, as it often was in the past. Rather, the presbyter is called to involve, facilitate and enable all other ministries in the community as that community gives due worship to its God through Christ. In addition, the presbyter/presider is to ensure and promote the full, active and conscious participation of all Christ's faithful in the church's public worship and, of course also, in the whole life of that church. This will require skills and talents in the presbyter as well as an appropriate attitude and openness. These will be skills and talents not often called into play in the past under the sacral model, e.g., the skill of presiding over a worshipping assembly, of co ordinating the various ministries in the liturgy, of encouraging active participation by all, of explaining the meaning and relevance of word and sacrament in the context of public worship.

Along with these two tasks the presbyter as understood in the ministerial model will be called to exercise pastoral leadership in his parish. This involves many things and extends to the various aspects of the moral and religious leadership of a Christian parish community. It does not, however, require the presbyter to do everything himself. On the contrary, he is envisaged as the one who is to inspire, encourage and facilitate the community in using its talents and energies as it attends, constructively and wholeheartedly, to the numerous activities that are called for in meeting the Christian needs of the community and in building it up to the fullest degree possible. These include religious formation and instruction at all levels, welfare concerns, justice demands, routine maintenance of the parish plant and fundraising.

To facilitate and enrich his whole ministry as just outlined the ordained minister will need to know his people in a personal manner. He cannot effectively lead or preside over a community he does not know well. Hence, he is called to walk daily among his people and also to walk with them in their commitments and interests, in their activities and meetings, in their joys and sorrows. In a word, he has to share their life and their lifestyle and at the same time be their Christian leader. He has to be one of them without being just one of the boys. Not an easy task!

The manner of presbyteral leadership

It would seem to follow from what has been said about the ministerial model that the manner in which the presbyter/priest should exercise his Christian leadership would not be as in the sacral model, but would rather be what may be called fraternal or collegial. He should be more chairman than chief, as it were, and, therefore, it would be quite likely that a parish would have a variety of groups and committees, many meetings and a great number of involved parishioners, as the whole community works as a unit to build up God's kingdom by building up the Christian community that is the parish. A pastoral or parish council would seem essential here, functioning perhaps in some sort of co ordinating and facilitating role. A finance committee would have an important place also, even as church law lays down. In a word, the presbyter/priest as servant leader of the parish community must exercise his ministry and the authority that goes with it in a thoroughly collegial manner, because that is the nature of his office and, anyway, things go better, if not easier, in that way for most groups of human beings.

The spirituality of the presbyter in this model

To preach, teach and give leadership in worship and in community life, as outlined here, it will be essential that the presbyter live the gospel message that he proclaims and the sacred mysteries that he presides over. This he must do and can only do in the community of disciples in which he finds himself and in and through the ministry he is engaged in. Consequently, his Christian attitudes, virtues and lifestyle will and must be shaped and inspired by his ministry and not by some regime that smacks of the monastery more than the parish. In other words, his must be a pastoral spirituality that emerges from his work as pastor in his particular parish in his particular time. This spirituality will in its turn influence all that the presbyter does and says in the exercise of his pastoral ministry.

The cleric in the ministerial model

The priest of today is still very much the cleric of the sacral model. In some important ways this can be less than helpful as the presbyter of today seeks to live and act in accordance with the ministerial model of the priesthood. It seems clear that many

214

priests are unhappy with their status as clerics, in the sense of that word already explained, and it is also clear that the reality of the priest cleric is changing rapidly in our day and, it would seem, fading out somewhat. It is possible to see signs of this in things like the decreasing popularity of clerical dress among many priests today, the freer and more personal relationships between priests and lay people at present, the more extensive social activities of priests in recent times and, above all perhaps, in the controversies about clerical celibacy, women priests and part time or full time clergy. We are, it seems, in a transition phase between the two models of priesthood and that is bound to be confusing, controversial and a far from cosy time for most priests. However, there does not seem to be any short cut out of this situation. We must live through it.

It may also be a sign of the declining popularity of the sacral model of priesthood that in the new Code of Canon Law (1983) the idea of the priest as a sacred person, whom it is a sacrilege to attack physically, has been dropped completely.

Symbolising the ministerial model: The presbyter as presider at the Eucharist
Just as the sacral model of priesthood was symbolised by the priest's role in the Tridentine Mass, so we may use his role in the 'new', post Vatican II Mass as a symbol of the ministerial model.

In the new rite the presider or the presbyter who leads the celebration of the Eucharist faces the congregation and is placed among them, ideally at least, as he presides at the table of the Lord. He is one of the assembly but also their leader in preaching, in ritual worship and in their living as a Christian community. He is now fully visible to his people as he presides at Mass. This may be taken as a symbol of the fact that today who the priest is as a person and as a Christian is important to his ministry. Also his qualities and skills will be called into play as he presides, preaches and leads the people entrusted to him. Hence, these qualities and skills are of great importance for the priestly ministry. So too his humanity and personality, his life experience and wisdom, his virtues and vices impinge on his ministry for good and for ill. Clearly then, the presbyter/priest today cannot be an anonymous ritualiser following the rubrics and submerging his humanity behind his role or function. What he is as a person, the quality of his Christian faith and living and his skills in Christian leadership will be decisive factors for the fruitfulness of his ministry as a presbyter / priest.

In this conception of the presbyter it can be seen that the mystery and the mystique of old don't count for much and are disappearing more and more from the presbyter people relationship. Today, in other words, the presbyter is off his pedestal and what counts is the quality of his service as Christian leader of his people. It is not hard to see that in this view of the presbyterate the role of the ordained minister is much more humanised and, hence, much more demanding than in the sacral model. Some presbyter / priests find this renewed role more difficult and even threatening; others find it more satisfying and enriching. Relevant here too is the affirmation of the laity but also their criticism of the presbyter as he lives out his ministry among them.

New model of church re-enforces this model of priesthood
We may add here without going into the matter in detail that the more recent model or models of the church that have come to prominence since Vatican II, namely, the church as community or communion, as people of God, as servant, as herald, etc. have provided a favourable and supportive context for the ministerial model of priesthood or presbyterate. They breathe a more collegial spirit, based on the clear affirmation of the basic equality of all church members in faith and the call to all to participate fully and actively, not just in the liturgy, but in all aspects of church life and especially in the life of the parish to which one belongs. We may, therefore, expect the ministerial model of the presbyterate to become more widely accepted as time goes on and as the model of church changes even more. This will, however, be made more difficult by the renewed focus on the Tridentine Mass and by the fact that many young priests are more traditional and committed to the pre-Vatican II understanding of the priesthood.

Strengths and weaknesses of the ministerial model
In relation to its strengths we may make the following points: a) This model recognises and arises within the context of the many

ministries and charisms in the church. b) It stresses the link between the presbyter and the community and integrates him into the community in a helpful and necessary way. c) It gives us a wider concept of priesthood, extending it to cover all aspects of the religious and moral life of the parish community. d) It highlights the presbyter's role as preacher of the word, which was rather neglected in the sacral model, in practice at least. e) The ministerial model is well rooted in the NT and the early church. f) It is in line with contemporary experience and appeals to many of today's Catholics, while being also strongly grounded in the teaching of Vatican II.

As for its weaknesses we may note the following items: a) It could lead to an over-emphasis on the leadership of the presbyter to the comparative neglect of the leadership roles and abilities of others in the community. b) It could be interpreted by some in a way that would tend to collapse the difference between the priest and the lay members of the church. c) It could cause some priests to experience some degree of loss of identity; since so many can minister in the church, what is so special about the presbyter/priest? Is he needed at all? d) The new model needs to develop a renewed spirituality for the diocesan priest to replace the old spirituality that is disappearing as the sacral model declines.

The representational model of priesthood

In recent times some theologians have put forward another model or basic concept of priesthood called the representational model. This may be understood as a separate model but one can also see it as complementing the ministerial model we have just described. As a complement to that view of the priesthood it is valuable since it brings into focus the unique and specific aspects of the priesthood.

In essence this understanding of the priesthood affirms that the priest by his ordination becomes an official representative of the church, an ecclesial person, who has a public role in the life of the church, especially in and through his sacramental ministry. As such the priest is authorised to speak and act officially in the name of the church and he does this principally in the celebration of the sacraments. Now, since the church is itself the sacrament of Christ, we may say that the church represents Christ in the world and does so above all in those official public actions we call sacraments. Because the priest is the church's public representative in this sacramental ministry, we may say that in it he represents Christ and acts in Christ's name, in persona Christi, as the old phrase has it.[1]

This representative role of the priest does not make him a sacred person or one superior to other members of the church; nor does it mean that he is the only one who exercises ministry in the church. It does, however, bestow on him a special ecclesial character that points up the specific nature of the priestly ministry. This representational character of the priest in no way implies that he replaces the church or Christ. Rather the role here assigned to the priest is a function he performs in the church but it goes deeper than just a function. It means also that the priest is now an ecclesial person. In other words, this role has an ontological as well as a functional dimension.

It may be added that, because the priest has a representational role in relation to Christ and the church, he is called to live a life that is conformed to that of Christ, that is Christ-like. Hence, the priestly vocation requires the priest to be a truly Christian person in faith, love and hope, or to be, simply, a holy man.

Evaluation
The advantages of this model or concept of priesthood may be listed as follows. It points to what is unique and specific about the priest and so it can help clarify the priest's identity. It describes a priesthood that is appropriate for all kinds of priests, diocesan and religious. It highlights the need for personal virtue and holiness in the priest. It leaves room for ministry that does not belong to priests and it avoids the taint of functionalism that may attach in the minds of some to the ministerial model.

As for its weaknesses or the risks involved in it, we may say that it could be in danger of being interpreted to mean that the priest is a sacred person and is also the exclusive mediator

---

1. In relation to the phrase in persona Christi see David N. Power, 'Representing Christ in Community and Sacrament', in Donald J. Goergen, Editor, *Being a Priest Today*, A Michael Glazier Book, The Liturgical Press, Collegeville, Minnesota, 1992, 97-122; Fáinche Ryan, 'Images of God, Images of Priest', in *Doctrine and Life*, July-August 2011, 28-45.

between God and God's people. As such it could lead to some devaluation of the lay vocation and the lay person's ministry. It might also lead some to move back again towards a purely cultic understanding of the priesthood. Finally, it tends to devalue the ministry of pastoral leadership in the community that is so prominent in the ministerial model.

CONCLUSION

In view of the variety of models that exist and others could be added to those here discussed it seems both difficult and unwise to construct a single tight definition of the presbyterate or priesthood. Each model has its values, though some models are better than others, as will be clear from our exposition above, particularly in regard to the sacral model. But no one model is fully adequate on its own. Hence, there may be a need to see a model like the ministerial one as requiring to be complemented by the representational model rather than seeing them and others as opposed to one another. There may, however, be real conflict between different models at a variety of points. In addition, in different times and ages different models will appeal and work more satisfactorily. Our age is no exception.

It is hoped that what has been said in this chapter will prove helpful in understanding what is happening to the priesthood and to some priests in the Church in our day. It may also act as a spur to deeper and more extensive reflection on the presbyterate and on the many other ministries in the Church in our time.

CHAPTER THIRTEEN

Structures of Authority in the Church

You would need to be a very unperceptive member or observer of the Roman Catholic Church in our day not to know that all is not well in that Church. Few can be unaware of the many sexual and other scandals and controversies that have been plaguing the Catholic Church in recent times and that have done much to damage the standing and influence of the hierarchy and the clergy and the church itself among the Catholic laity and in society in general. There is a host of controversial issues here that show no signs of going away and that concern a great many church members either directly or indirectly. These include such contentious matters as the following: the absolute ban on the admission to communion of anyone living in an irregular marital situation, i.e. mostly divorced and remarried people; the ordination of married men; the anomaly of former Anglican clergymen who are married, being ordained as Catholic priests, while Catholic priests who have left the active ministry and got married are excluded totally from priestly ministry; questions in sexual ethics like contraception, homosexual relationships and homosexual activity, artificial reproductive techniques and divorce; the issue of women in the Church and in particular the ordination of women; the appointment by the Vatican in recent years of very conservative bishops, often against the wishes of the local church; the disciplining of progressive theologians by the Vatican and the concomitant growth of an atmosphere of fear within the theological community; the imposition of a new oath of fidelity on nearly all important office holders in the Church and the extension of the profession of faith to include all the provisions of the Code of Canon Law and almost all papal teaching; the total rejection by the Vatican of all public dissent from any church teaching; the virtual elimination of all real collegiality in the higher levels of church government. And of course most recently and perhaps most damaging of all, the scandals of clerical sexual abuse of children and vulnerable adults and the grave mishandling of these issues by bishops and the Vatican.

Each of these specific issues has its own importance and gets significant public attention. The point that must claim our interest here, however, is that, underlying these issues there is another issue or set of issues that has/have a big bearing on whether and how these problems are or are not brought to resolution. This is the matter of authority in the Catholic Church and in particular the structures of that authority, i.e. the way in which power is located, distributed and used. In other words, the root issue or problem that must be addressed, if the Catholic Church is to deal adequately with the specific questions mentioned above, is a structural one involving the structures of authority in the Church. One writer puts it as follows: '… underlying the obvious issues is a hidden agenda that blocks the solution of those issues at every turn. The hidden agenda is not a matter of something that someone is trying to hide or is even aware of hiding. It is simply authority in the Church and our assumptions about it.'[1] In a nutshell this structural problem can be seen as religious monarchy threatening to overwhelm the beginnings of religious democratisation in the Catholic Church.[2]

This chapter will be devoted to a discussion of this issue and how it impacts on at least some of the specific problems of church teaching, law and policy already referred to.

When it comes to authority and its structures in the Catholic Church we tend to think automatically of the Pope and the Curia, and in particular perhaps of papal primacy and how it is exercised more even than papal infallibility, though what is often called 'creeping infallibility' presents its own problems. This is understandable and right, because there resides the highest authority in the Church in regard to both teaching and jurisdiction. However, the issue and our discussion cannot be confined to this papal dimension only. We need to look at the structures of authority at all levels of the church in relation to how they are and should be set up, understood and made use of. This will involve us looking at the papacy and in particular the Pope's primacy of jurisdiction and its relation to the bishops and

1. See Monica Hellwig, *What are the theologians saying NOW?* Gill & Macmillan, Dublin, 1992, 46.
2. Eugene C. Bianchi and Rosemary Radford Ruether, *A Democratic Catholic Church*, Crossroad, NY. 1993, 34.

local churches. We will also need to focus on the understanding and exercise of the episcopal ministry at the diocesan level and how it relates and should relate to the other structures of authority, actual or possible, within the diocese. Finally, we must concern ourselves with the parish, its clergy and laity, and how they interact, and what structures of authority do and should exist at that basic level of the Church.

Before we turn our attention to these issues, however, it will be helpful to examine some background matters in terms of history, the theology of Vatican II and post conciliar theological and pastoral developments that are relevant to our discussion.

Pre-Vatican II position on structures of authority
There is no disputing the fact that for a very long time before Vatican II and in particular from the time of Vatican I in 1869-70 the understanding or model of the church and so of its authority structures that was dominant was what is referred to today as the institutional or 'pyramid' model. This viewed the church from above, as it were; it was a high ecclesiology, one could say. In other words, it placed the main and almost exclusive emphasis on authority, its structures, role and powers. At all levels and especially at the level of the papacy the judgments of church authorities were unquestioned and indeed unquestionable. And corresponding to this the central virtue in Catholic practice at all levels was obedience, indeed even blind obedience. A big factor in consolidating this understanding and practice in the Church was the definition by Vatican I of the jurisdictional primacy of the Pope over the whole Church: the Roman Pontiff has full and supreme power of jurisdiction in the universal church. This power is truly episcopal, ordinary and immediate over each and all churches and over each and all the faithful. This was further re-enforced by the declaration of the Pope's infallibility. As a result of this latter, every act of the Pope became suffused with an aura of authority that went beyond what it had by its nature as papal teaching and jurisdiction and that some have referred to as creeping infallibility.[3] Thus the Church became even more centralised and its structures of authority even more

3. See Bishop Geoffrey Robinson, *Confronting Power and Sex in the Catholic Church – Reclaiming the Spirit of Jesus*, The Columba Press, Dublin 2007, 121-2.

institutional and pyramidal. And this percolated down to the levels of the diocese and the parish and was reflected in the manner in which bishops and priests in parishes exercised their authority and understood their role.

In this context collegiality, subsidiarity and similar participative and democratising attitudes and practices were given little role in theory or practice at any level in the Church's life. Practically all decisions, especially important ones, were made from above and handed down with little or no consultation or participation of interested parties, whether those were bishops, priests or lay people. And this was regarded as normal and no one questioned it. Thus bishops were appointed by the Vatican with little regard for the wishes of the diocese involved. And where consultative procedures for appointing bishops existed, as in Ireland up to the early twentieth century, they tended in time to be bypassed or to fade out. At diocesan level bishops made appointments to parishes and curacies, not merely without consulting the people the priests were being sent to, but usually without any attention to the preferences or wishes or even the talents of the priest being appointed. Within parishes priests frequently ran a one man show and what the laity thought or said was largely ignored. They were not infrequently reduced to the roles of paying, praying and obeying, and they accepted that that was the way things were in the Church.

Clearly in such a conception of the Church authority was highly centralised, concentrated at the top and totally clerical. The structures favoured authoritarian rule, and the vast majority of those affected by this rule were excluded from power and decision making and were passive recipients of whatever those at the top decided.

This understanding and operation of the structures of authority had and has important advantages and disadvantages. Its advantages are that it gives full power to those in authority at the top of the structure and this makes the exercise of that authority easier and more decisive. There is usually little questioning of the decisions made and so the whole community marches forward on the one step. Generally life in such a community is ordered by clear and definite rules that are rarely disputed. All the members have to do is to inform themselves of the decisions and rules of those in authority and obey them. There is usually little ambiguity and uncertainty and, hence, people tend to feel secure, sure of their identity and role and clear about what is expected of them as church members.

These advantages are, however, offset by not insignificant disadvantages. The main ones are that most people in the Church are reduced to a very passive state with no say in the running of the Church community; they are largely excluded from responsibility, decision making and active participation in church life, whether at episcopal, clerical or lay level. Thus, most church members are rendered exceedingly dependent on authority and as a result the process of their growth to Christian maturity is slowed down or even halted. In addition, scripture scholars and theologians have not been slow to point out that such a model of the church and its authority structures seems significantly at odds with the New Testament account of Jesus' exercise of authority and with the structures and exercise of authority in the early church.

In the light of all this the pyramid or institutional model and exercise of authority can be seen to be an historical development in the Church, and, hence, not necessarily unchangeable or of divine origin.

It may be added here that Vatican I's strong teaching on the primacy of the Pope was not altogether free from ambiguity and unhelpful implications. The main one referred (and still refers) to the relationship between the Pope's power within any particular diocese and that of the local bishop. Some put it starkly and wondered was the Pope not now the bishop of every diocese and was the local bishop not, then, dispensable or at best a mere agent of the papacy? Despite assurances that this is not so and that the Pope cannot replace or take over from the local bishop, it is not fully clear that papal primacy is fully respectful of the authority of local bishops in their own dioceses, at least in the way it is sometimes exercised. In the pontificate of John Paul II and the present one also, when papal interventions in local churches are more frequent than earlier and often controversial, this question is especially pressing. Even Vatican II did not resolve it, despite its extensive attention to the office of bishop in the Church and the relationship of the bishop to the Pope.

But, notwithstanding these points, Vatican II greatly developed, in profound and far-reaching ways, the Church's self understanding in general and especially in relation to authority and its structures and exercise.

Vatican II's teaching on authority and its structures

The central point of relevance here is that the Council's Constitution on the Church, *Lumen Gentium*, moved from seeing the institutional model of the Church as the dominant one to placing the idea of the Church as the People of God at the centre of its thinking in the area of ecclesiology. This has profound implications for authority in the Church and for its structures. No longer is it possible to equate the Church with the hierarchy or the papacy nor to view it as an absolute monarchy with the Pope as the repository of all power. Now it is clear that, in the first place, the Church is the community of disciples of Christ, the People of God, united by baptism and all having a fundamental dignity and equality as children of God and brothers and sisters of Christ in the Church.

Hence, each member, just because he/she is a member, has a role to play in the Church and is called to full, active and conscious participation, not just in the eucharist, but in the life of the Church generally. In addition, this Church is in history and is still on pilgrimage to its final goal, the kingdom of God in its fullness. Hence, the Church, as it exists at any time, is imperfect, and, so, it can and should grow, change and develop in important ways, even in its structures, as it has done significantly in the past.

Only when all this has been said does the Council come to discuss office and hierarchy in the Church. Office is to be understood in terms of service to God's People and not in terms of domination, as had been the case often in the past. In addition, the very significant idea of *collegiality* between the Pope and the bishops of the Church is firmly taught in *Lumen Gentium* 2, where reference is made to the collegial nature of the episcopal order. Here was the recovery of a very ancient concept and practice in the Church by which bishops are linked to one another and to the bishop of Rome by the bonds of unity, charity and peace. This collegial nature of the body of bishops is expressed chiefly in ecumenical councils but in other ways too. It means that all bishops have a corporate responsibility for the unity of faith and of communion in the universal Church. While continuing to affirm the primacy of the Pope in terms of Vatican I, the Council sees the order of bishops as the successor of the 'college' of the apostles in teaching authority and pastoral rule and, hence, as the subject of supreme and full power over the universal Church.

This teaching on collegiality resulted from a return to the NT, and from an openness to the ways authority was structured in the infant church and the early Christian centuries. But Vatican II only sketched out the broad lines of the principle of collegiality and didn't spell out what its implications and expressions might be. One could assume that it would be rich with consequences, especially in relation to structures of authority involving the bishops. This has indeed proved to be the case. Examples are the synod of bishops, episcopal conferences, diocesan pastoral councils, councils of priests, national conferences of priests, etc.

All that has been said so far about the teaching of Vatican II does not, however, give us the full picture. The other side of the coin, as it were, is that, understandably, the Council repeated all that Vatican I had taught about the papacy and in particular about the Pope's primacy of jurisdiction and his infallibility, while also developing Church teaching on the episcopal office.

Vatican I, as we noted earlier, left unresolved the problem of the relationship between the Pope and individual bishops in their dioceses.[4] Vatican II did likewise and may have added to

---

4. This issue would seem to have been illustrated by a recent incident involving the Vatican, a Croatian diocese and a Benedictine monastery in that diocese. The Vatican took the unusual step in mid-2011 of temporarily suspending the bishop of the diocese – for a mere matter of hours – and appointing in his place an envoy to push through a financial arrangement, forcing the diocese to give back the monastery and compensate the Benedictines for the loss of their lands, now sold to developers, something the local bishop had refused to do. [The Croatian state had given this property to the diocese in 1999 to undo the injustice of the earlier Communist regime in Yugoslavia, which had confiscated the property from the Benedictines in 1948.] In this case the Pope as-

the problem by its fuller theology of the episcopate. In addition to this, Vatican II by its teaching on collegiality raised another problem, namely, how to reconcile the fact that the Pope has supreme, full and universal authority over the Church with the fact that the college of bishops has the same power. In addition, the Council discussed collegiality as pertaining largely to the papal episcopal level, and while open to it at all levels, e.g., bishop and priests, priests and laity, it was not as clear and unequivocal about these other levels as one might have wished. This has given room to more conservative or authoritarian bishops, pastors and theologians to maintain their attitudes and the non participative structures they tend to prefer.

We may mention also in this context that, because Vatican II's Constitution on the Church is in important ways a compromise document as between the more conservative and the more progressive bishops at the Council – and the latter were the overwhelming majority, it is open to being quoted selectively to suit one's preference in relation to church structures. In consequence some have stressed the collegial, participative, democratising elements, while others re affirm the Vatican I perspectives that favour more monarchical, authoritarian attitudes and structures. Thus, Vatican II is invoked by both groups in the Church today, conservatives and progressives, for their conflicting purposes. As a result the Council is used in the contemporary Church in ways that have fuelled post conciliar debates and controversies about church structures as well as providing for all a basis for unity and enrichment in regard to our understanding of the Church itself.

---

sumed the local bishop's authority and powers to carry through the move just mentioned, thus showing that the Pope can overrule a local bishop *in the latter's diocese*, if the Pope decides to do so. As *The Tablet* reporter stated (6/8/11, p 30-1), 'the canonical sleight of hand the Vatican used to procure it [the property deal] should send chills up the spines of bishops'. But this wasn't the end of the story. Some weeks after the Vatican's intervention the Croatian Government itself intervened to reverse the Roman legal move and so by its own legal move restored the monastery and the property to the local diocese to the 'great astonishment' of the Vatican (*The Tablet*, 20/8/11, p 26).

Post conciliar developments: ambiguity and conflict

We have spoken just now of conflicting groups in the Church today, each using Vatican II's teaching to its own advantage and for its own purposes. This points to the fact that in important ways the Catholic Church in our day is split into a conservative wing and a progressive wing. There is, of course, a silent majority not aligned with either group's theological and political attitudes and activities and not very aware of them either. But the fact of a real polarisation in the Church at the present time is indisputable. This division is based ultimately on theological differences that are rooted in contrasting ecclesiologies and, in particular, in differing theologies of authority in the Church and of the nature and functioning of the Church's structures of authority. These differing theologies are both grounded in the teaching of Vatican II with all the ambiguities and differing emphases we have adverted to. Thus, it becomes clear that an important issue behind the issues in dispute (as enumerated in the introduction to this chapter) between the conservatives and the progressives is that of authority in the Church and how it should be understood, structured and used.[5]

It seems clear too that, in this conflict, the Pope and the Curia have in the pontificate of John Paul II and in the present pontificate aligned themselves with and indeed led the conservative tendency in the Church by taking up a strongly conservative attitude to the understanding, structuring and use of authority and especially papal authority in the Church today. The conservative wing can, then, frequently claim backing from the Vatican on some issues and are not slow to assert that their own position is 'the Church's' position. In all this we find a Vatican I perspective that is, of course, to be found in Vatican II but does not represent all or indeed the main thrusts of that Council.

The group of theologians, pastors and even bishops who are often referred to as progressives or, more derogatorily today, as liberals, base their thinking, attitudes and judgments on those teachings of Vatican II that are more characteristic of that Council. These are the teachings that emphasise the role and

5. Owen O'Sullivan OFM Cap. has written a book called *The Silent Schism – Renewal of Catholic Spirit and Structures*, Gill & Macmillan, Dublin 1997.

importance of the local church, that call us to greater respect for and use of the principles of collegiality and subsidiarity in the Church and that urge all to full, active and conscious participation in church life generally, that put high store on the ancient principle that what touches all as individuals should be discussed and approved by all, and so on.[6] In short the thrust of Vatican II towards democratisation in and of the Church is the current of thought that grounds the views of the progressive wing in relation to the Church itself, its structures of authority and its pastoral decisions and policies. In this stance, it seems that this group is more true to the intention and attitude of Vatican II than the conservative wing, which has in effect sidelined *Lumen Gentium* or at best pays lip service to its distinctive ecclesiology. In practice they go a long way towards replacing it by Vatican I's *Pastor Aeternus* with its monarchical and authoritarian attitudes, tendencies and practices.

Symbolising this conflict: attitudes to dissent
At this point, it may be useful to discuss briefly one issue in church life today that in important ways can function as a kind of symbol of the polarisation referred to above. This is the issue of theological and pastoral dissent or disagreement. The contrasting attitudes to it in the Church in our day mirror and sum up the contrasting ecclesiological attitudes and practices we have been outlining.

The Vatican, especially through the actions of the Congregation for the Doctrine of the Faith (CDF), headed by Cardinal Ratzinger (now Benedict XVI) has made it abundantly clear in recent years that it sees no place whatever for public dissent from the teachings of the Church's official Magisterium or Teaching Office. The CDF judges that such dissent is wrong and it has issued a variety of documents expressing this view clearly and strongly. In addition, the CDF has laid down and imposed disciplinary measures against those it regards as dissenting theologians and pastors, e.g., Hans Kung, Charles Curran, Leonardo Boff, Archbishop Hunthausen (USA) and Bishop Gaillot (France).

6. See John R. Quinn [Retired Archbishop of San Francisco], *The Reform of the papacy – The Costly Call to Christian Unity*, A Herder and Herder Book, The Crossroad Publishing Company, New York, 1999, 123.

Those whom I have been calling the conservative element in the Church and especially some articulate groups and individuals within it have been and are very vociferous in their support for the CDF's teaching and disciplinary actions in regard to public dissent and indeed they have not been slow to call for Vatican condemnation of any theologians or pastors they judge to be public dissenters. It seems clear that Rome has listened to many of these calls and has responded positively to them. Hence, the spate of cases where theologians have been removed from their teaching posts and declared no longer Catholic theologians, or have been silenced for a period. Hence, also, the cases where imprimaturs have been withdrawn from books of theology on the Vatican's orders and where even bishops have been removed from office or have had their ordinary powers curtailed significantly. It is in pursuit of their campaign to crack down on public dissent that the CDF has imposed a new and more extensive profession of faith on many office holders in the Church and now also requires an oath of loyalty from a great number of church personnel as they assume any of a great variety of offices in the Church. It does not seem too far fetched to surmise also that the 1994 *Catechism of the Catholic Church*, which was strongly advocated and called for by many conservative voices at and outside the special Synod of Bishops in 1985, was not written merely to provide 'a sure and authentic reference text for ... preparing local catechisms.' In the minds of at least some of its supporters and probably in that of the CDF also the compilation of such a universal catechism had and has a 'political' purpose, namely, to provide a norm or standard by which 'liberal' theologians and writers could be checked and judged and, then, appropriately disciplined.

All these attitudes and measures in relation to dissent today reflect an ecclesiology that breathes a spirit other than that of the main thrusts of *Lumen Gentium* and that seems to understand the relevant structures of authority in an institutional manner. Hence, any questioning of or inability to accept church teaching is rejected as damaging to the unity of the Church and as lacking the requisite loyalty and spirit of submission that all Catholics must have towards the Magisterium and its teaching, even non infallible teaching. In addition, this view asserts, the faithful, especially the so-called 'simple' faithful, have a right not to be confused about Church teaching by discordant and dissenting opinions from theologians and others. In consequence of this view such dissent is seen as wrong and as something that may well call for disciplinary measures. A common way in which those who dissent from any of the Church's official teachings are today labelled is to speak of them as á la carte Catholics, i.e. those who take only what they like and leave the teachings they do not fancy. In this view the truly loyal Catholic accepts and holds dear *all* the Church's official teachings. Those who dissent on any issue are, then, branded as disloyal. Some who are particularly fond of using a military model to understand the Church – they see the Church as the army of Christ sent to do battle in and against the world and its forces of evil – are not slow to suggest that those who cannot accept all the Church's teachings fully and, hence, are not fully obedient to the leaders of the Church, should simply leave the Church, there being a place in it, as in any army, only for those who can give total obedience.

Those who make up the so-called progressive group in the Church today see things rather differently. Viewing the Church as the pilgrim People of God, they see the search for the fullness of truth as ever ongoing and never complete. The whole Church is learning and has to learn continually, while in a real sense the whole church is a teaching church, as it socialises its new members and deepens the faith and understanding of all who belong to it. As the Church thus learns and teaches it will inevitably be the case that proposals and suggestions will be made in relation to particular religious and moral issues; some will be good and acceptable, while others will not survive discussion and debate. Occasionally church leaders may need to intervene to point out errors and give indications of the best paths to take in the search for truth. Warnings may even be necessary and at times the rejection of some moral or theological position. Disciplinary measures may occasionally be taken. But overall, the emphasis of the Church's leadership should be on promoting the search for truth in a positive manner and building an atmosphere of trust and cooperation between theologians and bishops and the Vatican, something like the harmonious and very fruitful relationship that existed between them at Vatican II itself.

In the light of these attitudes to dissent from Church teaching and the promotion of the search for fuller truth, it seems right to say that how one reacts to disagreement or dissent is indicative or symbolic of one's whole ecclesiology, of one's model of the church and especially of its structures of authority. Those who allow no place for public dissent of a responsible kind seem to be adhering strictly to the institutional model of the church and read Vatican II from a Vatican I perspective. The more progressive position sees disagreement as an element in the never ending search for truth that may be constructive and may be helpful to the pilgrim People of God on its journey towards the fullness of God's kingdom.

Democratic ethos and the principle of subsidiarity

One sometimes hears it said, especially by more conservative church people, and not infrequently in response to a call for greater participation in church life and decisions by the laity and especially by women, that the Church is not a democracy. This statement is, of course, true, but as used in these contexts and by more institutionally minded Catholics it tends to carry the meaning that in the Church authority really belongs to the hierarchy, not to the laity and, in particular, not to women, that it is up to those in authority at every level to make the decisions and that, at the end of the day, everyone else is called and indeed obliged to accept and obey these decisions. In short, the meaning conveyed by such an assertion as we have quoted is that the Church is hierarchical by and in its basic structure of authority and that that authority is exercised, basically, in a monarchical manner, i.e. by one person who is really the 'boss'.

But, while we agree the Church is not formally a democracy, in the sense in which societies in the Western World are nowadays democracies, there is every reason why, especially in the light of Vatican II, we should seek to develop in the Church what has been called an ethos of democracy. Such an ethos would espouse mutual respect, a readiness of members to make the common interest one's own and to listen to one another, and to ensure that all who are affected by a given decision are accorded a hearing. In a word, a democratic ethos calls for and involves the participation of all, dialogue and open communication at all levels and participation in all decisions that affect one as a church member. What is in question here, really, is making the principle of subsidiarity a reality in the church at all levels. This envisions and requires the formal enactment of norms and structures of consultation, collaboration, accountability and due process, even in the absence of a mechanism of elections[7] and, as Pius XI stated, ensuring that decisions are taken at the most appropriate level and not at a higher level than is necessary. Alas, however, it seems that the church, especially at its higher levels, is careful to exclude this principle from church life, even though it is strongly supported and advocated for use in society generally by Pope Benedict, by earlier popes and *The Catechism of the Catholic Church*, n. 1883, as noted in the present Pope's 2009 *Encyclical Caritas in Veritate*, paragraphs 57 and 58 and footnote 137).[8]

One can hardly doubt that the spirit and the letter of Vatican II favours and promotes such a process of democratisation throughout the Church and its structures of authority. We have seen this already and will discuss its details later. It may be added here that in democratic countries there is bound to be pressure on the Church to move in the direction of subsidiarity and solidarity. That is what we find today, especially in the Western World, but as we have also noted, this has been and is being resisted inside the Church at every level by powerful forces. However, it is very important for the credibility of the Church in democratic societies that this process continue and succeed. An overly monarchical and centralised bureaucracy in the Church distances itself from the faithful and loses contact with urgent pastoral needs. When the Church in and by its structures neglects consultation, collaboration, accountability and due process and when it assumes an adversarial and negative attitude, then its credibility and its moral authority with its own members and in society generally is lessened and gradually eroded. This would seem to have been happening in recent years, above all because of the episcopal and papal failures in regard to clerical sexual abuse.

---

7. See John A. Coleman, S.J., 'Not Democracy but Democratization', in Bianchi and Radford Ruether, 227-9.
8. See Bishop Kevin Dowling, (South Africa), 'The Current State of the Church', *The Furrow*, November 2010, 594-7. Also in *The Tablet*, 17 July 2011, 11.

Rome and local churches

Vatican II understood the Church as really a communion of local churches which together constitute the Church of Christ. This understanding tends to highlight the place and importance of the local church and so encourages local initiatives by bishops in their dioceses, by national and regional episcopal conferences and by the whole local church in any particular diocese or region. Vatican II's emphasis on collegiality is in line with this renewed significance given to the local church.

In the light of this, the immediate post conciliar period (the late 1960s and the early 1970s) was characterised by the Vatican giving more attention and weight to the voice of local churches in the appointment of bishops and, as a result, many bishops were ordained who approached their ministry with a Vatican II theology and pastoral attitude. In consequence a collegial spirit began to percolate through the Church in many dioceses and regions and great stress came to be placed on pastoral renewal, openness to the signs of the times and progress in ecumenism. Social justice and the option for the poor became living realities in many local churches, especially those in South America. Overall, the winds of change and growth, so powerfully encouraged by the Council, began to blow refreshingly through the local church and the church universal.

In this period, too, the synod of bishops was established and met regularly in Rome with very significant results, especially in the form of final documents on several important issues, e.g. the priesthood and justice in the world. The synod appeared to be a real and valuable exercise of collegiality between the college of bishops and its head, the Pope. In these years also national and regional episcopal conferences were set up and proved their value and importance, not merely as forums for discussing issues and exchanging ideas, but also as instruments of teaching and collective decision making on a range of topics that were of great significance for the local churches of the area. In addition, theologians, continuing the most fruitful relationship between them and the bishops that obtained at Vatican II, did very creative and enriching work on many fronts, while acting also as the best and most probing critics of each other's theological output.

In the last thirty or more years, however, and especially in the pontificates of John Paul II and Benedict XVI, a lot of this has changed. There is a definite rowing back from the Vatican II perspectives just mentioned and we are in the midst of a 'restoration' of pre Vatican II emphases and attitudes, something that is quite evident in the Vatican's relation to local churches around the world.[9] This is very clear in relation to many things. The appointment of bishops is, perhaps, the most widely known and debated example.[10] Numerous very conservative bishops have in recent years been appointed by the Vatican, especially to crucial positions in the hierarchy. These bishops place loyalty to the Holy See at the head of their ministerial priorities and are chosen because they are safe men who are judged by Rome to be 'sound', especially on the controversial issues of our day: contraception, the ordination of women and the law of celibacy and the social teaching of the church. These bishops tend to adopt an earlier other worldly perspective and to de emphasise social justice, the option for the poor and the Church's ministry in the political, social and economic areas. All this raises the issue of whether and why individual dioceses should not have a major say in appointing their own bishops, as in the early church, with Rome having, perhaps, a veto. There seems to be no good reason today why this should not be the case.[11]

Add to this the fact that many of these new conservative bishops have been created cardinals and in consequence the college of cardinals has now taken on a very restorationist and conservative hue. It appears that the last and the present Popes are preparing the ground for the election of a successor very much in their own image and likeness. Thus, while the language of Vatican II is regularly invoked, there is no doubt that many of its perspectives are less than popular in the Vatican and seem to have been effectively sidelined.

In relation to the synod of bishops one has to state with regret that it is now little more than tokenism as far as collegiality is concerned. It is so fully controlled by the Curia that it has only the appearance of being collegial. The bishops of the Church universal air their views on the topic under discussion (itself

9. See Quinn, chapter 3;
10. Quinn, chapter 4; O'Sullivan, 80-4.
11. Robinson, 279-82.

chosen by Rome) but they are not allowed to issue a final document to the Church in general. This is reserved to the Pope who, it seems, incorporates only what suits Vatican policy and thinking at the time. This is generally regretted, since this instrument of collegiality could be a very valuable one, if it were permitted to function in a truly collegial manner. One has to ask, what is the Church's central administration afraid of? Does Peter not trust his fellow bishops to work and speak for the good of the Church in a constructive and helpful way?[12]

We find a similar story in relation to episcopal conferences. In the early 1990s Cardinal Ratzinger in particular took steps to make it clear that these conferences do not have a teaching function. They are, the CDF has taught, merely practical instruments for bishops of a particular area to consult together and exchange views but they do not and cannot teach. Only individual bishops can do that or a group of bishops in which all have agreed to the statement being made. This seems hard to accept, especially in the light of experience, e.g. the US bishops' pastorals on peace and on economic justice were documents which did in fact teach, even outside the United States, in a very influential way, however much one seeks to deny this. In addition, Vatican II speaks of these conferences as places where bishops jointly exercise their pastoral office. Is this a case in which the Vatican fears that the Magisterium or teaching function of the local church would somehow take from the papal or curial Magisterium, rather than supporting and enhancing it?[13]

The issue of the Vatican silencing or dismissing theologians and removing even bishops from their office is now well known, and, as we have noted, highly controversial. It raises several questions in connection with authority and its structures. It appears that the Vatican acts, at least sometimes, without consultation with the local bishop. So we have to ask, who is bishop of the diocese in question? The question of respect for the principle of subsidiarity arises here. It seems difficult to accept that these Vatican interventions are fully respectful of it. In addition, one has to wonder whether such methods of suppressing dissent achieve much beyond creating an unhelpful and

12. Quinn, 110-16; Robinson, 125-7, 271-3.
13. Quinn, 102-10.

repressive climate of fear and suspicion. Many have criticised the procedures used by the CDF in these cases as unjust, falling far short of what exists in many secular democracies. It is a poor defence by the CDF to say that the fact that its procedures can be improved doesn't mean they are unjust. One fears that justice within the Church is not attended to with the same zeal and impartiality as church teaching regularly displays in relation to justice in the world. The 1971 synod of bishops implied as much.

Another Vatican document in the 1990s moved from seeing the Church as a communion of local churches to putting the emphasis again on the universal church and its leadership, thus highlighting the role of the papacy and the Curia. This de emphasising of the local church seems to be central to the thinking and policies at present operative in the Vatican. Until these change, we can only expect more of what the last thirty years have brought us.[14] The issue of the new Roman Missal (2010) that came into use in English-speaking countries in Advent 2011 also illustrates the trend towards an ever more centralised church and an authoritarian central leadership. In this case the Vatican has paid little if any attention to the wishes of local churches but simply imposed its will on them, despite widespread calls not to do so, and disregarding the work and planning already done and agreed on a revised Missal among the bishops in anglophone countries.

Clericalism

In this context where we are discussing authority in the church, its structures and exercise, it is appropriate to reflect a little on a factor that today is frequently mentioned as a significant influence on those in authority in the church and those under that authority. This is what is called clericalism. It pervades and even corrupts clerical culture and so is a powerful, though often unrecognised and/or unadmitted influence on the clergy – popes, bishops and priests – in their understanding and exercise of the authority and power they possess by reason of their office. Clerical culture may be described as follows: it is the constellation

---

14. See Cardinal Walter Kasper's article on 'the church – a friendly reply to Cardinal Ratzinger', *The Furrow*, June 2001, 323-32 on the relationship of the universal church to local churches and its implications for church life.

of relationships and the universe of ideas and material reality in which diocesan priests and bishops exercise their ministry and spend their lives.[15] Clericalism is a kind of parasite on clerical culture and may be described in these words:

> Clericalism is the conscious or unconscious concern to promote the particular interests of the clergy and to protect the privileges and powers that have traditionally been conceded to those in the clerical state. There are attitudinal, behavioural and institutional dimensions to the phenomenon of clericalism. … it is often reinforced by institutional structures. Among its chief manifestations are an authoritarian style of ministerial leadership, a rigidly hierarchical worldview, and a virtual identification of the holiness and grace of the church with the clerical state and thereby with the cleric himself.[16]

Clericalism is closely associated with a triumphal lifestyle.[17]

In popular terms clericalism means that the clergy at all levels of the church are put on a pedestal and this by their own insistence or acceptance and by the passive acquiescence or even encouragement of some or all of the faithful. In practice, then, this means that priests, bishops and popes are treated as superior people in the church; they are given great but in fact excessive deference and perhaps exaggerated respect. In consequence they are able to enforce the authority their office or ministry gives them without question from those at the lower levels of the church: all Catholics in relation to the pope, priests and all the faithful in relation to the bishop, and the parishioners in relation to the priest in the parish. This involves at times dictating to those under clerical authority, using one's office to get one's way whatever the merits of the case, being authoritarian and even tyrannical in one's dealings with those the cleric sees as his ecclesial and even social inferiors. And for these clerics there was and is no question of being accountable to those under his

---

15. Michael L. Papesh, *Clerical Culture – Contradiction and Transformation*, Liturgical Press, Collegeville, Minnesota, 2004, 17.
16. Donald Cozzens, *Sacred Silence – Denial and the Crisis in the Church*, The Liturgical Press, Collegeville, Minnesota, 2002, 118.
17. Kevin Seasoltz, 'Clericalism: A Sickness in the Church', *The Furrow*, March 2010, 135.

authority and only relatively little accountability upwards to one's superiors in the hierarchy. In other words, authority is thus understood as power and is exercised in a self-serving, clergy-promoting manner, though in the past and even today such an exercise of authority has been and often is euphemistically designated as service to God's people.

The triumphalist element of this clericalism shows itself at times in special forms of dress, in titles displayed or even flaunted, in demands for unquestioning deference and obedience, in assuming attitudes of superiority by clergy and imagining one's views and opinions are of superior quality and weight and even beyond questioning, in the issuing of orders and commands to so-called inferiors in an imperious fashion. 'From their elevated status', says Seasoltz (135), 'the ordained were able to load on lay men and women heavy moral burdens which they themselves did not at times carry with integrity.' This often applied and may still apply at the level of bishops in relation to priests and the Pope (and the Vatican) in relation to bishops and all other church members.

All this clericalist thinking and acting was and still is underpinned by an understanding of the church that sees it as an institution that has the shape of a pyramid, where those at the higher levels of authority and power are facilitated in their clericalist attitudes by the theology they hold and adhere to in relation to the nature and functioning of the church. Vatican II made significant contributions to the effort to promote a quite different model of the church, the People of God or community models. Here all are seen as equal members of the Christian community, all are encouraged to display full, conscious and active participation in the life of the church and priests, bishops and popes are to be and act as true servants of God's people in promoting their moral and spiritual lives and advancing God's kingdom.

All this conciliar theology has had a major impact on church thinking and living in the last fifty years and today also. But clericalism is far from a thing of the past. It is, alas, alive and well in the church today and seems even to be growing stronger at all levels of ecclesial life. Seasoltz gives some examples (136): 'we witness the celebration of so-called Tridentine Masses in which lay people are reduced to silent spectators, where there is a very limited proclamation of Scripture, where the Mass comes across simply as the priest's Mass, and where women are denied all ministries in the celebration.' We also witness cardinals wearing cappa magnas with very long trains carried by young boys. Flamboyant vestments, elaborate thrones, and lace surplices and albs are all in evidence at papal ceremonies. To many in our church this comes across as triumphalism … many seminarians and recently ordained priests favour the cultic model of priesthood and have adopted the traditional clerical lifestyle. They are preoccupied with clerical dress – with cassocks, birettas, capes, French cuffs, lace surplices and clerical vests. They see themselves as part of a separate [and superior] clerical caste and often resist the more collaborative approaches associated with the reforms of the Second Vatican Council. They generally espouse a very traditional classical theology, have scarcely any self-doubt and see themselves quite separated from older priests who are more attuned to the pluralism of contemporary theology' (141). In a word, we see clericalism reviving and being rejuvenated with much support at the highest level in the church.

This latter point may be illustrated by quoting a South African bishop: '… the curial authorities working in conjunction with the pope have appropriated the tasks of the episcopal college … what compounds this, for me, is the mystique which has in increasing measure surrounded the person of the pope in the last thirty years, such that any hint of critique or questioning of his policies, his way of thinking, his exercising of authority, etc. is equated with disloyalty. There is more than a perception, because of this mystique, that unquestioning obedience by the faithful to the pope is required and is a sign of the ethos and fidelity of a true Catholic. When the pope's authority is then intentionally extended to the Vatican curia, there exists a real possibility that unquestioning obedience to very human decisions … becomes a mark of one's fidelity as a Catholic.'[18]

All this makes it clear that clericalism and the triumphalism that often accompanies it are once again thriving in the Catholic Church, more in the spirit, alas, of Trent rather than Vatican II. The latter council called for full, conscious and active participation of

18. Bishop Kevin Dowling, 'The Current State of the Church', The Furrow, November 2010, 595.

all in the life of the church; it spoke of ministry in the church as a form of service to God's people and called for a noble simplicity in regard to liturgical vestments, clerical dress and lifestyle generally. It looks, however, that some of the pre-Vatican II attitudes and practices of the clergy are being restored as the clericalism of the past makes a comeback and moves us once again towards a two-tiered church where the clergy are dominant and on a pedestal and the laity are again in danger of being reduced to the pay, pray and obey mentality and practice of the Vatican I era and its aftermath.[19]

Diocesan structures of authority

The commonest and most talked about structure of authority at diocesan level is the Council of Priests. This post Vatican II institution has been established in most, if not all, dioceses in Ireland and, it would seem, elsewhere also. It is required by church law (C.495) and is intended to be representative of the diocesan presbyterium. Its purpose is to assist the bishop in the governance of the diocese.

One's impression is that, while the Council of Priests does some good work and is in ways a useful structure in a diocese, it is not, generally, viewed with great enthusiasm or approached with deep commitment either by bishops, its priest members or the clergy of the diocese as a whole. This seems to be the case for more than one reason, not all of which have to do with the bishop. A lot depends on the attitude of the bishop in relation to the Council of Priests: he may fear it will usurp some of his authority or that he won't be able to control it. He may also be less than enthusiastic about 'democratic' structures and/or may find it difficult to manage or work with such a body. Increasingly today bishops may be less collegially minded and so more difficulties may arise in regard to the Council of Priests. In addition, some priests may have a similar mindset. They may not be good at operating collegial structures, may chaff at the time needed to run them well and may feel it's not worth the effort, given the sometimes meagre fruit that results from their work. All this leads on many occasions to a lacklustre Council of Priests that is

19. See also Gerard O'Hanlon, S.J., 'Culture and the Present Crisis in the Church', *The Furrow*, December 2010, 655-8; Papesh, chapters 2–5; Cozzens, chapter 7.

greatly loved by few, though also seriously disliked by few. There seems to be no easy solution that will make the Council of Priests a really vibrant collegial structure. Both bishops and priests need to change in attitude and commitment and only then will the hopes placed in Councils of Priests by Vatican II be fulfilled.

Another collegial structure in a diocese is the college of consultors. This is chosen by the bishop from among the members of the Council of Priests. In practice it seems like an empty and non active body. In law it has no worthwhile functions and in effect is of little significance. One has to regret this, since this college could be a valuable organ of collegiality, if properly developed and operated.

In many dioceses in Ireland the Chapter of Canons, where it exists, seems to be moribund and nowadays to have no useful function even in regard to liturgy in the cathedral. It seems highly unlikely that this Chapter can be revitalised, so as to play any worthwhile part in the diocese.

Diocesan synods have been held in some dioceses in Ireland with, it would seem, mixed results. Much like the National Pastoral Congress in England in 1980 the preparation and the synod event itself tend to be truly collegial and even inspirational, though in some places the synod has degenerated into a bishop bashing session. The really difficult thing is the follow up or implementation of the synod and its resolutions and decisions. Here the fruits have been thin enough in general and often frustration and anger have been the outcome. How a richer harvest can be garnered in this area is not immediately clear. But one would imagine that a diocesan synod could, in the proper circumstances, and with adequate preparation and structuring, be a very significant event for bishop, priests and laity in a diocese.

Particularly in the circumstances of the present time in the Irish Church having a Diocesan Finance Committee, as mandated by the Code (C. 492), makes eminent sense. How it works in places where it exists will depend a lot on the bishop's openness and commitment to accountability and transparency. One assumes that most dioceses in Ireland do have these committees and that they are valuable collegial structures in and for today's church.

Another collegial structure that has its roots in Vatican II is what is called the Diocesan Pastoral Council. This is quite different from the Council of Priests and according to the code (C.511) may be established 'when pastoral circumstances suggest.' It is to be representative of the diocese, priests, religious and especially laity (C. 512), and its purpose is to study and weigh those matters which concern pastoral works in the diocese.

One hears relatively little about this kind of instrument of collegiality, at least in Ireland and one can assume that they have not been established in very many dioceses. What evidence exists points to the conclusion that the performance or success of these pastoral councils has been spotty, much like councils of priests. But it seems fair to state also that pastoral councils can function effectively, if they are encouraged and facilitated in their operation by the bishop and those in other positions of power and influence in the diocese. But here again old attitudes and styles of leadership and of being led die hard and, hence, many at all levels find it difficult to adjust to and to operate this collegial structure in the spirit it requires for real effectiveness.[20]

We may mention briefly also the position in the diocese that is referred to as the Vicar Forane or Rural Dean. Some efforts have been made in recent times to revamp this role and the Code (C. 555) gives this Vicar some important tasks to carry out, e.g. to promote and coordinate common pastoral action in his vicariate or deanery, to ensure that the liturgy is properly celebrated, the churches well kept and the registers in parishes maintained correctly and kept in a safe place.

As far as one can observe from experience, VFs, as these functionaries are often called, have a rather insignificant role in practice and often do not even attempt to carry out what the Code lays down for them. The reasons for this seem to be that priests generally do not expect or want the VF to do anything along the lines the Code specifies and VFs themselves seem to take a similar view. The bishop often doesn't encourage a different approach and so VFs end up as less than notable as far as their role is concerned. One feels that there is here room for

20. See John Beal, 'Towards a Democratic Church: The Canonical Heritage', in Bianchi and Radford Ruether, 71-3.

improvement, so that this structure of authority could be given life and real clout at deanery level. One can say the same thing about the deanery meetings within any particular diocese. Priests seem to feel about these much as they feel about the council of priests and, in consequence, while it does some useful work, it cannot be said to be really successful, at least as far as my experience goes.

One feels that here too diocesan clergy in general are not over enthusiastic for democratisation within the diocese, at least in practice, perhaps because they find it difficult, haven't got the skills to cope with it or just prefer the old institutional models and structures at diocesan and, perhaps, also at parish level. Bishops probably feel much the same and so on the ground not a great deal happens and enthusiasm is often lacking. Where collegial structures of authority operate well, one usually finds that it is due to the conviction and energy of individual bishops and/or priests. But unfortunately, such men are relatively scarce and perhaps getting scarcer.

One may mention in this context a structure of authority at diocesan level that is almost completely lacking in the Church both in law and in pastoral practice. This is a structure or *system of accountability* for bishops and for pastoral priests. It must surely be considered a scandal that bishops in dioceses and priests in parishes and in other ministries are accountable for their ministry and its quality to no one, except to God through their conscience. Hence, a priest or bishop can be, say twenty-five years, in a parish or diocese or other ministry, can do the minimum, do it badly and with an unhelpful, negative and non collegial (to put it no stronger) attitude and very little is or can be done about it. If such a pastor does not fall into heresy or schism, misappropriate parish or diocesan funds, regularly fail to celebrate the Mass or commit some grave misdemeanour like child sex abuse, he can carry on his bad work with scarcely any possibility of anyone doing anything about the situation. Of course bishops are accountable to the Pope and priests to their bishop. But these superiors are relatively at a distance and unlikely to intervene in the day to day pastoral activities of a bishop or priest. There is, however, almost no accountability downwards, as it were, that is, in the bishop's case to his priests or to the faithful of the diocese, and in a priest's case to his parishioners. In fact as Cozzens says, 'The idea of accountability to one's hierarchical inferiors is simply dismissed out of hand'.[21] This is unfortunate and wrong and can lead to arrogance and pomposity and not a few mistakes. Devising a structure of accountability in this regard is not at all easy but it is urgently needed. Finance committees are or can be one element of this accountability; so can liturgy groups, parish councils and the present arrangements about dealing with clerical sexual abuse in a diocese or parish. But an adequate overall structure does not yet exist.

Another structure of authority that is much needed at diocesan level is some system whereby newly ordained priests are supported and guided in the early years of their ministry. This would help them grow into their new work more easily, avoid many mistakes, cope better with difficulties and failures and, thus, maintain their priestly commitment, self esteem and good morale at a high level. Something like medical internship might be what is needed here or at least a pastoral supervision or mentoring system such as obtains in the helping professions in the secular world. One is not, however, optimistic on this score, as very little discussion seems to be taking place among diocesan clergy on these deficiencies in our diocesan pastoral system. In addition, many young priests are very conservative and often authoritarian in their outlook and pastoral approach and so are not likely to take kindly to any sort of supervising.

Structures of authority at parish level
At the level of individual parishes one finds that much of what has been said above about dioceses holds true as regards attitudes, collegial structures and their success or lack of it. And perhaps this is not surprising, since at both levels the same priests are involved. Since this is the case, we need look only very briefly at individual pastoral structures within the parish.

Parish pastoral councils
In 1980 the National Conference of Priests of Ireland expressed its concern about the general absence of effective Parish Pastoral Councils, and reports from individual dioceses confirmed this judgment.[22] Things have probably improved somewhat since

21. *Sacred Silence*, 29.
22. See *The Furrow*, March and April 1981.

then but one has the impression that a lot still remains to be done in this area, despite strong recommendations and urgings from many bishops. In recent years, however, there has been a notable push to get these councils established in some dioceses. A variety of committees or parish groups exist, ranging from building committees and finance groups through parish councils of various types to the full reality of a parish pastoral council. This latter is a parish version of the diocesan pastoral council and its purpose is similar. The reasons for the uphill struggle here are probably much the same as in the case of councils of priests and that means that the attitudes of the laity are not a whole lot different from those of the clergy in relation to such collegial structures.

Other structures at parish level

In some parishes there are many groups or committees working in the pastoral area. They deal with finance, liturgy, religious education, women's issues, youth work, ecumenism, justice questions and so on. At its best a parish can have a great number of such groups. Thus, e.g. the late Fr Jerry Joyce of Clogh parish, Co Kilkenny related in his book that his parish had thirty-six groups, organisations and services.[23] There are also many ecclesial groups in existence since Vatican II. Some are parish based and some are not. These too are signs of life or 'seeds of a new church', as they have been called. Twenty-two of them are described in one author's book, and they represent a great and rich variety of activities and involvements at the grassroots level of the Church in our day.[24] They are an encouraging and significant fruit of the conciliar renewal that Vatican II initiated and inspired.

Overall, however, one has to admit that at parish level there is a lot more that could be done. Many priests seem to function as basically maintenance men and, so, little happens except the basic sacramental services. These priests are in important ways sacristy or cultic ministers, as priests tended to be in medieval times. Many laity, perhaps most, are happy with this understanding of priesthood and seem not to be tuned in to Vatican II

22. See *The Furrow*, March and April 1981.
23. Jerry Joyce, *The Laity: Help or Hindrance? – A Pastoral Plan*, Mercier Press, 1994, 86.
24. John O'Brien, CSSp., *Seeds of a New Church*, The Columba Press, Dublin, 1994, 43-134.

and its theology of the Church, the parish, the priest and the laity. Until this tuning in happens at all levels, the present situation will not change greatly.

What has been said in this chapter will have made it clear that the issue of the Church's structures of authority is a basic one influencing how we view, approach and respond to many specific questions or matters of debate in the life of the Church today. In other words, our responses to these issues often have a theological depth that is not apparent at first sight and that is frequently the root or at least a root from which the disagreement that is so widespread in the Church at the present time springs. Clearly, then, one's ecclesiology or understanding of the Church itself has a very pervasive influence on one's position on the more practical issues that we have been discussing, e.g. synods, dissent, parish pastoral councils, involvement of the laity. In a real sense, then, the question of the structures of authority in the Church is the issue behind many specific issues in debate in the Church today. Unless we can overcome these differences and arrive at an ecclesiological outlook that brings the conflicting viewpoints into at least a substantial harmony, we are unlikely to get much beyond acrimonious debate, and we will be far from a meeting of minds in regard to what will best promote the welfare of the Church community.

However, given the present polarisation in the church and the Vatican-led movement for the 'reform of the reform', it is hard to be optimistic or even hopeful. But despite this drive towards 'restoration' that is so powerful in the Church even at the highest level in our day, we can still be grateful for the many seeds of renewal that are growing and bearing fruit in so many parts of the Church at all levels. These represent Vatican II coming to fruition and give grounds for real hope and confidence that the council will in God's good time, if not ours, produce fruit a hundredfold, in the way Pope John XXIII envisioned and desired.

CHAPTER FOURTEEN

The Diocesan Clerical System:
How it shapes the Clergy within it

In recent years there has been a great deal of comment on and criticism of the diocesan clergy (and that includes the bishops) of the Catholic Church in Ireland and elsewhere. While recognising the sincerity and wholeheartedness, the talents and the often effective ministry of priests and bishops, these critics, both inside and outside the Church, frequently reiterate a rather familiar list of shortcomings in the ministry and life of many clergy.

On this list one finds such things as the following: the poor quality of homilies, the slipshodness of the preparations for the week-end Masses in some places and the less than inspiring manner of celebrating the sacraments that some priests display. Also mentioned is the fact that the diocesan clergy don't seem to be overly interested in parish or diocesan renewal. They often seem to change things largely because they have been told to do so. Parish clergy in general seem to be largely uninterested in the things of the mind and are not noted for their interest in contemporary theological or biblical studies. Many seem to follow their pre-Vatican II counterparts in relying largely on their seminary courses to see them through their years in ministry. Some diocesan clergy seem to take their pastoral work at a leisurely pace and for some collegiality and collaboration are more theory than practice. As a result the leadership skills of diocesan priests and bishops are regularly called into question today and seem to the critics to be less than the times and many pastoral situations require. And of course we all know how the diocesan (and other) clergy have in recent years been vilified, often unfairly, in relation to child sexual abuse, thus paying a heavy price for the misdeeds of a small number of their priestly colleagues.

Now these clerical problems and deficiencies are listed here not to indulge in another bout of clergy bashing for the pleasure it gives, nor to give any impression of detachment or superiority by this clerical author. On the contrary, the purpose of the present observations on the diocesan clergy is to make a case for the view that perhaps it is not all a matter of the personal weaknesses and faults of individual priests and bishops. There may be and, I believe, there is a hidden factor here that contributes in no small way to the list of faults and failings outlined above and that may even have a significant influence in shaping, both before and after ordination, the men who become priests and bishops and who have such a central and often decisive role to play in leading and managing the parishes and dioceses of our Church. This chapter will focus on this factor which I am referring to as the diocesan clerical system. I will be trying to show how this system has powerful and in important ways negative and deleterious effects on the men who live and work within it and so on their ministry to God's people in the Church. Some relevant sociological factors that affect the church as a human organisation will be noted and their impact assessed.

What is the diocesan clerical system?
One may say that it consists of a series of arrangements or structures which together constitute the institutional framework or system within which diocesan priests and bishops live and carry out their ministry. These structures and the diocesan clerical system which they make up have evolved over the centuries and are now for the most part supported and mandated by church law and custom. Structure here is understood as an established mode of behaviour and the motivations supporting it.[1] Hence, system in this context refers to the sum total of these structures as they shape and control clerical life and ministry. Examples of these structures are: the rules and arrangements (including regulations, criteria and motivation) for appointing bishops and priests and for promoting and changing them to other ministries; the rules and arrangements for recruiting and training students for the priesthood; the system of authority and its exercise in dioceses and parishes; the consultation and collaboration arrangements there and the leadership structures involved at these levels; the arrangements for accountability of diocesan clergy and bishops; the rewards system within the diocesan clerical system; retirement rules and practices.

---

1. Andrew Greeley, 'A church still waiting for the spring', *The Tablet*, England, 13 November 2004, 22.

The appointment of diocesan bishops

Central to the diocesan clerical system is the appointment of bishops and the nature of their role in the diocese. The theological understanding of the episcopal vocation or ministry is, of course, basic. It will be assumed here that that understanding is along the lines of Vatican II, even though within that there is, as recent experience indicates, room for a wide variety of interpretations of what the bishop should be and how he should carry out his ministry in the diocese. The concern in the present context is about how bishops are appointed. Nowadays, priests become bishops by direct appointment from the Vatican, though this is a relatively recent development. After Vatican II the practice developed of the Vatican consulting local bishops about an appointment to a neighbouring diocese and the priests of that diocese were regularly given a worthwhile say in who should be their new bishop. This way of doing things tended to result in many progressive, Vatican II-minded, pastoral bishops being given the mitre. Often they were priests of the diocese in question and so tended to be in tune with the presbyterate of which they had long been members. The general verdict on this arrangement among clergy and bishops was favourable, even though not all the resulting bishops were pastorally successful.

This method of choosing candidates for the episcopacy has undergone significant change in recent years under Popes John Paul II and Benedict XVI. New bishops nowadays tend to be appointed by the Vatican with not much more than token consultation with some clergy and other bishops. Archbishop Quinn says: '… it is the papal representative who draws up the list of names that is sent to Rome, and … the Pope … is free to choose someone who does not appear on the list at all. In recent years even [this] modicum of consultation … has largely disappeared.'[2] The reason for this change of attitude in the Vatican would seem to be a change of emphasis in Vatican ecclesiology. It would seem that the Vatican today wants as bishops only men who conform strictly to its doctrinally and legally conservative

---

2. John R. Quinn, *The Reform of the Papacy – The Costly Call to Christian Unity*, A Herder and Herder Book, The Crossroad Publishing Company, New York, 1999, 129.

and safe model of bishop.[3] In addition, it seems that at the centre of the church there is less weight given to the wishes and opinions of the local church. This has resulted in the appointment of many less than inspiring bishops in terms of pastoral leadership, bishops who, anyway, are tightly controlled by the Vatican.[4]

The consequences of this change in policy in regard to the appointment of bishops are noteworthy and rather negative. One result has been a tendency for bishops to be distanced from their priests as they look first to Rome and strict compliance with its wishes. Another result has been to make pastoral cooperation between bishop and priests less easy. Not unexpectedly, there has been a tendency for some bishops to act and be experienced as simply 'the boss' rather than as the servant-leader or true chief pastor of the priests and people of the diocese. In such a context the bishop may not be well placed to care for his priests in a genuinely pastoral and personal manner and he may tend to approach his pastoral tasks and relationships with an attitude somewhat removed from that of a 'good shepherd'.

In consequence of these developments there will tend to be a lowering of priestly morale due to a feeling that the priests do not count so much any more, that they find themselves implementing policies into which they have had little real input and conforming to and imposing rules and regulations that, more often than not, have every appearance of turning the clock back. It seems unlikely that the Vatican will change the present system of appointing bishops, recent though it is. One may note that up to 1925 the system in Ireland called for the Parish Priests to meet, choose three names of priests they considered suitable to be bishops and send them to Rome for the Pope to appoint one of them.[5] It can be seen from these remarks that the present system of appointing bishops can impact negatively on the priests of a diocese.

---

4. Brendan Hoban, *Change or Decay – Irish Catholicism in Crisis*, Banley House, Kilglass, Co Sligo, Ireland, 2004, 123-30. O'Sullivan, 30, 80-4; Geoffrey Robinson, *Confronting Power and Sex in the Catholic Church – Reclaiming the Spirit of Jesus*, The Columba Press, Dublin 2007, 279-82.
5. See Quinn, chapter 4.

The appointment of priests to parishes

The system for appointing priests to pastoral and other roles in a diocese is well established, well known and quite simple. The bishop as chief pastor is invested with all the authority and power required for the exercise of his office. This includes the power to appoint priests to the pastoral offices of parish priest and curate, and also to specific ministries like catechetics, teaching, vocations director, pastoral development officer, etc. The duration of these appointments is also at the bishop's discretion and in relation to parochial ministries is generally unspecified. In the post-Vatican II period bishops have tended to consult priests about their appointment and at least in some dioceses few priests are placed or left in pastoral positions they are unsuited for or don't like.

In practice priests in parochial ministry are appointed to that ministry from the date of their ordination until, in accordance with law, they retire at seventy-five years of age. During those fifty or so years priests will usually have served in several different parishes as curate and parish priest. Most priests will attain the rank of parish priest after serving for a substantial number of years as a curate or assistant priest or in some other pastoral or academic role. In most dioceses, particularly the smaller ones, priests are chosen for the office of parish priest on the basis of the seniority system, that is, the priest who is the senior priest by virtue of the date of his ordination will be appointed as parish priest to the parish that next becomes vacant, and so on down the line of priests over the years.

This system has obvious advantages, e.g. it rules out jockeying for 'better' parishes and helps to keep those over-zealous to climb the clerical ladder in check. It largely avoids the problem of cronyism on the part of the bishop and it allows a priest to know roughly when he will become a parish priest. This will help the priests to avoid having unrealistic expectations or unnecessary fears about the level and timing of their change of ministry.

Of course the seniority system has equally obvious weaknesses that are behind the not infrequent calls for its modification or even abolition. Such weaknesses are the following. This system, when fully implemented, tends to exclude merit or talent as the basis for appointment to a parish as parish priest. It can, then, reward mediocrity or even indolence or simple endurance, while ignoring diligence, commitment and real ability and talent for pastoral leadership. This may tend to encourage the mentality 'stick around and you'll get there' in relation to becoming a parish priest rather than that of spending oneself ever more in the service of God's people. In addition, attaining the office of parish priest exclusively on the basis of seniority removes any encouragement to work harder in one's priestly ministry in the hope of getting an opportunity to use one's gifts and energy in the exercise of greater pastoral responsibility elsewhere in the diocese.[6]

Some suggest that the process of incardination by which a priest commits himself at ordination to one diocese and to that alone can be a limiting factor, especially in a small rural diocese, in relation to diversity of ministry and opportunity for developing one's talents for pastoral leadership. While there may be some truth in this view, the decline in the number of priests today will work against any such change, and anyway, not very many diocesan priests seem eager to move in this direction.

Here the experience of another Christian denomination may be instructive. In the Church of Ireland when a new rector is needed for a parish, the position is advertised in church circles and included is a brief job description. Applicants for the position need not necessarily come from the diocese in which the vacant rectorship happens to be; ministers/priests from anywhere in the Anglican Communion can apply. Interviews are held by a group including clergy and laity; a nomination is made to the bishop and he appoints the new rector.

There would seem to be some wisdom in this arrangement. In the search for the best person for the position it casts its net very widely, it attends to the qualities and commitment of the priest to be appointed, and it involves the laity of the parish in the choosing of their new pastor.

All this makes it clear that the present way of appointing priests to parishes in the present diocesan clerical system can shape the outlook and attitudes of the clergy in the diocese, often in a significantly negative manner.

---

6. See Hoban, 131-2; O'Sullivan, 79-80.

Formation in the seminary system

The seminary system in which young men who believe they have a vocation to the priesthood are trained for priestly ministry in a particular diocese (or religious congregation), involves a six or seven year programme of formation. This is formation primarily in intellectual (philosophy and theology) and spiritual (meditation and prayer, both personal and liturgical) matters with also a much increased and very necessary emphasis on acquiring pastoral experience during the seminary years. Nowadays too seminary formation endeavours to promote the psychological and emotional growth of candidates for the priesthood and hence also their development as sexual persons called to live the virtue of chastity in its celibate form. There can be little doubt, though, that the emphasis in the seminary system today as in the past is on producing intellectually informed and orthodox young priests who also have a solid spiritual or prayer life. These seminary priests are and are intended to be what one could call clerical GPs rather than theologians, philosophers or experts in liturgy or spirituality. As such they are considered suitable to run the parishes of their dioceses, pasturing the flock entrusted to them in accordance with the present understanding of priesthood and within the diocesan clerical system that is the subject of our reflections here.

If one wishes to enumerate other probable characteristics of those ordained after seminary training, one may mention the following which are likely to be very influential in the young priest's ministry and pastoral relationships.

If one can judge by the experience of diocesan priests generally, one can say that, as in the past, diocesan clergy tend to be priests who as a rule after ordination are not inclined to pursue their studies very assiduously. There are quite a few exceptions to this but overall priests in parishes don't do much professional reading or study. They seem to function on the assumption that what they learned in the seminary is basically adequate to see them through their years of pastoral ministry. This tends to have the effect that diocesan clergy are often less than enthusiastic about continuing renewal and can become resistant to new ideas and quite conservative in their theology and pastoral attitudes and practices. Few will contest this assertion. It would seem to provide at least a partial explanation for the generally accepted fact that the standard of preaching in parishes is quite low and that, as has already been noted, diocesan priests are less open to renewal than most other clergy and very obviously less than religious sisters.

It often happens that people who, like diocesan priests generally, are conservative may also have a tendency to act, at least sometimes, in an authoritarian fashion. This would seem to be true of a good number of diocesan priests and bishops, though of course in varying degrees. This is in spite of all the teaching about collegiality and collaborative ministry in the seminary and outside of it. In a way, though, this is not very surprising, since the way in which priestly ministry is structured, even in these post-Vatican II times, allows the priest, if he is so minded, to function in this highhanded manner. It may even encourage it. Perhaps also it is not going too far to say that the seminary, with the central place it still gives to the lecture system and the all-knowing answer man (or woman) on the rostrum, somehow inculcates the idea that the man in charge of the parish, the priest, knows it all, thus sowing the seeds of a one-man-band attitude in the priest that can at times express itself in an authoritarian and perhaps a centralising approach to parish leadership. And it is a sad fact that for some years now the church authorities at the highest level have been providing a model both for negative attitudes to progressive ideas and for authoritarian and centralising attitudes and practices, particularly in relation to local churches and their bishops, priests and people. It is scarcely a surprise, then, to learn that a large percentage of young priests and seminarians today are quite conservative in their ecclesial attitudes and, not infrequently, authoritarian in their style of pastoral leadership.

As in the past, today's seminary seems to turn out some priests who appear to have a significant element of the 'lone ranger' about them. This is probably related to the point made in the preceding paragraph as well as to the theology and structure of the priestly role in the parish and to one parish's independence from other parishes. Perhaps also it is influenced by the fact that priests are celibate and so are in a real sense alone and belonging to no family in the parish. Thus they may learn to do their own thing in a way that can easily turn into an excessive independence to the detriment of the inter-dependence that is so important and necessary for a truly collaborative and fruitful ministry.

It is the belief of many that one effect of six or seven years in seminary formation, in which students are prepared for a celibate lifestyle, is that young priests emerge in a rather immature state both emotionally and sexually.[7] US studies in the early 1970s found in fact that priests were not as mature as their comparably educated male counterparts.[8] This is not altogether surprising, even in the more open seminary system of today. From the time when they enter the seminary the students, whether they come directly from secondary school or from university or from some form of employment, are in practice bound to celibacy. They may not go dating, have a girlfriend or seek to have one; they are denied much of the experience of close interpersonal relationships with the other sex that the majority of males of their age have and need, if they are to mature emotionally and sexually in the normal way. The not unexpected result is a retarding of their emotional and sexual development and in some cases repression in these areas. Thus the intimacy needs of these young men may not be adequately met and that may well occasion immature attitudes and conduct in relation to women or, for some, undue preoccupation with possessions, money, status and power.[9] Another possibility is that such a priest may adopt a style or approach of non-involvement in his ministry because of the difficulty in relating to people, or he may take on an aggressive style that seeks to dominate those he encounters in ministry.[10] In extreme cases this deficit in emotional and sexual

7. Michael L. Papesh, *Clerical Culture – Contradiction and Transformation*, Liturgical Press, Collegeville, Minnesota, 2004, 13, 69-71.
8. Donald B. Cozzens, 'The Spirituality of the Diocesan Priest', Donald J. Goergen, Editor, *Being a Priest Today*, A Michael Glazier Book, The Liturgical Press, Collegeville, Minnesota, USA, 1992, 58.
9. Donald B. Cozzens, *The Changing Face of the Priesthood – A Reflection on the Priest's Crisis of Soul*, The Liturgical Press, Collegeville, Minnesota, USA, 2000, 31.
10. Patricia H. Livingston, 'Intimacy and Priestly Life', Donald J. Goergen, Editor, *Being a Priest Today*, A Michael Glazier Book, The Liturgical Press, Collegeville, Minnesota, USA, 1992, 143.

maturity may contribute to a particular priest engaging in child sexual abuse.[11] Whatever the outcome, the principle is well established: the quality of priestly ministry is directly related to the quality of personal development in the priest, and the seminary system may not promote that development as adequately as one might hope.[12]

The seminary even today tends to put a strong emphasis on conformity to rules and obedience to superiors and, of course, to church teaching. This is a necessary emphasis but it can have negative, even if unintended, side effects. It may give rise to attitudes in seminarians and young priests in which passivity is prized, initiative is de-emphasised and pleasing and keeping on the right side of those in charge take priority. This may make life easier for bishops and other authority figures but it would seem to make a maintenance rather than a mission approach to pastoral ministry much more likely as well as fostering, perhaps, an attitude which expects unquestioning compliance from parishioners in a parish and from clergy and laity in a diocese.

The priest as cleric
Over the centuries the ordained presbyter / priest has come to be also a cleric. This means that in addition to being the pastoral leader of his congregation, the priest (or bishop) has acquired features or characteristics that, when taken together, make him, in addition, a cleric. These features, which are not necessarily elements of the priestly or presbyteral vocation and lifestyle, are the following. The priest wears a special uniform which is called clerical dress. He is given special titles like 'reverend', 'father', 'canon', etc. He has no secular employment but is full-time in his role as pastoral minister. And, most importantly, he is bound to a celibate way of life. These features of the priestly lifestyle ensure that the presbyter / priest is set apart, ecclesially and socially, from the laity generally and from the members of his own congregation. Thus is the presbyter / priest constituted as a cleric, put on a pedestal and seen as in some sense a sacred person.[13]

---

11. Donald B. Cozzens, *Sacred Silence – Denial and the Crisis in the Church*, The Liturgical Press, Collegeville, Minnesota, USA, 2002, 103.
12. Livingston, 140.
13. Chapter 12 above, Models of the Priesthood.

This fact that the priest is also a cleric is in practice an important feature of the diocesan clerical system. It has a notable impact on the priest's relationships with his congregation, on their perception of their priest and on how he understands and lives his priestly life and ministry. This impact and its elements will be discussed later.

Sociological factors influencing the diocesan clerical system
It will be important to point out that, sociologically speaking, we are here talking about a church or denomination, not a sect or a cult. From the viewpoint of this chapter this fact has three significant implications:

i) It means, firstly, that the Catholic community as a church / denomination in the sociological sense will tend to have a relatively positive, accepting attitude to society and to the societal status quo, unlike sects and cults which tend towards a negative stance vis-à-vis society. At the same time society will tend to approve and accept the church and will consider it quite normal for its citizens to be members of the Catholic (or other) denomination. This means that church members will tend to be significantly influenced and indeed shaped by their society and its values and practices and so in a real sense these members will be both in and of 'the world'. Of course the influence can sometimes go the other way as the church / denomination has an impact on society through its teaching or the authoritative pronouncements of one or more of its leaders.

Priests are not exempt from this denominational-societal dynamic. Hence, it will tend to be the case sociologically that the diocesan clergy, bishops included, will in a real sense be 'secular', or 'worldly', that is, men of their society and time, though perhaps, like their church / denomination, not uncritically or without some tension in relation to the society or culture in which they live. The likely outcome of this situation will be that, like their church / denomination, the diocesan clergy will tend to be socially conservative and in consequence accepting of society itself and of the main values and attitudes that are dominant in their culture at any particular time.

ii) The second implication of the Catholic community being sociologically a denomination is that it accepts an ordinary level of religiosity or religious commitment. This contrasts with sects and cults which demand total and full-time commitment from their members. They require those who belong to them to be religious virtuosi striving for religious perfection, and are not satisfied with the normal levels of religiosity that the mass of church or denomination members settle for. So, for example, the Hare Krishna lifestyle involves two hours of chanting during the night, one hour of corporate worship in the temple, complete vegetarianism and abstention from alcohol, tea, coffee, cigarettes and drugs, while sex is allowed strictly for procreation.[14] In the Catholic church this level of intensity in religious commitment is matched only by members of monastic communities. These are the religious virtuosi in the church. They are not satisfied with ordinary religiosity as lived by the mass of church members but demand an intense level of it that requires the individual member to leave everything to follow this way of life. Thus the Religious Order and, more particularly, the monastic community may be said to be the ultimate social organisation of virtuoso religion.[15]

In contrast to this - and this is the focus of our interest here – the rest of the church/denomination members including the diocesan clergy live a much less intense religious lifestyle. The church itself accepts and the great bulk of church members accept and live a sort of mass standard of religious commitment, even though they too are called to the ideal of perfection and total commitment to Christ and the Christian way of living. The level of commitment here, in terms of intensity and time, resembles the ordinary church member's commitment to other voluntary organisations like a political party, a charitable group or a sporting club. This holds too for the diocesan clergy, even though they are full time in religious ministry, are bound to a celibate lifestyle, and are urged to be examples of Christian living to the faithful. It follows that diocesan priests generally will tend to attain a level of religious commitment that approximates to the mass standard that has been mentioned. While there will

14. Ginnie Kennerly, 'The Cults and Christianity', *Doctrine and Life*, Dublin, Ireland, May-June 1984, 252-63.
15. Meredith B. Maguire, *Religion: The Social Context*, Wadsworth Publishing Company, Belmont, California, 1987, 128.

be exceptions (e.g. the Curé of Ars), experience would seem to bear this out as would the relative scarcity of diocesan priests (and bishops) among the formally beatified and canonised in the Catholic church.

In consequence of accepting and living this mass or ordinary standard (in terms of intensity and time) of religious commitment it would seem likely that diocesan priests and bishops would tend in their ministry to settle for a less intense degree of religious dedication and pastoral involvement. As a kind of pastoral or clerical GP the priest in a parish and the bishop in a diocese will be equipped to keep the show going, as it were, but, since not much more will be demanded of them by their role and the system they operate, it will be likely that the majority of diocesan clerics will content themselves with that maintenance role and won't reach for the stars, as one might say, in terms of religiosity, pastoral endeavour and initiatives for renewal and growth.

iii) A denomination also accepts and facilitates the religious role of its members as one segmented from other aspects of life. This means that the members' religious activity is limited to a rather restricted time and has to find its place alongside their other activities and involvements like work, family, community and charitable activity, recreation, politics, etc. This is a situation we are quite familiar with as Catholic Christians in the church and we take it for granted as the way things normally are. It contrasts, however, with how things are in many sects and cults and also in Catholic monastic communities. It differs radically also from how the Christian church was in its origins as portrayed in the *Acts of the Apostles*. Then the Christian community was effectively a sect within Judaism. In consequence the religious role of its members was their master role, pervading and dominating all other aspects of their lives (See *Acts* 2.4-7, 4.32-35). This is very different from our ordinary Christian lifestyle today, not just because social, cultural, economic, political and religious conditions have changed radically, but crucially because now the Christian community is no longer a sect but is, from the sociological viewpoint, a church/denomination. As a result the religious role of church members is but one of many that these members are involved in.

This segmentation of roles will tend to have a significant impact on the lifestyle of diocesan priests and bishops. In practice it will mean that the clergy will tend to have notable social roles in the parish, the diocese and beyond. Thus their interests and involvements will be broadened, leaving them less energy and time for their essential ministerial work. So the diocesan priest and bishop will generally tend to live a middle class lifestyle. They will regularly be involved in social activities of a recreational, sporting and charitable nature as well as maintaining a socially supportive and personally necessary circle of relatives and friends. In these ways the diocesan clergy will have a style of life that has many resemblances to that of their parishioners. While their religious role will be central, their other roles will exist side by side with it and make for a significant segmentation of the diocesan priest's time, energy and commitment. It will be important to note too that the cleric's role in the parish or diocese will involve him in extensive administrative functions and activities and these will tend to increase the segmentation in question here. The result usually is to confine his strictly pastoral role within even tighter limits of both energy and time. All this does not mean that the priest's religious/pastoral role is unimportant but it does mean that it will be much less pervasive than that of the monk or sect member and will have less influence in the total picture of the priest's daily life. This multiple-role lifestyle of the diocesan priest may be conducive to clerical burn-out and stress. But it may also foster a tendency, given the other demands on the priest's time and energy, to settle pastorally for the tried and true, to adopt a maintenance attitude to pastoral life and so to give a lower priority to initiatives, renewal and development.

Clearly, then, the sociological situation of the church and its clergy and in particular the three influences that have been noted here will and do shape in important ways the spirituality, pastoral attitudes and practice of diocesan priests and bishops, and in doing so will tend to reinforce the impact of the diocesan clerical system as we will see in what follows.

Advantages of the diocesan clerical system
The diocesan clerical system which has been described in the preceding pages of this chapter is well established and firmly in

place in the Catholic Church. It has, as one can well imagine, many advantages and positive aspects which one should note.

It provides a real definiteness and stability for those involved in it, particularly for bishops and priests. It ensures that the religious and moral needs of the parishioners are well and continuously met by the presence or at least the ministry of a priest or priests in each parish. The presence and ministry of the bishop in the diocese ensures pastoral leadership, the celebration of the sacraments proper to a bishop and a visible link to the universal church in the person of the bishop. The system also enables all the priests of the diocese to exercise the ministry they chose in their earlier life and so to have the possibility of finding satisfaction and fulfilment as human beings, as Christians and as ordained ministers in their work of service of God and God's people.

This clerical system also provides some room for a priest to prove himself capable of taking on greater responsibility or a more demanding service in the pastoral sphere, or, in secular and for the Christian, rather inappropriate, terms, to gain some promotion, e.g. by becoming a senior curate, a parish priest, a Vicar Forane, a canon, a Vicar General, a monsignor or, for the few, a bishop.

It is also true that the pastoral ministry within a parish or diocese gives real space and opportunity for the priests there to exercise their initiative and use their talents in creative ways, often in a collaborative mode, for the pastoral and spiritual benefit of the parishioners. The fact that each parish is independent of other parishes in regard to its ministry facilitates this creativity and provides scope for ideas and programmes tailored to the needs of the individual parish community. This is not, however, to deny that the separateness of parishes from their neighbouring parishes has its drawbacks in terms of isolation, lone rangerism and difficulty in cooperation when that would be valuable.

The diocesan clerical system also goes a good way towards avoiding or sidelining any canvassing for positions within the structures of the diocese. Since the bishop makes the appointments and he is normally a man committed to the good of the diocese and to choosing the best man for any particular pastoral role, there will rarely be any room for favouritism or cronyism or for seeking to influence the bishop's choice in any specific direction. In any case the culture obtaining among the diocesan clergy usually won't tolerate any moves by a bishop or by individual priests towards influencing particular appointments. There is, also of course, the fact that not every bishop is outstanding in the deployment of the priests available to serve in the diocese he leads, but that is not often a problem, especially if the bishop is wise enough to take advice in this area.

Another advantage of the clerical system we are discussing is that it provides quite a lot of support for the individual priests who work within it, both ministerially and personally. This support is found at the parish level among the group of priests serving there and at deanery level, i.e. the group of parishes in a particular area which are regarded as a pastoral unit. It can come also from relationships within structures like the council of priests and often from lay friends and at times from the bishop. In addition, the camaraderie and friendships that usually obtain among priests within an individual diocese not infrequently lend some real personal support to individual priests and can be a great help, especially when the going gets tough for whatever reason. At the same time this support has real limits as is made clear all too often when an individual priest runs into serious personal difficulty and perhaps later complains that the priestly support he so much needed was not forthcoming. The result sometimes is that he seeks and finds the needed support elsewhere, not infrequently from some empathic woman, who provides a listening ear more sensitive and understanding than the man's priestly colleagues.

Some negative effects of the diocesan clerical system
In this section the emphasis will be on the disadvantages or the downside of the diocesan clerical system, particularly in regard to its influence on the clergy within it and the ways in which it shapes their spirituality and pastoral outlook and activity. This will be done by considering nine areas or influences of the system on the clergy. As the reader will notice some of these points will have been mentioned in passing earlier in this chapter:

1. Because the diocesan clergy will tend to be both socially and ecclesiastically conservative, it would seem right to expect that they will tend to be less than fully enthusiastic about renewal and

innovation at parish and diocesan levels. This would seem to be borne out by the experience in the years since Vatican II. Both diocesan bishops and priests were taken by surprise by the renewal mandated by the Council. They were not ready for it, understood what was involved only very imperfectly and in general were less than enthusiastic in implementing the changes the Council required, though they did obediently do so. There were, of course, many exceptions to this but overall the diocesan clerical system provided a notable weight in favour of maintaining the status quo.

This tendency to drag clerical feet because of the conservatism inculcated in the clergy by the very system within which they work has received powerful support in recent years from John Paul II's Vatican congregations and the Pope himself and also in the present pontificate. While praising the Council for its great work for the renewal of the church, the tendency at the highest level in the church seems to be to criticise the way many have interpreted the Council's teachings and programme of renewal and in consequence to take a series of steps to reverse, not just what are considered abuses or faulty interpretations, but what are in fact trends and changes made in response to the Council and in implementing its teaching. This is especially clear in relation to the responsibility for the translation of liturgical texts and the manner in which these translations are made. It is visible also in regard to the role of the laity in carrying out various ministries in the Mass. And of course collegiality, which is so central in the teaching of the Council, remains still in many places, as one author has said, a sleeping princess ever awaiting her prince charming to breathe life into her.[16] In this context it is hardly surprising that many candidates offering themselves for training for the priesthood are of a very conservative frame of mind, much more so than their more senior colleagues who were ordained around and immediately after the time of Vatican II. Thus is the innate conservatism of the diocesan clerical system being strengthened as we move on into the twenty-first century.

16. See Quinn, 229-34; Enda McDonagh, 'A Dual Lament', *The Furrow*, Maynooth, Ireland, May 2005, 275-8; John A. Coleman, S. J., 'Not Democracy but Democratization', in *A Democratic Catholic Church – The Reconstruction of Roman Catholicism*, Edited by Eugene C. Bianchi and Rosemary Radford Ruether, Crossroad, New York, 1993, 229-34.

2. As we saw in relation to the spirituality of the clergy working within the diocesan clerical system so in regard to their commitment to the pastoral life of the diocese and parish. The system basically demands only a maintenance approach or role, requiring merely that the bishop or priest in his ministry provide the fundamental religious services, keep the plant in reasonable shape and do the essential administrative work to ensure a viable diocese or parish whose survival is not in question. This is obviously essential and important work and many priests (and bishops) who do it conscientiously and well find themselves very busy. Of course the diocesan clerical system does allow the cleric to adopt a more proactive attitude or role in which to some extent at least he ministers in a way that is more mission than just maintenance. Not a few diocesan bishops and priests are zealous enough to adopt this more demanding and positive form of ministry as has been demonstrated in many places in the post-conciliar period. Still, most of us are content to meet the demands the clerical system places on us and to settle for that. We live down, one might say, to what the system we operate requires of us, so that many dioceses and parishes would seem to be in maintenance mode most of the time. This makes for a static, routine form of ministry that is rather uninspiring and probably involves the members of the diocese and of the parish in fairly minimal and somewhat utilitarian types of active participation. Thus does the clerical system contribute to shaping the intensity and quality of the ministry of diocesan bishops and priests.

3. Earlier it was mentioned that the diocesan clerical system provides some room for the exercise of increasing responsibility by individual priests and bishops. However, in the system as it works nowadays this room seems a diminishing entity. These days, says Papesh (105), what constitutes advancement or recognition among priests is unclear. In some dioceses at least it is no big deal to be or become a senior curate, especially when one is ministering in a rural parish and doing so in a position that requires only one curate. Similarly with becoming a parish priest. A large parish can be simply more work.[17] And with

---

17. Papesh, 105, 92.

salary systems for priests becoming more common in dioceses today there are now few 'better' or 'plum' parishes to ambition. In addition, team ministry is becoming more a reality in various places, and, because there are now fewer priests than heretofore, the number of one-priest parishes is increasing rapidly with the result that parish priests are under more pressure and some priests, understandably, are reluctant to go to such parishes. Also in some rural areas especially there is no major difference between what a parish priest has to do and can do ministerially and what his curate a few miles down the road is engaged in. A relatively new development here is the refusal of some priests to move from their present appointment. There is usually a variety of reasons and motives for this, some good, some more self-serving. On the other hand, it is sometimes true that the case a bishop makes for moving a particular priest from A to B is far from convincing, being largely concerned with filling a gap, which could equally well be filled by any one of two or three other priests who could possibly move.

Nowadays also, titles like canon, archdeacon, dean, etc. have in many dioceses lost much of their significance even as honorary positions. In fact in some places they have disappeared altogether or are reduced to not much more that mere labels signifying little – except perhaps the approach of the grim reaper! (In one Irish diocese it is reported that the bishop cannot get any priest to agree to becoming a canon!) Some still covet the papal honour of being made a monsignor, but it is just a title of honour and gives one no extra responsibility or even clout at least at the parish level. In some dioceses VFs or rural deans play only a minor role, despite what canon law lays down. Even VGs may have been given only a temporary position and may find themselves performing duties that are less than noteworthy. Effectively, then, what one may call the honours system or list has in many dioceses of the Catholic church withered away to virtual insignificance.[18] It is not, then, much of an exaggeration to say that the only worthwhile increase in pastoral responsibility a diocesan priest is likely to get over his fifty years of parish ministry is becoming a bishop and only very few indeed make it to that episcopal level. Indeed, for many priests even becoming

18. Hoban, 60-61.

a bishop is of no interest, because it opens one to considerable pressure, headaches and politicking in what is the most difficult and stressful ministry in the Church.[19]

In spite of this shrinkage of the external rewards system or the promotional prospects, as it were, for diocesan priests, it would seem that some priests are still ambitious about honours and titles. It is not likely that such motivation and hopes and the manoeuvring that can often accompany them will do much for pastoral commitment and effectiveness. But the good news is that the number of such priests seems to be diminishing of late as realism dawns and the service of God's people comes to be understood in a more authentic and less self-serving manner.

As a result of all this it will be clear that the diocesan clerical system affords very little opportunity for a priest to rise to a position of greater pastoral responsibility or, in secular terms, to gain promotion. Hence, many priests may find their positions in parish life dull and unchallenging. One may, then, opt for the relatively undemanding life that the system presents one with or he may turn to hobbies or occupations that interest him or he may leave the priesthood for greener and more challenging and more satisfying pastures.

4. While what has just been said about opportunities for greater responsibility in the pastoral life is important at the ministerial and personal levels in terms of providing motivation for diocesan priests, it must also be kept in mind that the really powerful motivators for anyone, the clergy included, are not external rewards such as have been mentioned just now. Rather what really motivates people and gives the deepest personal satisfaction are factors internal to their work. One survey found that the ultimate sources of satisfaction and what was most rewarding for those interviewed was the creative challenge and stimulation of their work itself and the chance to keep learning.[20] When one finds one's work enjoyable and even exhilarating, one does one's best work and then one has the most powerful motivation that there is for continuing it, namely, the sheer delight of doing it. It has been found too that people feel better

19. Papesh, 105.
20. Daniel Goleman, *Working with Emotional Intelligence*, Bloomsbury, London, 1999, 106.

doing work they love rather than work they do only because they are rewarded financially for it. Status appears very low down on the list of motivators for work and financial gain comes even lower.[21]

One can presume that diocesan priests and bishops in general find their work or ministry as pastors satisfying, though survey findings on the matter are hard to come by. At the same time the generally accepted fact that 100,000 or more priests have left the priesthood in the last fifty or so years does raise a question. Did they all leave because of celibacy? Authority figures and others have been at pains to answer 'no'. Could other reasons for the exodus have been things like lack of a worthwhile challenge in the pastoral ministry or too little responsibility in the exercise of one's priesthood or finding that authority figures higher up the ecclesiastical ladder had lost their nerve and were veering in a conservative direction away from the Council's agenda and spirit? Or just getting bored from years of doing much the same things in much the same situations for much the same people?

What about those who have stayed? Here we don't really know either. The diocesan clerical system certainly does give stability and a ministry to pursue all one's active priestly life till retirement. Do priests generally enjoy and get satisfaction from their ministry? Are they well rewarded by the sheer delight of ministering to God's people? One would hope so and anecdotal evidence would seem to indicate that many do, to some degree at least. But given that we are at present in a period of decline at least in the western church, that diocesan priests and bishops live a celibate lifestyle and that the opportunities for extra responsibility or challenge are rather limited, as has been noted, and that, therefore, priests are more dependent than most on their priestly ministry itself to provide them with the sense of satisfaction and fulfilment that they need to make life worth living, one may wonder, in the light of all that has been said up to now about the diocesan clerical system and its limitations and drawbacks, if at least some priests and bishops are not struggling to find the joy, contentment and peace in their priestly lives that one would expect and hope for as one who preaches the good news and ministers to God's people.

---

21. Goleman, 106.

5. One of the major lacks in the diocesan clerical system is to be found in the area of accountability. There is no adequate system or structure of accountability for diocesan bishops or priests. While there is some accountability upwards, to Rome for the bishop and to the bishop for the priest, basically, these pastors are accountable for their ministry and its quality only to God through their conscience and that can often be less than objective and sensitive. So it can happen that a priest or a bishop can be, say, twenty-five years in a parish or diocese or other ministry; he can do the minimum, do it badly and with an unhelpful, negative and non-collegial attitude, and very little is or can be done about it. If such a pastor does not fall into heresy or schism, misappropriate parish or diocesan funds, regularly fail to celebrate Mass or commit some grave misdemeanour like beating up his superior or desecrating the sacred species or become a child sex abuser, then he can carry on his inadequate ministerial work with scarcely any possibility of anyone doing anything about the situation. The experience of many testifies to this. Such a diocesan minister can even reverse the pastoral policies and practices of a predecessor in, e.g. an authoritarian or conservative direction and get away with it, however many people or priests may object. In short then there is in the daily run of the pastoral ministry little real accountability for the diocesan bishop or priest. While this gives the bishop or priest in question almost a carte blanche in his pastoral sphere for better or for worse, it also means that he lacks any incentive from within the clerical system to stretch himself, to do more and to do better. Almost everything depends, then, on his own motivation, interests, talents and disposition. These may at times be excellent but not always. As a result mediocrity can reign, eccentricity can have a field day, negativity can dominate and the people of God are likely to be the main victims of the largely unaccountable cleric.[22]

6. The diocesan clerical system places nearly all responsibility and decision-making power in the hands of the clergy. They run the show at diocesan and parish level. In the light of the

22. Robinson, 290-2; Paul Lakeland, *Catholicism at the Crossroads – How the Laity can save the Church*, Continuum, New York & London, 2007, chapter 3.

previous points one is inclined to suspect that that is where the power will very likely stay. Again the clerical system hasn't any significant built-in mechanisms for distributing responsibility or power especially to the laity or to priests in a diocese, and it doesn't furnish those in charge with any ready method or compelling incentive to do so. Hence, it must be said that the system is weighted against democratisation or power-sharing. And the fact that seminary formation still seems to turn out a·great many priests of a conservative and even authoritarian and lone ranger mentality in regard to ministry indicates that this situation seems likely to continue.

One effect of this clerical control of the levers of authority, decision-making and power in the church is the creation and the perpetuation of the vast gulf between the clergy and the laity. This is the root of the widespread attitude among the laity that anything to do with liturgy and religious services generally and with the pastoral side of diocesan and parish life is the business of the cleric in charge. This is even still a deeply entrenched attitude and seems set to remain so as long as the clergy remain the fonts of almost all responsibility and decision-making on the pastoral scene. It is hardly necessary to add that such an almost total exclusion of lay people from authority and power continues to ensure that lay people will remain amateurs as far as the church goes, whatever their expertise in other areas of their lives. This in turn impacts quite negatively on the motivation of the laity in regard to involvement in pastoral activity. In companies in the business world the principle is established: no involvement, no commitment.[23] There is no reason to think that this doesn't apply to the church too. The implication will be clear. The more clergy reserve responsibility to themselves, the more it will be left to them as lay people refuse – quite reasonably from their viewpoint - to buy into structures, policies and plans in which they have little or no say. In this context one begins to suspect that today this exclusion of the laity may be at least for some lay people an element in their decision to abandon religious practice and perhaps also in the choice of a growing number to leave the church altogether. It may also help to

23. Stephen R. Covey, *The Seven Habits of Highly Effective People – Restoring the Character Ethic*, Simon & Schuster, London, 1989, 1992, 143.

explain why mere exhortation to become involved in church activity so frequently falls on deaf ears. Such calls are no doubt well intentioned but they are bound to be ineffective when the ethos and the structures of the parish and the diocese silently but powerfully proclaim that such involvement is not really wanted.[24]

7. There is no doubt that the art of leadership is very difficult to practise in any group or organisation. Pastoral leadership is no different and so one regularly hears criticism of diocesan priests and bishops in this regard. This is not surprising, not just because of the intrinsic difficulty of being a leader in a parish or a diocese but also because of the diocesan clerical system that is being considered here.

This system provides the diocesan priest and bishop with a well defined community of disciples for whom he is called to provide spiritual or Christian leadership. Some do this very well. Most seem not to be overly successful, just as in society itself and especially in politics the proportion of really good and successful leaders is very small. The church's tradition and the authority structures of centuries and even of today have given and continue to give the priest and bishop almost complete authority and power in the parish and the diocese. In addition, this tradition and these structures have allowed and still allow priests (and bishops) to exercise their leadership role in an authoritarian manner with the laity largely excluded from responsibility. In effect it may be said that the emphasis has been on control more than leadership. This was reinforced for the priest in the parish by the controlling and often the domineering attitude of the bishop, who in turn felt the weight of Vatican control mechanisms.

Perhaps the widespread lack of success in pastoral leadership as distinct from rigid control is explained in part at least by the fact that there was little or no training or formation in the seminary precisely in leadership and the character and skills required to exercise it effectively on the pastoral scene. One has to hope that the seminary today does a better job in this area than its pre-Vatican II predecessor, though the attitudes of some younger

---

24. Covey, 206, 229-32.

priests today, as already noted, serve to raise questions about how successful the contemporary seminary is in this matter.

Vatican II in its renewed ecclesiology provided the inspiration for big steps forward in pastoral leadership and its exercise. This has had a big impact on clergy and bishops in the pastoral sphere and many priests and bishops have made valiant efforts to be more collegial and democratic in their leadership style, with parish councils, liturgy groups, pastoral councils, etc. playing important new roles in parish and diocesan life in many places. However, Vatican II seems to have had little effect on the leadership style of some clergy and, with the law still placing almost full authority in their hands, it is not surprising that the authoritarian, controlling style of leadership is very much alive and in the ascendant in some parishes and dioceses. With the recent resurgence of a more conservative and authoritarian attitude in the Vatican in relation to local churches and diocesan bishops this style of leadership is being reinforced at the highest level of the church. The appointment of many more conservative bishops during the pontificates of John Paul II and that of the present Pope too means that men of a more authoritarian mentality are now in charge in more and more dioceses. At parish level the arrival on the scene of more and more conservative young priests seems to presage a return in many places to a style of leadership where the emphasis will again be on clerical control and power rather than on lay responsibility, active participation and collaboration with the lay members of the church.

8. The diocesan clerical system can operate negatively in another way in relation to pastoral commitment and effectiveness. Priests (and bishops) know that, in the ordinary run of things, they are guaranteed a ministerial position for their working life till retirement at seventy-five. This is obviously a good thing in itself. But it is not hard to imagine that it might also give rise to a certain complacency in some priests (and bishops) who might in consequence be inclined to rest on their oars, as one might say, and adopt a maintenance mentality such as was discussed earlier. This may have a deadening effect on the parish or diocese due to the cleric in charge running out of steam, as it were. There may ensue, then, a long stint of less than inspiring or dynamic leadership and,

perhaps, a relationship with the priest or bishop that might be far from affirming and could be a source of frustration, annoyance and even alienation from the church as an institution.

One way out of this would be to appoint bishops and priests for a limited number of years, say ten, to any particular pastoral position. It might even be a good idea to adopt the practice in many religious congregations whereby after some years of leadership one returns to the ranks.

It might be noted too that seventy-five is a rather high age for retirement. Perhaps it should be made possible for bishops and priests to retire earlier with full entitlements.

9. A few words may be added here about the impact on the priest and his people of the fact that, as explained earlier, the priest is also a cleric.

Making the presbyter/priest a cleric had the effect of separating the priest from the laity and placing him on a level of his own, in a sacred caste, on a pedestal, removed to a large extent from 'the world' and superior in status and holiness to those to whom he ministered. Thus the priest was seen as a sacred person standing as a mediator between God and his people and having the role of an *alter Christus*. All this gave the priest greater standing and increased his authority and control over his people, often enough facilitating the priest, if he were so minded, in exercising that authority in an authoritarian and centralising manner.

Today, however, the priest as cleric is more widely perceived as distant from his people, cut off from large slices of their daily experience (marriage, family life as a parent, and having a job in the workplace like other adults) and, therefore, as less in tune with and less understanding of their lifestyle with its blessings and its problems. Thus, in our day the priest's status as cleric has become problematic and is viewed by many, including big numbers of priests themselves, as less than helpful to the priest's (and bishop's) ministry and as contributing in some real degree to the personal problems and ministerial difficulties many priests have been experiencing in the last forty or so years, most notably in the matter of obligatory celibacy.[25]

---

25. See chapter 12 above.

CONCLUSION

The rather lengthy discussion of the diocesan clerical system that has been presented in this chapter is aimed, not at clergy or church bashing, but at highlighting and explaining the system and its notable influence. This is necessary, because people frequently ignore these structures or this system and put all the blame on bishops or priests individually or collectively. The point here is: the system does matter and its power should be recognised.

A related and equally important aim of the discussion here is to make the point that, if one seeks to renew and improve the commitment, the theology and the pastoral practice of the diocesan clergy, then it won't do just to say: pray more, work harder, read more theological, liturgical and pastoral books, attend more courses, etc. One must also try to renew the system. This is likely to be both difficult and controversial. But only by engaging in this difficult and radical form of renewal can one hope to make a real difference at the pastoral level and enable diocesan bishops, priests and lay people also to reach their full potential and be freed to minister together in the service of God's people in a more collegial, challenging and enriching manner.

In conclusion the words of Donald Cozzens may be quoted:

> Institutions ... display an institutional instinct that makes their first priority the enhancement of the organisation and the reinforcement of the organisation's authority ... [The church] behaves instinctively the way institutions behave.[26]

> We need to acknowledge, candidly and without fear, the systemic and personal realities that so shape today's ministerial priesthood. [T]he structural changes needed to bring about a renewed priesthood ... will meet significant resistance. ... Even though honest questioning is necessary in the face of the present crisis, it will be judged by some as an act of disloyalty. The real disloyalty, I believe, is the refusal to move beyond the denial and downplaying of the priesthood's problems.[27]

---

26. Sacred Silence, 30.
27. Cozzens *The Tablet*, 5 August 2000, 1044-5.

CHAPTER FIFTEEN

The Cost of Discipleship

In 1937 the German Lutheran theologian Dietrich Bonhoeffer
(executed by the Nazis in 1945, aged thirty-nine) wrote a book
with the above title. Then and later it made a significant impact,
not just in Lutheran but in Catholic and other religious circles.
Prominent in Bonhoeffer's thought here is his criticism of the
idea of 'cheap grace' and his insistence on the fact that
Christianity and Christian discipleship involve and require
'costly grace'. 'Cheap grace' really relieves one of the obligations
of discipleship, because it tends towards the position that it is
enough for a church or an individual Christian to hold the correct doctrines or truths and that doing so gives one a part of that
grace. But such a viewpoint really provides a cheap covering for
the world's and one's own sins, while requiring no contrition
and still less any real desire to be delivered from sin. In reality,
however, it is 'costly grace' that accompanies a life of Christian
discipleship. Such grace is costly, because it calls us to follow
Christ and in doing so it costs a person one's life.[1]

In this chapter an attempt will be made to spell out, even if
briefly, what is involved in this costliness of Christian discipleship. It is not intended to present a full account of discipleship
but to focus on the demands, the struggle or challenging dimension of being a follower of Jesus.

Jesus' vocation: God's love and Jesus' personal struggle
The obvious place to begin is with Jesus and his experience of
God, Abba, in his own life. This experience may be summarised
in two basic statements or as having two fundamental elements.
Firstly, Jesus in his teaching uses metaphors, images and stories
to convey his basic insights about God. He experiences and presents the Father as a God who is an utterly gracious and compassionate Father. Jesus' own deepest experience of Abba must
have been an overwhelming experience of being loved and
heard. What he lived and preached was his own experience of

---

1. Franklin Sherman, , 'Dietrich Bonhoeffer' *A Handbook of Christian
Theologians* , Edited by Marty, Martin, E. and Pearman, Dean G.,
Cambridge, USA: Lutterworth Press, 1984, 64-7.

God as Abba and he is convinced that Abba is passionately in love with all God's children.[2]

In presenting God the Father in these terms through metaphor, image and story Jesus is proclaiming the coming of God's kingdom, which is essentially about God's love of and graciousness and compassion towards all. Jesus acts in the name of a King who is utterly gracious in his way of acting and he speaks in the name of a Father who is infinitely compassionate. This is indeed good news, it is happening now and all are called to respond in kind to this graciousness of Abba, the living and forgiving Father.[3] It is clear from the gospels that Jesus himself responded to Abba, his heavenly Father, with his whole heart and soul, going even to death on the cross in response to the Father's call and the mission entrusted to Jesus, the Father's well beloved Son.

But the second fundamental element of Jesus' experience in his earthly ministry is quite different from this positive experience of God as loving and compassionate Father. This second element may be characterised as a test or trial or struggle.[4] This is imaginatively expressed and symbolised in the gospel accounts of Jesus' temptation, or, more accurately, testing in the desert after his baptism (Mt 4.1-11; Lk 4.1-13; Mk 1.12-13). These testing/temptation stories should not be taken in isolation from Jesus' ministry.[5] In fact they may be seen as summarising in the apocalyptic thought patterns of the time the testing of Jesus' faith engendered by the conflicts he encountered as he preached the kingdom.[6] In other words, we can view the entire ministry of Jesus under the rubric of 'test' or 'trial', as study of the gospels makes clear.[7] Jesus spoke of both an accomplished victory over the forces of evil, achieved before he began his ministry, and an ongoing struggle (peirasmos) with these forces of evil in daily

2. Eamonn Bredin,. *Disturbing the Peace – The Way of Disciples*, Second, revised edition, Dublin: The Columba Press, 1986, 93-4.

3. Bredin, 95-6.

4. Bredin, 65.

5. Bredin, 66.

6. Brown, Raymond E., S.S., Fitzmeyer, Joseph A., S.J., and Murphy, Roland E., O. Carm., Editors, *The New Jerome Biblical Commentary*, London: Geoffrey Chapman, 1989, 688.

7. Bredin, 65.

life in which Jesus is trying to bring God to humankind and humankind to God. In this testing Jesus has to search for Abba's will and future as they emerge out of everyday occurrences. He must wrestle with the possibilities that confront him and be on his guard for the tester who is always awaiting an opportune time (Lk 4.13).[8] So, the testing/temptation stories draw together and symbolise all that could obstruct Jesus or divert him from following through the role he saw for himself in relation to Abba.[9]

It will be clear from what has been said here on these two fundamental elements of Jesus' earthly experience that being loved by God and being called to love the Father was for Jesus both a gift or blessing and a task or challenge, or, more precisely, a gift involving a task. These are two sides of the same coin, as it were. They are essential dimensions of the vocation Jesus had to incarnate and preach the kingdom of God. It is clear, then, that for Jesus the fulfilment of his mission was a costly experience, one costing not less than everything.

It is also clear from the gospels that Jesus responded supremely well to the testing, struggle and challenge involved in this dimension of his earthly life. Metaphorically speaking, he carried the crosses of life with a heart full of love for the Father in heaven and for us sinful human beings. His literal carrying of his cross to Calvary serves as the final and definitive proof of this love. So, one may say that Jesus' response to the Father's call to him is for us the model or exemplar of how we are to live as Jesus' disciples and as children of Abba, the Father. This is true in relation to both dimensions of Jesus' response, that to the Father's graciousness and that to the test or struggle Jesus encountered in his earthly life.

The costliness of Christian discipleship
In the life of the church community and of the individual Christian disciple one can discover the two fundamental elements that we noted in the life experience and the teaching of Jesus. Firstly and primarily, there is the presence and experience of the Father's gracious and forgiving love, particularly as that love is incarnated and lived out in the life and death of Jesus.

8. Bredin, 65-6.
9. Bredin, 73; see 66-73 for a more detailed account.

This is the heavenly reality which Jesus has made available to all people and especially to the community of his disciples, the Church and to individual Christians and which transforms us into new creations. This is good news for all and constitutes the ultimate enrichment of human existence and all people. Discipleship is essentially appreciating and responding to this divine love and doing so after the manner and in imitation of Jesus.

The second dimension of Christian discipleship, as of Jesus' life on earth, can be characterised as the test, trial or struggle it involves and that we as Christians experience in our daily lives. It is important to be clear that this dimension of our Christian lives is not separate from its first dimension just mentioned. Rather, as experience teaches, the Christian life of love of God and the neighbour necessarily implies and brings with it an inescapable element of test and struggle. This latter element has been given a variety of names in the Christian spiritual tradition, including the following: self-denial, mortification, carrying one's cross, sacrificing self, asceticism. Here we refer to it as the asceticism of daily living. It may be noted that this aspect of our Christian lives as here understood has often been given inadequate attention or even largely overlooked as spiritual teachers, writers and preachers too concerned themselves overmuch with particular practices designed to restrain our bodily appetites, especially in the sexual area, or presented an excessively negative view of what is involved in living as a Christian with emphasis on what is forbidden or is to be avoided. As already indicated, this asceticism of daily living is a built-in, essential and unavoidable feature of the Christian life, one that makes its demands every day as one seeks to live as a Christian should. It involves and requires effort, struggle, self-sacrifice and self-discipline. It will prove testing for even the best of us and will constitute a trial of our Christian virtue at many points in the journey of life. One could say that, as in the case of Jesus, this ascetical dimension of our lives as disciples is the reverse side of the coin of Christian love. It is the cost the Christian disciple must pay as (s)he loves the neighbour and God as Jesus did. It will be important, then, to spell out in a little detail what is involved in this asceticism of daily living which is under consideration here.

The asceticism of daily living: where and how it is costly

If we look, firstly, at our relationships, it will be clear that living morally and especially living as a disciple of Jesus is very demanding and costly in terms of personal effort and self-sacrifice. It involves, not merely avoiding what is immoral, but will also require one to forego many good and wholesome things as well as putting aside on numerous occasions one's own wishes, preferences and plans, as one seeks to nourish some particular relationship and avoid damaging conflict. A parent, for example, finds that (s)he has many significant duties to fulfil. These will make demands in terms of time and energy, of care and attention and may involve sacrifices and expenses often of major proportions, especially when a child falls ill or has a permanent disability. A spouse may find that her/his marriage partner has limitations, problems or faults that are very trying and can stretch one's patience, tolerance, loyalty and love to breaking point, e.g. continuing to act as 'one of the boys' after marriage, being given to extravagance in the use of money, talking endlessly about one's own private experiences and preoccupations, having alcoholic or excessive gambling tendencies, being inclined towards violence or aggressiveness, having a 'me-first' attitude, being moody, bossy or jealous. Similar trials may confront one in one's friendships and general social relationships, whether in the workplace, the neighbourhood, on the sports field or among one's relatives. The single or celibate person will have his/her own costly demands to face, perhaps loneliness, social isolation, awkwardness and even suspicion at social events, and, not surprisingly perhaps, emotional and sexual tension and even frustration. The struggle to avoid the bachelor or spinster syndrome with its self-centredness, rigidity of attitude and habit, and even lack of care for oneself emotionally, physically and socially, will be ever present and ongoing for the unmarried person, if (s)he is to remain an open and caring, a warm and loving individual in the mould of a true disciple of Jesus.

If one looks now at the area of career or work, one finds also how costly being a true disciple of Jesus or even just a good person will often be. Even those who enjoy their work or ministry - and there are many who don't! - find it a struggle in important ways. Just to be there regularly and on time is no easy thing and quite a few don't manage it consistently. To be tuned in to what one is about and to direct one's energies to the task in hand at any particular time can prove very difficult, and experience shows we don't always rise to it. To carry through and complete a task efficiently and well, whether it is in the office, at the sales counter, in the factory, on the farm or at the altar, may take concentration and effort that is, not infrequently, as much or more than one can summon up. Routine, tiredness, distraction or sheer laziness can get in the way here on quite a few occasions and mar the performance in notable ways. We don't always take the means or make the sacrifices necessary to do such things in the way we know they should be done. A farmer has to cope with the uncertainties of the weather and of the markets as well as putting in the effort to sow, attend to and reap the crops, look after the cattle, etc. as (s)he seeks to make a living from the land. A student at college must make the sacrifices required to do his/her studies and complete her/his education, at the cost of not a little anxiety and of resisting the temptation to engage in a lively social life or simply taking it easy and just getting by. A priest is called on to make the sacrifices involved in being and remaining celibate as well as those needed to ensure that his ministry is dedicated, caring and fruitful. Many of us find the struggle to care for our health rather demanding at least at times and not everyone succeeds very well in doing what they know to be the right thing in this area.

One can look at the costliness of discipleship from another and in some ways overlapping angle. This will help one to be clearer about the asceticism involved in being a good and loving follower of Christ. This may be discussed under six headings.

1. The Christian disciple is called to engage in the usually lifelong struggle to overcome his/her sinfulness. This will require one to uproot all the sinful attitudes and habits one has, correcting the false and faulty values and priorities that may be part of one's personal moral lifestyle, and putting aside all the thoughts, words and deeds that are selfish and sinful. All this is very difficult and demanding. It will necessitate growth in self-awareness, in sensitivity to others, in tenderness of conscience and in conversion of heart in perhaps many areas of one's life.

2. Costly also will be the dedicated effort required to grow in virtue and goodness all one's days. This is more than getting rid

of one's sinfulness. It requires positive growth, especially in the virtues one most lacks, e.g. patience, meekness (maturity in managing anger and aggression), truthfulness, empathy, individual, social and ecological justice, chastity, etc. Unfortunately, it would seem from experience that few adults make much notable progress in this matter of growth in virtue. Indeed in some cases the movement would seem to be in the opposite direction.

3. To facilitate and indeed to enable the above two major tasks and obligations the Christian disciple may well find it necessary to set about healing the emotional wounds inflicted in one's early life and which are frequently at the root of one's sinful attitudes, habits and tendencies. Some examples of such wounds may be mentioned here: low self-esteem, emotional insecurity, poor self-image, feelings of inferiority or superiority or jealousy, attention seeking or domineering tendencies, etc. Not many people are even aware of these roots of their sinfulness and even fewer make significant efforts to undertake and carry through the emotional healing process needed to arrive at the emotional maturity that is essential, if moral maturity in the areas of life just mentioned is to be reached.

4. Everyone has to cope with some of what might be called the trials and tribulations of life. These are things like illness or injury, old age with its problems and limitations, failure, loss of one's job and/or wealth or property, loss of reputation, death in the family or some other tragedy, loneliness, worry, stress, marriage breakdown, divorce, alcoholism, substance abuse, scandal, etc. Some people seem to be faced with more than their fair share of these trials and tribulations. But even if this is not the case, such events will tax the best of us. To cope courageously and in an adult manner with even one of these crosses that life can on occasion force us to carry is seldom easy and can at times involve an asceticism of virtually heroic proportions. Experience teaches us that here is a major element of the asceticism of daily life. Responding well to it will be part of what being a strong human being and a mature Christian requires.

5. Jesus calls us to love our enemies. Few of us are lucky or virtuous enough to have none. The rest of us know from experience how difficult this loving of our enemies can be. To be kind,

patient and even helpful towards those who get on our nerves, whom we have fallen out with, who hate the sight of us, who despise everything we stand for or vice versa is no mean achievement. Few of us do it well consistently. And to turn these enemies into friends or at least people we are on friendly terms with can demand almost saint-like goodness, which few if any of us possess. Yet this loving our enemies is what we Christians are expected to do as an essential element of our Christian spirituality. Clearly here a very demanding asceticism presents itself and it is without doubt an asceticism of daily living which is not optional, if we are to love others in the manner in which Jesus did.

6. Especially in today's more secular world it will often be a far from easy struggle for the Christian disciple to remain faithful to his/her regular religious practice. When so many around us are forsaking important elements of their religious duties as church members, it requires strength of character and courage to maintain one's up to now firm commitment to the prayer forms, liturgical and personal, that it was so much easier to practise in an earlier more supportive environment. This too can be counted as part or a form of the asceticism of daily living in our contemporary social milieu and even in the once much trumpeted 'holy' Ireland.

Christian discipleship – gift involving task
From this effort to explain what is involved in the asceticism of daily living it is quite clear that the Christian disciple, if (s)he is to be counted as a genuine follower of Christ, cannot avoid taking up the cross every day. To be a truly loving and caring person after the manner of Jesus and so to live out one's Christian spirituality as one should one cannot and should not avoid the costly and demanding dimension of Christian living that has here been spelled out. To put this in other words one can say that the asceticism of daily living is the other side of the coin of Christian love and as such cannot be split off from Jesus' example and command to love God and other people as he himself did. It can then be said that the Christian life and its spirituality, whether in the monastery or the workplace, whether clerical or lay, is both gift and task, or, more accurately, a gift involving a task. It is a gift or blessing to be invited to live human life as it

should be lived. But Christian discipleship is also a task or challenge as has just been explained. The disciple, then, needs single-mindedness, courage and readiness to give him/herself without counting the cost, and, as we have seen, this cost is indeed considerable.

It may be added here too that being a very ascetical, disciplined and detached person is, of course, a very good thing. It would be more in line with our present line of thinking here, however, if one sought, first and primarily, to become a loving person, that is, an understanding, compassionate, wholehearted, forgiving, humble, yet firm and strong, person. Then one would be well placed and indeed far advanced in undertaking and coping with the asceticism of daily living, which is, as already indicated, an essential dimension of loving God and other people, of being a Christian disciple.

Ascetical practices voluntarily undertaken

It is likely that if one were to ask Christians generally about the cost of discipleship, many would make reference to well-known and traditional penitential practices like fasting, almsgiving, the spiritual and corporal works of mercy, giving up things like alcohol, cigarettes, chocolate, sweets, going on a penitential pilgrimage to Lough Derg or Croagh Patrick or taking on, perhaps in Lent, something like getting up earlier, taking a long reflective walk regularly, giving more time to prayer or meditation, doing more work, reading a spiritual book, etc. These and similar practices have usually been thought of as penitential or ascetical; people tend to see them as forms of mortification or self-denial. And of course they have long been made use of in the Catholic tradition and highly esteemed as valuable aids in the struggle against sin and the effort to promote personal virtue.

In the light of what has been said above about the asceticism of daily living, however, it must be emphasised that these ascetical or penitential practices must be considered secondary to that built-in, necessary and unavoidable dimension of our Christian lives. They are also optional or voluntary and, therefore, less than central in one's Christian life. Here some brief reflections on their undoubted value will be presented.

It would seem correct to say that these voluntarily assumed ascetical practices are of value for Christian living insofar as they are of help to one in overcoming one's sinful habits and tendencies, in growing in virtue and so in coping better with the demands of the asceticism of daily living. It has usually been assumed that these practices are valuable in this way and so they have long been highly prized in the Church. It is, however, hard to measure the good effects of these ascetical practices. At times it will be difficult to discern any significant improvement in one's own or another's Christian living, despite engaging in some of these practices for quite a while. The question must, then, be asked: is the particular ascetical practice suitable for the end in view? Or is the person assuming that, because it is difficult, it is, therefore, spiritually good for him/her? If, for example, one engages in fasting in an effort to help one control one's aggression or tendency to be domineering, one has to fear that the person may be missing the point and wasting his/her energy, perhaps because (s)he does not understand the root cause of this aggressiveness or bossiness. Or if one prays more, without taking any other steps, in an effort to inculcate moderation in the use of alcohol or in relation to one's attachment to material things, one may suspect that little improvement will be forthcoming, because the means taken are not by themselves adequate to the task in hand.

The increased psychological knowledge of recent times has made this point clearer, and this is reinforced by our experience, that some very ascetical people continue to have significant faults and weaknesses that seem largely unaffected by the ascetical practices in which they engage.

The practical conclusion from all this is that voluntarily assumed ascetical practices, despite their long-attested value, which no one would want to dispute, may not at times be very helpful in fostering the asceticism of daily living. To make real progress in this latter area and to grow as a loving person, it may well be necessary to take on some ascetical practice or difficult healing process or therapy which is directly contrary to or focused on the root of the particular fault or weakness one is struggling with, rather than being content with what seems to be viewed by some as a kind of cure-all ascetical practice, made use of in the possibly vain hope of uprooting some specific fault or promoting growth in some virtue.

CONCLUSION

Bonhoeffer would agree, one can hope, that the present account of the cost of discipleship eschews any notion of 'cheap grace' and makes clear that being a disciple of Jesus involves 'costly grace' – one is called to follow Christ and the doing of that costs a person his/her life. At the same time one must keep in mind that Christian discipleship is, fundamentally, the Christian's response to God's love incarnate in and lived out in the life, death and resurrection of Jesus. As such it is a way of life that is in its essence one of love, love of God and the neighbour, but one that costs not less than everything.

CHAPTER SIXTEEN

Understanding Baptism: Changes of Emphasis Today

It is widely known among laity and clergy at parish level and beyond that in recent years there have been notable developments in relation to the sacrament of baptism, both theologically and socially. In relation to theology, where the most important changes have taken place, the Church today understands baptism rather differently, at least in regard to priorities, from how it was understood during the centuries up to Vatican II and its aftermath (1962-5). From the social viewpoint the baptising of a child in Ireland and, presumably, in the western world generally, has evolved into a fairly significant social event in the life of the family concerned. In this brief chapter these developments will be noted and explained with the emphasis on the theological aspect of the sacrament.

The emphasis within baptism before Vatican II
Up to the council in the 1960s and for some years afterwards having a child baptised in the Catholic Church was a very small and private event in a family. It usually took place the day after the birth of the child or even on the very day of birth, if it happened that the child was born in the early hours. Because of this quick resort to baptism, the mother of the newborn could not be present and few beyond the father and the godparents (sponsors) would have attended. Any social celebration there might be would have been very low key indeed.

If one asks, why this haste in having one's child baptised?, the following reasons were important and indeed decisive. In a time when obstetrical procedures and care weren't nearly as good as they are nowadays, there was often some danger that the child might die before (s)he could be baptised. And if this were to happen, serious theological and practical consequences would follow – apart from the natural distress and grief that such a death would cause in a family. These consequences were the real reasons why parents, back then, brought their children for baptism so soon after birth.

The basic issue here was the understanding or theology of baptism, certainly as it was viewed at the pastoral level. At that time baptism was understood as the sacrament that takes away original sin. It was then and from the beginning also taught that baptism makes one a member of the Church and a child of God in a special sense. But these latter points of doctrine, essential though they were to the Church's teaching about this sacrament, were in practice given a lesser priority than the fact that baptism had the effect of taking away original sin. If, in those circumstances, the child didn't get baptised and so remained in the state of original sin, then after death (s)he was excluded from heaven for all eternity and assigned to limbo. In addition, the unbaptised child would not be buried in consecrated ground but in a plot specially reserved for those who had not been baptised.

To incur such a fate represented to the ordinary good Catholic a terrible trauma and was a source of grave spiritual and indeed social distress. It was, consequently, of great importance for any family to do all possible to avoid such an eventuality. Hence, the haste to ensure one's child was baptised as soon as possible after birth, a very understandable haste in the time and circumstances.

The changed emphasis within baptism in the Church today
The most obvious thing about the celebration of baptism nowadays, apart from it being conducted in the vernacular, is that it usually takes place some weeks and even months after the child's birth. This trend began shortly after Vatican II and has continued and grown in the intervening years. This has the advantage that it enables the mother of the child to be present and to participate. It facilitates any pastoral preparation that may be envisaged by the parish or deanery and also any social event the family may wish to have to celebrate the new family member.

But of course the fundamental reason for postponing baptism for some weeks after the arrival of the child and the consequent abandonment of the rush to the font is again theological. It has to do with the change of emphasis in the pastoral presentation of the theology of baptism at the present time. Unlike in the pre-conciliar period which has been discussed above, the main emphasis today is clearly and unambiguously on the fact that baptism makes one a member of the Church. By being baptised one becomes, officially, a Christian, a disciple of Christ in the community of his disciples, the Church. Far from being new, however, this emphasis represents a recovery of the early understanding of the sacrament in the first Christian centuries. Back then, when many new members coming into the Christian Church were adults turning from some form of paganism or perhaps Judaism, it was rather easy to grasp the point that being baptised was the ritual by which the Christian Church incorporated new members into its ranks. But in the centuries when most of those being baptised were children and their parents were already church members, and especially when the teaching on original sin had received, not just its name, but also new development, emphasis and authority, particularly from the theology of St Augustine (AD 354 - 430),[1] then it became the common teaching and pastoral practice to understand baptism as having as its primary effect the taking away of original sin.

This understanding persisted over the centuries and down to the time of the Second Vatican Council in the 1960s. Today, however, the emphasis has reverted to that of the early centuries, as has just been pointed out.

The consequences of this change of emphasis
It will be important to outline here some of the pastoral consequences or implications of putting the main emphasis in understanding baptism on the fact that it makes one a member of the Church. We are, of course, concerned only with the baptism of infants, since nearly all baptisms in Ireland and the western world generally involve the newly born. Also the focus will be on pastoral matters additional to those already mentioned about the interval between birth and the celebration of this sacrament.

i) Parents are expected to request baptism
As in the case of most clubs or organisations it is the person who wishes to join and become a member who normally should take the initiative in relation to that membership. In the case of the baptism of an infant it is and has to be the parents' decision that their child become a member of the Church. Hence, it is to be expected that they will approach their local priest with this

---

1. See 'original sin' in Richard P. McBrien, General Editor, *Encyclopedia of Catholicism*, HarperCollins Publishers, New York, 1995, 943.

request. It is not, then, the priest's job to raise the issue with the parents. Indeed in the present circumstances where one hears repeated complaints from priests in parishes and others that many coming for the baptism of their children are not churchgoers, it would seem wise to abstain from urging people to bring their child to the font, lest the priest thereby increase the number of parents who seldom, if ever, darken the door of the church but yet want their child baptised.

ii) The responsibility of the parents

Implied in what has just been said is the point that it is the responsibility of the parents to ensure that after being baptised their child becomes a member of the Church in fact as well as in name. There is no need to argue the point that parents are the primary educators and formatters of their children socially, culturally, morally and religiously. If the parents do a good job in this regard, then, religiously and morally, their child will be formed deeply in the Christian way. (S)he will have had passed on to him/her the faith of the Church with its religious and moral vision of life, including especially its religious beliefs and practices and its moral values and principles. In such a situation the work of the parish and the school can support and supplement the formative influence of the parents. If, however, the parents fail significantly in their duty as Christian parents, then there will usually be little hope that their child or children will benefit from the faith being passed on to them in any way that will make a significant difference in their lives.

Of course in the baptismal ceremony parents make a commitment to pass on the light of faith to their child. They solemnly make their baptismal promises to do so. One hopes that such a formal and public commitment will make some impact on the parents, especially those whose connection with the Church leaves something to be desired. But experience would seem to indicate that this is not to be expected in the majority of cases, even when there has been some pastoral preparation of parents for the baptism of their child.

(iii) The responsibility of the priest

The fact that the important responsibilities just mentioned belong to the parents doesn't mean the priest in the parish is without responsibility in relation to the baptisms he celebrates in his parish. Apart from his duty to celebrate this sacrament according to the liturgical norms and in a pastorally dignified and helpful manner, the priest should visit the family or have them visited,[2] and prepare them for the baptism of their child so as to help them to carry out the task of education which they undertake during the celebration of the sacrament.[3] In addition, in the present circumstances where quite a number of parishioners are not churchgoers, may be weak in their attachment to the Church and even to their faith, the priest has the duty to assure himself that there is a well-founded hope that this baptism will bear fruit.[4] This means that he must get from the parents or close relatives assurances that an authentic education in the faith and Christian life will be given to the child.[5] The assurances required here will be considered sufficient if they amount to 'any pledge giving a well-founded hope for the Christian upbringing of the children'.[6] In practice it would seem that, when uncertain about this, many priests give the parents the benefit of the doubt. But as the official church instruction on this issue states, 'if these assurances are not really serious there may be grounds for delaying the sacrament, and if they are certainly non-existent the sacrament should even be refused'.[7] One has the impression, however, that in general priests rarely refuse to baptise a child and, especially if there has been pastoral preparation, they rather seldom seek to delay the sacrament. At times this approach would seem to be motivated, less by the hope that the parents will abide by their assurances than by the fear that, if one delays the baptism or refuses it altogether, the parents will be even more completely alienated from the Church or will simply go elsewhere to a priest who will be more accommodating.

2. Sacred Congregation of Divine Worship, *Introduction to the Rite of Infant Baptism*, 24 June 1973, n. 5, (1) in Vatican Collection, Volume 2: *Vatican Council II – More Post-Conciliar Documents*, General Editor: Austin Flannery, O.P. Fowler Wright Books Ltd., Leominster, Herefordshire, 1982, 30.

3. Ibid., n. 7, (1), Flannery, 31.

4. Sacred Congregation of the Doctrine of the Faith, *Instruction on Infant Baptism*, 20 October 1980, n. 30, Flannery, 113.

5. Ibid., n. 28, 2; Flannery, 113.

6. Ibid., n.31; Flannery, 113.

7. Ibid., n.28, 2; Flannery, 112.

What about original sin in this context?
As has already been stated, baptism takes away original sin. This remains true, though it is nowadays given a lesser priority than formerly in the pastoral celebration of baptism.

Original sin is sin only by analogy, that is, it is like a personal sin but different in that it is a state not an act of the person who has it. So it is 'contracted' rather than 'committed'.[8] It consists in 'a deprivation of original holiness and justice',[9] that is, the sanctifying grace one would have had, if Adam hadn't fallen. Now baptism gives one this grace or love of God and, hence, it is true to say that the sacrament takes away original sin.

It is important to add here that being a member of the Church through being baptised and living in the Church in a truly Christian manner is the best way to overcome what the Catechism calls the consequences of original sin and of all men's personal and social sins, that is, what St John describes as 'the sin of the world'(John 1.29).[10] So, being a member of the Church, the community of grace, helps one, more than anything else, to combat these consequences of original, personal and social sin. Living in the Church provides one with all the means of grace necessary to resist the powers of Satan, the forces of evil, in other words, to overcome all sin and the evils that flow from sinful situations and actions. Because of this, it is right and important to stress that the primary effect of baptism is to make one a member of the Church and a child of God and that, belonging to the Church, one is best armed, as it were, to deal with the harmful effects of original sin

In the light of this it is clear that the top priority in baptism must go to the fact that it incorporates one into the Body of Christ. The removal of original sin and its consequences will then take its appropriate place at a lower level of priority and as something that is best brought about in and through membership of the Church, a membership which is lived out as one journeys on the Christian pilgrimage towards the kingdom of God. As one author says, "To say 'Baptism takes away original sin' is to express one aspect of 'Baptism incorporates into Christ'.[11]

8. *Catechism of the Catholic Church*, Geoffrey Chapman, London, 1994, n. 404.
9. Ibid., 405.
10. Ibid., n. 408.
11. Paul Turner in *The New Dictionary of Sacramental Worship*, Editor: Peter E. Fink, S.J., Gill & Macmillan, Dublin, 1990, 81.

CHAPTER SEVENTEEN

Concelebration: Values and Drawbacks

When concelebration was restored after Vatican II it was warm-
ly welcomed as a vast improvement on the previous practice of
every priest going to a different altar to say his own 'private'
Mass, a practice that now looks like liturgical individualism at
its worst and is quite anomalous in relation to the nature of the
Eucharist as community worship. Concelebration was then seen
and rightly as a better symbol of the unity of the local community and of the priesthood and more in accordance with the nature
of the eucharist as the sacrament of unity of the church with God
in Christ and of the diocese, parish or religious community. As
such this form of celebrating the eucharist was welcomed and
became and remains very popular, especially among the clergy.

In recent years, however, there seems to be some unease in
some quarters at least about concelebration and criticisms of it
are voiced at the pastoral level, among liturgical experts and
among theologians also.

Criticisms of concelebration
Here we may outline some of the main points that are made by
the critics in relation to concelebration. Perhaps others may
emerge in the time to come, especially as the Pope and the
Vatican are clearly unhappy with many of the liturgical reforms
that were implemented after the Council and very conservative
prelates are being appointed to major Curia positions with
power to take further steps in the 'the reform of the reform', as it
is sometimes called. The present critical remarks are, however,
made from the viewpoint of people who are promoting the developments arising from the Council's Liturgy Constitution but
see some drawbacks in regard to the practice and theology of
concelebration.

i) At the level of aesthetic impression one finds that concelebration as a ceremony is often badly performed: from the viewpoint
of liturgical dress it can be a shambles, the babble of voices during the eucharistic prayer can often sound cacophonous and can
make audibility difficult; the placing of the concelebrants in the

sanctuary area and their over-large number on some occasions are less than helpful and can make the assembly appear a bit top heavy, as it were; at times too communicating under both species by the concelebrants can be long-drawn out and tedious.[1]

ii) From the viewpoint of *liturgical symbolism* concelebration can contradict what it is intended to signify. It can be or appear as a sign or re-affirmation of the dominance of the clergy. It can point up their privileged status and power in relation or even in opposition to the lay faithful, who may seem silent, secondary and on the periphery of the 'real' action. Sadly, this impression or appearance does still reflect the reality of clergy-laity relations in many cases, since, despite Vatican II and its promotion of the laity and their role and ministry in the church, the clergy are still the dominant ecclesial group with all the authority and jurisdiction, while lay people have at best an advisory role.

Concelebration also has the drawback that it can emphasise or appear to emphasise the male dominance in the church. This can and regularly today does make many women feel excluded and unimportant in regard to church matters and especially the eucharist. Sadly again, this merely reflects the reality of women's position and powerlessness in the church and to that extent these concelebrations are a sign of the imbalance there is ecclesially between the role of women in our church and that of the male clerics. Thus, though concelebration is understood theologically as a symbol of the unity of the priesthood, it often appears as signifying and highlighting division and inequality in the Christian community and so can do more harm than good and be counter-productive.

Some also wonder what is the point of having more than one presider in the eucharistic assembly? It only needs one and in fact has only one, who is called the chief celebrant or presider. The others are superfluous, do not really preside and in fact have no role in relation to the ministry of president of the eucharistic assembly.[2]

---

1. John M. Huels, 'Concelebration', in *Disputed Questions in the Liturgy Today*. Liturgy Training Publications, Chicago, 1988, 39-40.
2. Huels, 40-41.

iii) At the theological level there are questions about the concept of priesthood at work in this form of concelebration. Some priests, it seems, have an older notion of priesthood, which makes them feel they must exercise 'their' priestly powers or orders every time they are at Mass, irrespective almost of the community and its need for the eucharist. Related to this there are some priests who feel called to say Mass every day as part of their personal piety, and concelebration provides an opportunity for this. For them Mass seems to be a personal devotion rather than a community celebration. There are also priests who are not happy just to join the congregation at Mass, because they seem to think that only the chief celebrant and the concelebrants 'really' celebrate the eucharist, while those in the congregation are somehow not celebrating. Finally, it appears that for some priests having a Mass intention arising from a Mass offering they have received provides a good reason for joining in a concelebration.[3]

Rethinking and re-presenting concelebration
In the light of what has here been said it would seem that some rethinking is called for in relation to concelebration and, in consequence, perhaps some changes might be suggested at all three levels.

At the theological level there seems to be a conflict of two theologies of the eucharist and of the priesthood in the thinking about concelebration. The older one has already been discussed above. The more popular one in contemporary theology sees the eucharist as the sacrament of the unity of the local church or Christian community and considers that all present in the congregation truly celebrate the Mass. This unity is seen then as the primary value in the liturgical situation. The unity of the priesthood is an important value in the situation also but is secondary to the unity of the assembly and must not supplant it. In addition, the contemporary understanding of priesthood envisages the priest as the leader of the eucharistic assembly celebrating with all present as their presider or president. The unity of the community gathered to celebrate the eucharist is better served, then, by having one presider with everyone else being simply part of the congregation.

---

3. Huels, 41-42.

In this context it would seem better to understand concelebration in its present form as at best a transitional arrangement or a feature of liturgical life that is acceptable as a step away from the pre-Vatican II situation of every priest for himself, as it were, to a more ideal situation, which prevailed in the early church, in which the whole eucharistic assembly, priests included, would celebrate as a single community with one priest filling the indispensable role of presider. In such a situation the words 'celebrant' and 'concelebrant' would be unnecessary or would acquire a different meaning: all would be seen as celebrating or even concelebrating under a single presider, the priest. The latter is no longer spoken of as simply 'the celebrant', since now the whole assembly are celebrants in a true sense. Hence, the use of the word 'presider'.

At present, however, we are only in this transitional phase and, hence, concelebration as we now know it will find its place and have its value, though these will only be of secondary importance. It would seem, then, that concelebration should be comparatively rare, at least in parish life, but would be suitable for special occasions like the visit of the bishop for confirmation, an ordination, a special anniversary or feast, and perhaps a particular funeral. Gatherings of priests might also be included here, though why they couldn't all take their places in the congregation under the presidency of one of their number might be hard to see and justify.[4]

Here arises the obscure question about what is the theological and liturgical (as distinct from the legal and rubrical) difference between concelebrating and participating in the Mass as a member of the congregation. It seems to be an issue of not great importance and most priests don't seem to put any great weight on the difference. One can hope that priests will come eventually to the view that it is better theologically and liturgically to join in the congregation and not seek to concelebrate except on special occasions.

One can hope also that priests will come to see that, if one does concelebrate, it is better not to take a Mass offering, if one is not the chief celebrant, since to do so is a purely private matter for the individual priest and not an element of the communal

---

4. Huels, 42, 45.

celebration and could be said to have the appearance of that priest celebrating his own 'private' Mass in the midst of an otherwise public eucharistic celebration.

At the liturgical level the main emphasis must be on highlighting the unity of the eucharistic community. Nothing should be done as regards the concelebration that detracts from that or gives faulty impressions or puts other values ahead of that primary one. Hence, great sensitivity is needed to avoid anything that could be seen as a display of clerical or male dominance or that looks as if one believes that the assembly needs to have more than one presider or is better if it is many-headed! No impression should be given, either, that detracts from the basic fact that *all* who are present in the congregation do in fact celebrate the eucharist, though, obviously, not all have the same role to play in it.

At the level of aesthetic impression a good master of ceremonies will be helpful, at least in the planning of a particular eucharistic celebration, so as to avoid the faults mentioned just now. Vast numbers of priests crammed around the sanctuary or filling the front seats won't help and, as the law says, the chief celebrant's voice should be clearly audible and not drowned out by a cacophony of other voices, very often not in unison, and so making the words and meaning of the liturgical text almost unintelligible. It seems that many concelebrants nowadays speak their shared parts in a very low voice and so avoid this annoying practice. It will help also to ensure that the concelebrants are vested with care, wear the appropriate liturgical colour and follow the appropriate norms. This will enhance the dignity and the liturgical quality of the celebration. Care must be taken also that the concelebrants do not block off the view of the rest of the congregation by inappropriate positioning. It is liturgically more appropriate if the concelebrants do not each take the consecrated elements for themselves but have them administered to them by another minister. Some suggest as well that as a sign of hospitality the concelebrants might receive communion after the rest of the assembly or at least not have the distribution of communion to the members of the congregation delayed unduly through waiting for all the concelebrants to receive under both kinds. If, in a particular parish lay eucharistic ministers have been appointed to distribute communion at the Mass being celebrated, it would seem wrong for any of the concelebrants to usurp their function, especially if these concelebrants have appeared unexpectedly or after such arrangements have been made by the local clergy.

CONCLUSION

It will be clear from what has been said here that an unthinking and indiscriminate recourse to concelebration is far from the ideal and may at times be unhelpful or even liturgically inappropriate. The law of the church seeks to rule such an approach out. Hence, it is important that clergy have a good theological and liturgical understanding of concelebration and what it involves. This will provide the basis for a dignified and truly appropriate concelebration on the special occasions when it is suitable to make use of it.

CHAPTER EIGHTEEN

Eucharistic Devotions: Understanding their Decline

In this chapter our aim is to discuss the fact that eucharistic devotions have declined notably in the years since Vatican II
(1962-5). We will look at what seems to be a main cause of this
decline and ask, whether in the light of history and of the
Council, this decline should be seen as a significant spiritual and
devotional loss or whether it is to be expected in the post-conciliar liturgical situation and is in consequence not the disaster
some make it out to be.

The facts
Most Catholics are clearly aware of the fact that in recent
decades there has been a major fading out of the very familiar
devotional practices that we have for centuries associated with
the Mass and the blessed sacrament reserved in our tabernacles.
We are referring here to such practices or devotions as: private
visits to the blessed sacrament, benediction, exposition of the
blessed sacrament, perpetual adoration, processions with the
blessed sacrament as on the feast of Corpus Christi, 'private'
Masses, getting Mass said for a particular intention while making a Mass offering to the priest, sodalities, etc. These forms of
eucharistic devotions, while still a long way from being dead
and gone, have notably declined in our churches, even in rural
areas, though in recent years there has been a notable increase in
the practice of Exposition of the Blessed Sacrament. When a
priest today decides to put on or celebrate one of these devotions, it not infrequently happens that very few people attend
and those who do are mostly the elderly members of the congregation and predominantly female ones. Evening devotions on a
Sunday are a thing of the past, even in the Irish countryside.
Benediction, even in its renewed form, is a rare enough event
and holy hours before the blessed sacrament exposed are very
infrequent apart from retreat houses, monasteries and convents.
Corpus Christi processions in our towns and villages are also
feeling the pinch and are becoming harder to stage as the

numbers of participants drop more and more. It is noticeable that, even in the lives of very committed and devout Catholics, including bishops, priests, nuns and brothers, these devotions no longer hold the same place they once had. And while many regret their passing, few consider themselves less holy or spiritually very deprived, because they no longer practise or take part in these eucharistic devotions as they did in the past. In the case of younger Catholics these devotions are all but unknown.

(A similar major decline is in evidence also in relation to non-eucharistic devotions like the rosary, the stations of the cross, prayer to the saints, the Blessed Virgin and the Sacred Heart, gaining indulgences, devotional (or indeed any) confession, etc. These are not, however, our concern here.)

A look at history[1]

It will be instructive to look briefly at the history of eucharistic devotions, so as to note their origin and the reasons why they emerged in the first place and became popular.

The eucharistic devotions we are concerned with here came into existence mostly in or about the thirteenth century, when several factors contributed to their emergence. The main reason they developed and became widespread was because of the way in which the Mass itself was understood and celebrated up to and at that time.

In the thirteenth century (and in the preceding and following ones also) the Mass was, essentially, the priest's business; the laity were excluded almost completely from participation in it. What the priest did at the altar was for all practical purposes the eucharist, while the lay people in the congregation were basically spectators, looking on from afar. Even the long narrow shape of medieval churches in which the altar was quite distant from the congregation made this clear. In addition, the priest had his back to the people, the Mass was said in Latin and the faithful went very infrequently to communion. Add to this the facts that communion in the hand and communion from the chalice had

---

1. Everett A. Diederich, S.J., 'Eucharistic Worship Outside the Mass' in Peter E. Fink, S.J., Editor, *The New Dictionary of Sacramental Worship*, Gill & Macmillan, Dublin, 1990, 459-61. Also Eugene Laverdiere, S.S.S., Editor, *The New Dictionary of Catholic Spirituality*, Gill & Macmillan, Dublin, 1993, 360-1.

been discontinued and forbidden long before the thirteenth century, and you get a very attenuated form of participation in the Mass by the laity. In a word, the only form of participation in the Mass that was in practice available to lay people was participation by looking. Because of this and because of the emphasis on the full presence of Christ in the host alone (as distinct from the chalice), the custom grew up in the Europe of the twelfth and thirteenth centuries of elevating the consecrated host during the Mass, so that the congregation could see and adore it. Up to that time there had been no elevation, as it called, in the Mass. An extension of this practice, which seems very strange to us today, was that members of the congregation used to run from church to church to see a second and a third elevation, so much did this participation by vision appeal to people in the absence of any other form of participation in the Mass. In this context it was no great surprise that stories abounded about bleeding hosts, apparitions of Christ at the elevation, cures when one gazed on the elevated host, etc. And of course in the wake of these developments superstitious ideas were not too far behind, e.g., that gazing on the host would cure you, keep you youthful, make you prosperous, etc.

From the perspective of today we can well understand that this very minimal form of participation in the eucharist was not at all adequate to meet the profound religious needs of the Catholics of those centuries. It gave little opportunity for the development and expression of the affective dimension of our Catholic faith and piety, something that is now seen to be essential to a living and vibrant religious faith. As a result of this serious lack one could expect that the Catholic community would sooner or later devise ways and means by which this devotional deficit of the official liturgy of the church would be met and the affective religious needs of the faithful satisfied. Eucharistic devotions were the main way by which this was achieved and it was especially in the thirteenth century that these devotions began to proliferate and gain popularity. Though at times they became quite separate from the Mass itself, they came into being to supplement and at times even to replace the official liturgical services of the church in the devotional lives of many Catholics. In contrast to the official liturgy these eucharistic devotions expressed, catered for and fostered devotion, that is, the religious feelings and affections of pious Catholics which were not adequately recognised and nourished in the Mass and the sacraments as then celebrated.

An important contributing factor to the emergence of these eucharistic devotions was a strong emphasis, from the twelfth century onwards, on the humanity of Christ, something that was not very evident in the Mass itself, where the focus was more on the divinity of the Saviour.

Thus, especially from the thirteenth century on, there emerged, not just an increased stress on the long-standing practice of visiting churches to pray privately before the blessed sacrament, but also new devotions or religious practices like public processions with the consecrated host, the feast of Corpus Christi, and, then, in the fourteenth century, exposition and benediction. And these practices continued to maintain their prominent positions in the devotional lives of many Catholics right down to the recent decline that we are discussing.

Reflection on this history

The important point to note here is that these eucharistic devotions arose in the context of and in response to a non-participatory understanding and practice of the Mass, an individualistic and privatised theology and liturgy of the eucharist that was conducive to a passive, non-involving eucharistic piety. Given that kind of practice and experience of the Mass, these eucharistic devotions met a real need of the Christian people of those centuries and down to our own time. They were, therefore, very important, valuable and necessary as they supplied the affective and devotional dimensions of Catholic worship and prayer that the Mass itself in its form at that time did not and could not provide. Not surprisingly, they flourished and enjoyed widespread popularity for all the centuries during which the medieval Mass, as already described, remained the official form that the eucharist took in the Catholic church. The implication here, is clearly that, if that theology and liturgy of the Mass were changed or even replaced by a more participatory and communal understanding and celebration of the Mass, then one could expect that the eucharistic devotions which it gave rise to might

themselves suffer some eclipse and decline perhaps significantly in popularity and in their value in the Catholic community.
Devotions, including eucharistic ones, come and go in the history of the church, arising in particular times and places, because
of particular needs, and later falling by the wayside or giving
way to newer devotional practices.

It seems clear from what has here been said that we have
pointed up a major factor in the decline of the medieval devotions that has occurred in our own time. The replacement of this
medieval Mass at Vatican II was bound to bring in its wake the
kind of withering of these devotional practices that we have
been experiencing in the decades since the Council in the 1960s.

Contemporary influences
It must be added, however, that in recent times there have been
other factors at work that have contributed to the decline of the
devotions, both eucharistic and non-eucharistic, in the Catholic
church. Some of these are social factors, others pertain to the
church itself and its internal life. In relation to the former two
very obvious influences may be mentioned. They are, simply,
television and the motor car. These have made significant differences in our social lives, differences that in our time often mili-
tate against the practice of the devotions of the past. Many people are occupied watching television in the evenings and travel
has been massively facilitated by having a car that enables one
to travel great distances. In addition, in very recent times society
even in Ireland has become less favourable to religion and its
devotional practices. Negative attitudes have grown stronger
and some of the media seem to foster this negativity. Many people also say that western society including Irish society has become more secular than in earlier times with predictable consequences for religion, church and churchgoing. As a result of
these social changes religious devotions have taken a hit and
have seen their decline accelerated. Indeed, even Mass-going
has been seriously affected by what has been happening in
western and Irish society, as is very obvious to all.

As for factors within the church the general drop in religious
practice in the western world has taken its toll, in relation to the
Mass and even more so in regard to the eucharistic and

non-eucharistic devotions we are concerned about here. And of course the clerical sex abuse scandals and the cover-ups of them at the episcopal level have dealt a grievous blow to church allegiance generally and to Mass-going and devotional practice too. However, we must now focus on what would seem to be a main reason for the decline of eucharistic devotions in recent decades, the new Vatican II Mass.

The eucharist in and after Vatican II
Since it will be unnecessary here to set out a full theological and liturgical understanding of the Mass as Vatican II saw it, we may concentrate on a few significant points that are relevant in the present context.

The eucharist, as understood by Vatican II, is, above all, a participatory celebration, that is, its theology and liturgy call for and facilitate full, active and conscious participation by the whole liturgical assembly in the Mass. This is especially clear from the facts that the Mass is now in the language of the people, the priest faces the people as he presides at the altar or table of the Lord and many of the members of the congregation are actively involved in various roles or ministries during the course of the celebration. Hence, the Mass is no longer the preserve of the priest but has as its chief celebrant the assembly itself, that is, the whole congregation with the priest as leader or presider. Clearly, then, the medieval Mass is transformed and a much more communal understanding and structuring of the eucharist is embraced in the church's official vision of the Lord's Supper.

The question now is: how is this renewed vision and celebration of the Mass likely to impact on the eucharistic devotions that we have associated with the medieval or Tridentine or pre-Vatican II Mass? And will it spark a new crop of eucharistic devotional practices suitable to the church and the spirit of Vatican II? We will treat these questions in turn.

Impact on eucharistic devotions
It would seem likely, prima facie, that a participatory understanding and celebration of the eucharist would not be experienced by the Catholic faithful, priests and bishops included, as supporting the eucharistic devotions that sprang up in the

situation where the Mass was celebrated in a non-participatory manner. It would be likely too that the liturgical community would find the participatory Mass of Vatican II to be a ritual celebration that would go a long way to meeting its deep religious and especially affective needs. The reason for this is that it calls for the community to be involved; it enables the congregation to feel welcome and at home in the liturgical assembly, and also to be active, creative and to take initiatives in their liturgy. It also nourishes their faith through the liturgy of the word, which all can now understand, and through the liturgy of the eucharist which is now spoken aloud, is in the vernacular and facilitates active participation, above all by reception of communion as the climax of that participation.

Music and hymn-singing are also encouraged and these greatly enhance the eucharist liturgically and also affectively. In this context participation by looking is not at all the only or the most important way in which people can take part in the Mass. Rather is it subsumed into the fully personal and communal form of participation which Vatican II fosters and requires.

It would seem likely, then, that the Catholic community would experience a decline in the popularity of the eucharistic devotions of medieval times, precisely because of the renewed theology and liturgy of the Mass itself. This is what we find in practice, as is well known over the decades since the Council. It should be clear to all, however, that such a decline was not at all the purpose or aim of the Council in its renewal of the Mass. But it is equally clear that the decline we are discussing has been to some extent at least a consequence of the conciliar renewal, and in the light of what has been said above, understandably so. It would be incorrect, though, to blame the Council or those who implemented it for the decline in question here. The root of the problem is, rather, the medieval Mass itself and its major deficiencies in regard to congregational participation and to meeting the affective and devotional needs of the Catholic community.

All this does not imply that the Vatican II Mass is perfect or that it is celebrated perfectly in all the Catholic churches around the world. It too has its weaknesses and inadequacies and its celebration in many churches can leave a lot to be desired. Still, one may express the opinion that the recent widening of the availability of the Tridentine/medieval or pre-Vatican II rite or form of the Mass will not have any appreciable impact on the restoration of the older devotions, since in Ireland and indeed in most countries only a very tiny minority of Catholics are committed to attending Tridentine Masses, despite the obvious support for it by the Pope and major figures in the Vatican.

Nevertheless, the basic understanding and structure of the Mass is, as has been pointed out, conducive to congregational participation. Because of this, it can be expected to go a long way towards meeting the deep religious needs of the faithful today, just as they were met to a significant extent in the past by the medieval eucharistic devotions we have been discussing.

At the same time it seems right to say that priests may have tended in recent decades to resort too frequently to the Mass to the comparative neglect of devotions like benediction, exposition, holy hour, etc. No doubt people will come to a Mass more readily than to such devotions but it could be said that priests in recent years have not made a sufficient effort to keep these devotions alive and frequently used, and may have resorted to the Mass on too many occasions when a religious service was appropriate.

New Eucharistic Devotions

A natural question arises at this point. Has the Mass of Vatican II helped in any way to facilitate and foster the emergence of new eucharistic (or indeed non-eucharistic) devotions that are suitable to the Catholics of the present century? Or will history repeat itself, so that we will see eucharistic devotions emerging that owe little to the conciliar Mass but seek to meet the spiritual and affective needs of today's Catholics that have not been satisfied by the celebration of the present form of the eucharist?

The answer to these questions is not easy to give with any certainty. It took centuries for the earlier devotional forms to develop, so we cannot provide definitive verdicts on this matter after less than fifty years. There is at present a widespread movement that promotes eucharistic adoration before the blessed sacrament exposed. This is to be found in very many of the parishes of Ireland and no doubt other countries too. It is difficult to say, however, whether it has developed because of a nostalgia for the past or a lack in the present form of eucharistic celebration or both or neither. In some cases it seems to be promoted by some people on the traditional wing of the Catholic church, even at times by some who desire a 'reform of the [conciliar] reform', as it is called nowadays. Some might say also that there could be a connection between this revived devotional practice as well as others like the charismatic movement and the perceived deficiencies in the Vatican II Mass. It is pointed out by some that the Mass today is too wordy and lacks a reflective or contemplative dimension; that it appeals too much to the intellect and not enough to one's imagination or affections; that the sense of mystery so obvious in the medieval Mass has all but disappeared; that the reverence appropriate at Mass is much diluted in churches today.

One could hazard a guess that these perceived weaknesses in the Mass today could occasion in time the emergence of new eucharistic devotions in the years ahead. But, as they say, it is early days yet in this matter. One notes also the phenomenon of apparitions in places like Medjugorje, the popularity of pilgrimages in our day, no doubt facilitated greatly by the improved means of travel and the higher standard of living in our world, the growth of various types of prayer groups in Catholic circles, the continuing popularity of retreats and days of prayer in many places. These are positive developments and help no doubt to fill the gaps left by the demise of the traditional devotions we have been discussing.

CONCLUSION

Vatican II insisted that the eucharist is the primary form of Catholic worship and all other forms of eucharistic worship are to be seen as derived from this central liturgy and leading back to it.[2] But until the new liturgy is relieved of the burden of total responsibility for people's devotional needs and until new devotional forms complementary to the revised liturgy emerge, the work of Vatican II will be incomplete.[3]

2. Raymond Moloney, S.J., 'Eucharistic Devotions Today', *The Furrow*, September 1994, 503.
3. Donal Flanagan, 'A People in Search of Devotions', *The Furrow*, September 1990, 499.

CHAPTER NINETEEN

Mass Offerings:
Issues in Theology and Practice

A recent discussion of Mass Offerings[1] has raised an important, very practical and yet controversial topic. There are questions about the money involved in getting a Mass said by a priest, as the comments made in the discussion show. There are deeper issues about the theological nature and meaning of Mass Offerings (MO) and then also the pastoral issues about what to do in a parish or Religious Order in relation to MOs.

Some reflections on these matters may throw a little light on the points in debate.

Celebrating Mass and the Offerings: loosening the link
The first point to make concerns the name for the giving of money in connection with requesting that a Mass be celebrated for a particular intention. For a very long number of centuries this sum of money had been referred to as a stipend and some still use the word. Now, the word 'stipend' means a payment for a service rendered and fits into the category of legal contract. Hence, the matter becomes an issue of justice: I pay you (the priest) to perform a service for me, namely, celebrating a Mass. So it was held that the priest was bound in justice to celebrate a Mass for the intention specified and church law still sees the matter in this way.

This was a legal view of the MO, an approach that was understandable in the centuries when the whole Christian moral message and life were understood in legal categories. But this model of the Christian moral life is now seen as a valid but very defective way of presenting the Christian ethic. So too with regard to MOs. Hence, the 1983 *Code of Canon Law* replaced the legal view of MOs by dropping the word 'stipend' and speaking of the reality in question as an offering. Now this is not purely a matter of nomenclature. Rather it indicates a shift from the legal to the more personal and relational understanding of MOs. In practice

---

1. *The Furrow*, October, 2007, 563-4, November 2007, 627-8 and December 2007, 680-1.

this means that the money given to the priest in the context of re-questing a Mass to be celebrated must be understood, not as a payment for a service rendered, but as a gift or donation.[2]

This has significant implications for the priest and the donor. It means that the priest or parish or Religious Order is not at lib-erty to demand a minimum amount of money as the sum the donor *must* give. Because the MO is a gift, it is up to the donor to give what he/she decides is appropriate and the priest should accept this. Experience indicates that in some places at least this does not result in lesser sums being offered. Despite this change, however, it seems many priests still think in the pre-Code cate-gories with all their implications.

Of course there is the practical necessity, which arises on some rare occasions of deciding what to do when a person gives or leaves money "for Masses" without specifying how many. The diocese or Order usually makes a practical decision here by deciding that X is the appropriate amount for a MO (C.950). This problem can arise also in the practice of transferring Masses and the accompanying offerings to another priest or to the Missions (C.955). But it would seem right to say that this doesn't justify an individual priest in a parish or elsewhere in insisting that a par-ticular minimum offering be given.

Also it is implied in this approach to MOs that the priest who accepts a MO incurs a moral obligation to fulfil his commitment to celebrate the Mass. This seems best characterised as an oblig-ation in fidelity, not one in justice, despite church authority still presenting the matter in those terms (1991 Decree on Multi-Intentional Masses, art. 1).

It can be said then in the light of all this that the change from stipend to offering helps somewhat to lessen the appearance of 'buying a Mass' and to that extent loosens the link or bond between celebrating the Mass and giving a donation. This is an advance.

A second step along this path is the system of multi-inten-tional or shared Masses which was approved by the Vatican in 1991 (See *The Furrow*, June 1991, pp 385-7 for the full text). In essence this decree approves the practice of celebrating one Mass for many intentions, intentions that have been specified

---

2. John M. Huels, 'Mass Intentions' in *Disputed Questions in the Liturgy Today*, Liturgy Training Publications, Chicago, 1988, 48.

and requested by donors, with each donor giving an offering. This is, however, subject to the rule that the priest may retain for himself the offering for one Mass only (C. 951, par. 1 and the 1991 Decree, par. 1 and art. 3, par. 2), and other rules about getting the explicit consent of each donor beforehand, announcing when and where each of these Masses is to be celebrated and not having more than two of them in a church in any one week (1991 Decree, art. 2, par. 1 & 2). This new arrangement, which is officially described as an exception to the law about MOs, introduces the idea of the shared Mass or the collective Mass intention and in so doing indicates that there is no theological objection to satisfying many intentions in one Mass as happens in practice in many Masses anyway. This rules out the idea in this context that one person can, as it were, claim a Mass for a single intention in an exclusive manner. Far from being able to 'buy a Mass', one can here at most request a share in the community's public worship and pray with the assembly for God's grace for one's intention. In addition, the priest is reminded by the rule about the offerings that the Mass is not an occasion for making money and that the spiritual dimension must always be kept in mind.

Other helpful developments in loosening the connection between the Mass intention and the offering include that mentioned by An tAthair Leon O Mórcháin.[3] In the situation he mentions Mass is celebrated for a particular intention and the person who requests the Mass commits him/herself to participate in that Mass. But there is no question of money changing hands; no offering is given or accepted. This rather radical proposal is implemented in some parishes and is well accepted by clergy and laity. A fourth step that may help here is where specially worded Mass cards are made available to the faithful who can fill one in, sign it and send it to the family of, say, a deceased person, thereby committing the sender to participate in a Mass for the intention specified on the card. The priest is not involved and no money is given to any priest or any cause.[4]

One may suggest that these new ideas and practices in relation to MOs are moving in the right direction and further weakening the link between celebrating the Mass for particular intentions and the giving of money.

3. *The Furrow*, November, 2007, 627-8
4. See below 'New Mass Cards'.

But the tradition of giving money on the occasion of request-ing a Mass for a particular intention is centuries old, officially sanctioned as an approved custom by church authority (C.945, par. 1), deeply rooted in parish life and seems to meet real spiri-tual and material needs of many of the faithful, clerical and lay. Hence, it is not to be expected that it will disappear any time soon, though there is no doubt that the inherited system has sig-nificant defects and weaknesses. Some of these, which occur at the deeper level of the theology implied in the longstanding practice, will now be outlined.

THE DEEPER ISSUES: THEOLOGY PAST AND PRESENT

Mass Offerings : a little theological history
When our present system of MOs emerged in the eighth century it was profoundly influenced by the understanding and practice of the Eucharist that was dominant at the time. In this matter as in so many others in the Church practice went ahead of and gave rise to theory or theology, so that the medieval theology of Mass stipends was basically an explanation and a justification of the practice that was already well established. Undetected weak-nesses in the practice were likely to be reflected in the theology.

In the eighth century the Mass was, essentially, a clerical pre-serve from which the congregation was almost totally excluded. In effect the priest alone offered the Mass and the laity didn't participate in any meaningful or active way, even by receiving Holy Communion. In addition, from the seventh century on, only unleavened bread was permitted in the Eucharist and this made even the production of the bread for the Mass something that was in practice reserved to the clergy and monks. As a re-sult the laity ceased to present bread and wine for the celebra-tion of the Eucharist; instead they tended to bring and offer money.

This offering of money soon ceased to be a substitute for the offerings of bread and wine and ceased also to be an expression of the donor's participation in the Mass. So, instead of being a sign of participation in the Mass by a person who was already part of the celebrating assembly, the offering of money to the priest-celebrant became an effort by a person who was basically excluded from the celebration of the Eucharist to gain access to at least some of its graces or fruits by requesting the priest to offer the Mass for his/her intention. Since the priest was effectively the sole offerer of the Mass, he was seen as having control over these fruits of the Mass in such a way as to be able to direct them to the intention of the donor of the stipend and to that intention alone.[5]

From the eighth century on the Mass stipend came more and more to be given outside and apart from participation by the donor in the Mass, so that very often the priest offered the Mass in the absence of the donor. This became the common practice, when the so-called private Mass with only the priest and the server present became an established feature of the Church's liturgy. In fact the existence of the Mass stipend system hastened the emergence of the private Mass. The physical presence of the donor at the Mass was not required and in practice donors were often not present.

It is implied here that the congregation or assembly were basically spectators. Consequently, it was not considered important that the congregation, if it was present, knew about the intention the donor wanted the Mass offered for. It sufficed that the priest knew. Also it came to be accepted that the taking of a stipend was a legal thing that gave rise to a contract. Thus the stipend came to be viewed as a payment for a service rendered, a stipend in the strict sense. This highly legal understanding of the stipend prevailed down to recent times. Thus emerged the Mass stipend properly so-called. It came to be defined in the words of Jungmann as an offering or honorarium paid in advance to obligate a priest to offer a Mass exclusively for the intention of the donor.

The medieval theory of the three fruits of the Mass[6] which was accepted down almost to our own time was worked out by the theologian Scotus in the thirteenth century and was, fundamentally, an effort to explain and justify the system of Mass

5. Huels, 49.
6. This theory may be stated as follows: The fruits of the Mass, which are limited at least in practice, may be shared in a threefold way: i) by the universal church in a most general way; ii) by the priest-celebrant in a most special way; iii) by the intention for which the Mass is offered and the stipend given in a special way.

stipends which has just been outlined. This theory was readily accepted, because it made sense of the practice of Mass stipends in use since the eighth century.[7]

This theory presupposed the validity of the Mass stipend system and did not at all alter its fundamental elements. Hence, leaving aside the theory, as has been done by Church authorities and by theologians in recent years, does not really change anything in the system. What this leaving aside does do is raise the question of who the beneficiaries of the Mass stipend are as the Mass is understood in our day.

The theological understanding of MOs today

In the light of the present renewed understanding of the Eucharist and especially the roles of the faithful and the priest in it some comments are called for in relation to MOs and the system of which they are part and how they are to be understood in the contemporary Church.

i) The Mass – a community celebration

Contemporary church teaching and theology understand the Mass to be public community worship which is celebrated or offered by the liturgical assembly or congregation present and participating with the priest in the essential role of presider. It is clear then that the whole assembly is the celebrant and it is an anomaly when a Mass is celebrated without a congregation. It follows that the priest alone does not celebrate the Mass, as was the view when MOs first emerged in the eighth century and for many centuries afterwards.

It would seem right then to say that the normal practice should be for the intention of the donor to be inserted in the Prayer of the Faithful so that the assembly can make it/them their own and celebrate the Mass for it/them. This would seem to be confirmed by the language of the Mass itself where many people and groups are prayed for. It would then be out of line

---

7. See William Dalton, 'Mass Stipends, Mass Offerings, Mass Cards', *The Furrow*, September 1990, 501-5; John P. Beal, James A. Coriden and Thomas J. Green, Editors, *New Commentary on the Code of Canon Law*, commissioned by The Canon Law Society of America, (Paulist Press, New York, 2000), 1129-30; William Cosgrave, 'Mass Offerings: Theological and Pastoral Rethinking Today', *Doctrine and Life*, October 1992, 502-4; Huels, 50.

with the nature of the Eucharist for the priest himself to pray for the intention(s) privately or silently during the Mass or to announce the intention at the beginning of Mass and not include it/them in the Prayer of the Faithful.

ii) The beneficiaries of the MO[8]

If we now ask, who benefits from the giving of a MO for a particular intention? The answer would seem to be along the following lines as official church documents indicate.

The Code of Canon Law (C. 946) says that the faithful who make an offering so that Mass can be celebrated for their intention contribute to the good of the Church, and by that offering they share in the Church's concern for the support of its ministers and its activities. Trent had earlier stated that the Mass offered for a particular intention is beneficial for those for whom it is offered and that through this offering some grace of remission of sin flows. However, all that this entails and how it is accomplished remain matters of theological opinion.[9]

It is noteworthy here that the latest official Vatican documents including the Code do not repeat the statement of Trent about the spiritual benefits for the intention for which the Mass is celebrated. Rather the official position puts the emphasis on the benefits to the donor, namely, he/she contributes to the good of the Church and provides material support for its ministers and its activities (C. 946). So, the 1991 decree on multi-intentional Masses views the MO as primarily a form of participation in the Mass by the donor in which he/she makes a sacrifice and thus contributes in a particular way to the needs of the Church and especially to the sustenance of its ministers (*The Furrow*, June 1991, p 385). The second beneficiary here is clearly the priest-presider or concelebrant or the local church who/which receives the money offered for the Mass intention.

What then is one to say about the benefits for the intention for which the Mass is offered? There is no mention of such benefits in the official documents of recent years. This may be taken to indicate a definitive abandonment of the medieval theory of the fruits of the Mass and how they were said to be divided, as already referred to. So, it seems that the intention prayed for is not

8. Huels, 50-1.
9. Beal, Coriden and Green, 1130.

now said to benefit in the Mass by any special graces. But, since the local church prays in the Mass for this and other intentions, one may be certain that God's grace and help are granted for the benefit of the intention for which the donor requested the Mass.

iii) One Mass, one MO?

If one asks why does church law still hold to the principle that only one MO should normally be accepted for any one Mass, it would now seem that this is a prudential regulation about money and not a theological statement based on the nature of the Eucharist. This would seem to be clear from the very existence of multi-intentional Masses and their official approval, even if only by way of exception, in the 1991 decree. There is, then, no theological or liturgical objection in principle to praying for or offering a particular Mass for more than one intention arising from MOs.

MOs in the practice of the Church today : suggestions

A few practical points or suggestions may be made at this stage in an endeavour to connect with the concerns expressed in the recent contributions to *The Furrow*, as mentioned at the beginning, and also to indicate some of the pastoral implications of the theological considerations outlined above.

It should be quite clear that no priest or parishioner is obliged to use the MO system with the money element included. The system is merely an approved custom (C. 945, par.1), not a law or a legal imposition. Hence, one may celebrate Mass for particular intentions without any money changing hands. This is more desirable and easier to do in a time of affluence, when the priest's material needs, at least in the western world, are generally well provided for from other sources.

In the light of the present emphasis on the benefits to the donor of a MO, it would seem right to urge donors to do all possible to be present at the Mass which is being celebrated for their intention as expressed in the MO they have given to the priest-presider or concelebrant.

It may be reiterated here that the intention for which a Mass is being celebrated should be included in the Prayer of the Faithful and not reserved privately to the priest or announced at the beginning of the Mass.

From the theological point of view it would seem preferable to include many intentions arising from MOs in any Mass. This would help to avoid the impression that a particular Mass is being celebrated for one intention *in an exclusive manner*. But, whether a Mass is being offered for one or more intentions, it would seem best to announce or make clear in the wording of the Prayer of the Faithful that the Mass is being celebrated *especially* for X (and Y) rather than simply saying it is being offered for X (and Y). Again this signals the difference between exclusiveness and inclusiveness.[10]

One may wonder about the practice of the *Missa pro Populo* (Mass for the People) which parish priests are legally obliged to celebrate every Sunday and Holyday for their parishioners (C.534). It would seem correct to say that every parish Mass, and especially those celebrated on Sundays and Holydays, is celebrated both by and for the local congregation or parish community. To state that only one such Mass is celebrated 'for the people' would seem to imply that the others are not so celebrated. This can hardly be correct. In practice then the *Missa pro Populo* would seem to be an unnecessary duplication with its roots in the medieval conception of the Mass and its fruits. If, however, it is desired to offer a Mass or pray especially for the people in a parish Mass on a Sunday or Holyday, that intention can be very appropriately accommodated by inserting it into the Prayer of the Faithful.

In relation to concelebrants of a Mass taking a MO it would seem to be at odds with the nature of the Mass as now understood, since it is a purely private spiritual practice quite unknown to the congregation and even to the other concelebrants. It could appear as if the priest is celebrating his own private Mass as the community celebrates around him. Hence, it is hard to see how it is appropriate to take a MO in these circumstances, though there is no reason why a priest may not pray privately for an intention as he concelebrates.

The problem of pre-signed Mass Cards[11]
The controversy about Mass cards in recent times in Ireland has focused largely on the selling of these cards in commercial outlets after they have been signed by a priest. The problem has

---

10. Huels, 51-2.
11. See *Intercom*, May 2011, 17.

THE CHALLENGE OF CHRISTIAN DISCIPLESHIP

been that there were doubts in certain cases about where the money offered by the donor went. Did it all go to the priest whose name was signed on the card or was some or most of it diverted into the shop till or into the pocket of the person who had promoted the sale of these cards? In addition, there have been questions in certain situations about who the priest, whose name was on the card, actually was. Was he a real ordained person, said to live in some far away country like India, or was he deceased or was the name on the card that of a non-existent person supposedly resident in some missionary territory? In some cases the name of the priest was so illegible as to be beyond recognition and so further suspicions were aroused.

In an effort to overcome these problems the Irish Bishops' Conference along with the Missionary Religious Congregations successfully requested the Irish Government to include in the 2009 Charities Act a regulation to the following effect: It is a criminal offence to sell a signed Mass card without the sale being authorised by a Catholic bishop or the Superior of a Religious Congregation.

There can be no doubt that this regulation was necessary in the circumstances and it may be said that it has gone some way towards removing the abuses outlined above. It is not clear, however, that the problem has been fully solved as some of the people involved in providing pre-signed Mass cards for sale are adept at finding ways around the law.

The use of Mass cards today
The custom of giving or sending Mass cards is relatively recent and has become a common practice only in the last few decades, even in dioceses like Ferns, the diocese in which I serve, where there were no Funeral Offerings such as Bishop Colm O'Reilly of the diocese of Ardagh and Clonmacnoise mentions in his article in *Intercom*.[12]

It must be said immediately that the use of these Mass cards is simply an approved practice that, though now widespread, is completely optional. There is no obligation of any sort to make use of them. In important ways it would be better if people dropped the practice and made a personal visit to the family of

12. February, 2011, 33.

the deceased or to the one for whom the Mass has being request-ed. But this is not always possible and so the best that can be done may be to send or give the card. Of course it often happens too that a person will go to a wake or a funeral and actually bring a Mass card with them, thus showing their sympathy by their pres-ence and by prayer. On such occasions also priests in parishes are, not infrequently, called on to sign such Mass cards, thus clearly avoiding the problems of the pre-signed Mass cards that are in question here and that are the real issue in this whole context.

New Mass Cards
In more recent years one notices a new kind of Mass card for the deceased and for the living that in important ways resolves or avoids the problem being discussed here. This card is one that commits the person who sends it to go to Mass for the inten-tion/person named on the card. In other words, the sender of-fers a Mass he/she is participating in for the person or intention that has been specified on the card. This card does not require the signature of a priest nor is a priest asked to celebrate Mass for the intention involved. Rather a person purchases one of these cards for, say, a euro, writes in the intention, signs the card and sends or gives it to the person or family in question.

These cards can easily be made available in a parish as the priest or parish council there can arrange for a local printer to produce them along with the envelopes needed, while the priest or council also supply an appropriate wording to appear on the cards for the living on one version of the card and for the dead on another version. The cost of printing can be offset by the price charged for the cards but in a non-profit-making manner.

In this context it may be mentioned that it is very desirable and important that a donor who requests a priest to celebrate for a particular intention should do all possible to attend and participate in that Mass.

CONCLUDING REMARKS
In the light of the above theological and liturgical observations one seems justified in saying that the issue about MOs nowa-days revolves almost completely about money rather than the-ology. This was the focus of the recent discussion about MOs in *The Furrow* mentioned at the beginning and understandably so.

Some recent efforts to lessen this problem have been adverted to above. The radical step of refusing all monetary rewards for celebrating a Mass for a particular intention is, of course, available to every priest and in ways would seem the best course to take. It seems unlikely, however, that it will gain widespread acceptance in the short or even the medium term. If this is the case, then it is appropriate and necessary to regulate the practice of MOs and especially the money aspect of it along the lines of present church law.

It is regrettable, though, that official church thinking today seems to see MOs as chiefly a way of funding the clergy. These MOs are no doubt necessary and very welcome in the poorer areas of the Church like the Missions, where the churches and the priests are very needy.[13] But, still, it would seem a pity that the material aspect of the system should take precedence over the spiritual realities involved.[14] Such an emphasis probably helps to ensure that the monetary side of the MO system will remain prominent, while the spiritual benefits may tend to be given less attention. In this context one has to wonder whether better ways of funding poorer churches could not be devised and whether it wouldn't be preferable, all things considered, to discontinue the present MO system, because of the prominence given to its material dimension and the moral and spiritual consequences such an emphasis could well foster in both clergy and laity.

---

13. See the letter from Fr Michael Walsh, OSA, *Intercom*, July / August 2011, 6.
14. See Dalton, *The Furrow*, September 1990, 505.